Research-Based Readers' Advisory

ALA READERS' ADVISORY SERIES

Research-Based Readers' Advisory

JESSICA E. MOYER

WITH CONTRIBUTIONS BY

Amanda Blau | Heather Booth | Sarah Statz Cords

Nanette Wargo Donohue | Katie Dunneback

Neil Hollands | Jane Jorgenson | Cynthia Orr

Joyce Saricks | Andrew Smith | Kaite Mediatore Stover

Joan Bessman Taylor | Mary Wilkes Towner

Barry Trott | David Wright

American Library Association
Chicago   2008

While extensive effort has gone into ensuring the reliability of information appearing in this book, the publisher makes no warranty, express or implied, on the accuracy or reliability of the information, and does not assume and hereby disclaims any liability to any person for any loss or damage caused by errors or omissions in this publication.

The paper used in this publication meets the minimum requirements of American National Standard for Information Sciences—Permanence of Paper for Printed Library Materials, ANSI Z39.48-1992.∞

Library of Congress Cataloging-in-Publication Data
Moyer, Jessica E.
    Research-based readers' advisory / Jessica E. Moyer ; with contributions by Amanda Blau . . . [et al.].
      p. cm.
    Includes bibliographical references and index.
    ISBN-13: 978-0-8389-0959-1 (alk. paper)
    ISBN-10: 0-8389-0959-0 (alk. paper)
    1. Readers' advisory services. I. Moyer, Jessica E. II. Blau, Amanda.
Z711.55.M69 2008
025.5′4—dc22   2007049421

ISBN-13: 978-0-8389-0959-1
ISBN-10: 0-8389-0959-0

Printed in the United States of America

12 11 10 09 08   5 4 3 2 1

CONTENTS

PREFACE

Welcome to *Research-Based Readers' Advisory*. This book is unique to the world of library science publications because it is meant for and written by both researchers and practitioners. In fact, eleven of the twelve chapters in the book (the exception is the introductory chapter) were written by both a researcher and a librarian, in a format never seen before. Let me tell you a little more about the structure of this book.

Chapter 1, the introductory chapter, is by readers' advisory experts Joyce Saricks and Barry Trott. Both winners of the Allie Beth Martin Award for their outstanding work in readers' advisory services, Saricks and Trott discuss the major developments in readers' advisory services, the current state of the service, and the concept of the reflective practitioner.

Using the same format, chapters 2 through 10 look at adult readers, nonfiction readers and nonfiction advisory, audiovisual advisory, children and young adult readers and readers' advisory, book groups, romance and genre readers, the readers' advisory interview, tools for advisors, cataloging and classification, and collection development and collection management.

The first section in each chapter, approximately half of the chapter, is the "Research Review"—a thorough and critical review of the existing research related to an area of readers' advisory services. Each Research Review notes the gaps in the existing research and works that need to be updated to reflect the many changes brought on by recent technological developments. Written with the busy advisor in mind, these sections often extensively summarize important works to make the full findings available to the reader who may not be able to access or read the original work. By the end of each Research Review, advisors all over the world will be systematically exposed to the key researchers, publications, and findings in each area of readers' advisory. The reviews, though focused on scholarly research, are written in such a way as to be accessible to all practicing advisors as well as library and information science students of all types.

The second section of each chapter is the "Librarian's View." Approximately the same length as the preceding Research Review, the Librarian's View is written by a practicing librarian and readers' advisor with interest and experience in that particular aspect of readers' advisory services.

Less formalized and structured than the previous section, the Librarian's View focuses on the practical aspects of the selected area of readers' advisory services. The Librarian's View also includes some response to the Research Review from a practitioner's point of view, as well as personal experiences from the advisor's interest and expertise.

Chapter 12, about the future of readers' advisory, is a collaborative chapter coauthored by Neil Hollands, reader services librarian at Williamsburg Regional Library, and me. We focus on a recent publication about the history of readers' advisory and outline some directions for future developments and changes in readers' advisory research and practice.

Above all, I hope that you enjoy the book and find it useful in your work as an advisor. And if you are a student reading this book, then I hope you are inspired to work as an advisor.

Acknowledgments

The creation of a book is never the work of one person, and this book was no different. I would first like to thank my many coauthors who not only listened to my ideas but agreed to write a chapter for me, despite their busy personal and professional lives. I thank Juanita Ball, interlibrary loan technical assistant at Richland Community College, who spent many hours obtaining most of the articles and book chapters referenced in this book, as well as all of the interlibrary loan staff and student workers at Milne Library, SUNY Oneonta, who filled in the missing pieces. Joyce Saricks and Laura Pelehach were the first people to hear my ideas for this book, which without their encouragement and thoughtful feedback never would have been written. Finally, I extend my gratitude to my family: my husband, Christopher, for dealing with me (and doing the housework) while I wrote and for listening to me ramble on every time I had a new idea or problem; and my cats, past and present, Tornado Max, Charlotte, Mitt, Tiggy, and Smokey, for keeping me company while I worked.

1

READERS' ADVISORY SERVICES: THE STATE OF THE PRACTICE

by Joyce Saricks and Barry Trott

How We Got There

Since the last quarter of the nineteenth century, when the public library as we think of it today was being established, librarians have realized the value to the library that comes from working with readers. In his 1876 article in the first volume of *Library Journal,* Samuel S. Green called for the development of what he described in the title of the article as "Personal Relations between Libraries and Readers."[1] Here, Green outlined the ways that librarians could connect with readers (of both fiction and nonfiction) and set the stage for the development of both reference and readers' advisory services in the public library over the next century and a quarter. Green's article noted the ways that libraries benefit from the development of a relationship between the librarian and the library user. These benefits should all sound familiar to contemporary librarians and, in particular, to readers' advisors:

Joyce Saricks developed and directed the readers' advisory department at the Downers Grove Public Library in Illinois from 1983 to 2004. She has written two books on readers' advisory. Saricks currently serves as NoveList's read-alike coordinator as well as columnist and audio reviewer for Booklist. *In her spare time, she teaches at Dominican University Graduate School of Library Science.*

Barry Trott is the director of adult services at the Williamsburg (Virginia) Regional Library, where has also worked as a reference and reader services librarian. Barry is the past chair of the RUSA CODES Readers' Advisory Committee for ALA, edits the readers' advisory column for Reference and User Services Quarterly, *and writes for the NoveList* readers' advisory database. *In 2007 he was awarded both the Public Library Association's Allie Beth Martin Award and the ALA Reference and User Services Association's Margaret E. Monroe Library Adult Services Award in recognition of his work in readers' advisory services.*

- If you gain the respect and confidence of readers, and they find you easy to get at and pleasant to talk with, great opportunities are afforded of stimulating the love of study and of directing investigators to the best sources of information.

- You find out what books the actual users of the library need, and your judgment improves in regard to the kind of books it is best to add to it.

- One of the best means of making a library *popular* is to mingle freely with its users and help them in every way.

Here Green has captured the opportunities readers' advisory services offer to the library and to the advisor. First, he recognizes the chance to build an ongoing relationship with library users. This connection between reader and librarian is at the heart of readers' advisory services. Second, Green notes the connection of this relationship between the library and its readers to the building of successful collections. As he observes, working directly with the readers in the community should inform the library's collection development process. A close understanding of the reading interests of both individuals and the broader community in general ensures that the library has a collection that reflects its readers' interests. Finally, Green reminds us that these personal connections between the library and its users serve to make the library valued in its community. As libraries are increasingly under fiscal pressures, they recognize that gaining more support from users translates into financial support.

Librarians have built on Green's call to service with varying degrees of intensity in the ensuing years, and readers' advisory services have waxed and waned as trends in librarianship have come and gone. Readers interested in an outline of the history of readers' advisory services should see Bill Crowley's essay "A History of Readers' Advisory Service in the Public Library" in *Nonfiction Reader's Advisory*. Or, for a somewhat more controversial view on the development of readers' advisory, see *Readers' Advisory Service in North American Public Libraries, 1870–2005: A History and Critical Analysis,* by Juris Dilevko and Candice F. C. Magowan.[2] A more extended discussion of the latter work can be found in the final chapter of this book.

In the last quarter century, there has been a blossoming of interest in readers' advisory services. Although this has mostly been centered on public library service to adult fiction readers, the burgeoning awareness of the value and importance to the success of the library that results from working with fiction readers has expanded the definition of readers' advisory to include working with nonfiction readers and with groups, including library- and community-sponsored book groups. There has also been increasing interest in the development of readers' services focused on children and young adult readers. Most recently, advisory for nonprint formats has gained attention. All of these (and other important areas) are discussed in upcoming chapters. None of these expansions and new interests would have been possible without the several key moments in readers' advisory services discussed below.

One of the earliest developments in the renaissance of readers' advisory work was the publication in 1982 of the first edition of *Genreflecting*—one of the first attempts to define and describe genres and offer librarians a straightforward tool for building their knowledge of important authors and titles—under the editorship of Betty Rosenberg.[3] As Joyce Saricks points out, the open-minded approach taken by Rosenberg and her successor, Diana Tixier Herald, proved to be invaluable to the development of readers' advisory skills.[4] For the first time, genre fiction was not being relegated to the dark corners of the library collection but rather celebrated and encouraged.

In many ways, a key moment in the resurgence of interest in readers' advisory services in the late twentieth century was the establishment of the Chicago area Adult Reading Round Table (ARRT) in 1984. Early promoters of readers' services such as Saricks, Vivian Mortensen, Merle Jacob, Ted Balcom, and others came together out of a frustration with the "lack of continuing education available on both the national and local level relevant to their specific area of librarianship: readers' advisory service for adults."[5] The success of the ARRT in developing and promoting training for readers' advisors cannot be underestimated. The Chicago area continues to be known as a center for readers' services, and the ARRT model has been adapted by librarians throughout the country to bring together readers' advisors to build their skills and improve their practice.

A third crucial point in the development of contemporary readers' advisory services, also from the Chicago area, was the publication in 1989 of the first edition of *Readers' Advisory Service in the Public Library*, by Joyce Saricks and Nancy Brown. Now in its third edition, Saricks and Brown's book became the bible for a developing generation of readers' advisors. The key to the success of the book was its recognition and explication of the use of "appeal factors" as the source for providing readers with suggestions for titles that might interest them. Prior to Saricks and Brown's work, the concept of providing suggestions to readers was frequently grounded in the subject matter of the book. Although subject can be an important piece of why a reader is drawn to a particular book, it is only one piece of the picture, and often not the most important. As defined by Saricks in the most recent edition of her book, "*appeal* refers to those elements in a book, whether definable or just understood, that make readers enjoy the book."[6] Shifting the focus to these appeal elements, arranged into four categories (pacing, characterization, storyline, and frame), allowed readers' advisors to make connections between books in new ways. The emphasis on the appeal of the book enabled the advisor to focus on what the reader enjoyed and sought in a new book, rather than simply relying on what the advisor thought was a "good book" for that reader. By defining and describing appeal factors, Saricks and Brown also gave both readers and advisors the ability to articulate more clearly what made a book enjoyable. Readers' advisors could use this new way of looking at books to make connections between titles and across genres that might not otherwise have come to light.

The establishment of the ARRT and publication of *Genreflecting* and *Readers' Advisory Service in the Public Library* laid the groundwork for a rapid expansion in the development of readers' advisory services in the 1990s that has continued into the early twenty-first century. This expansion has included the development of a wide range of tools for readers' advisors, both print and electronic; the establishment of professional groups focused on readers' services; and the growth of opportunities for readers' advisory training across the United States. Some of the landmark developments included the publication of *Developing Readers' Advisory Services: Concepts and Commitments,* by Kathleen de la Peña McCook and Gary O. Rolstad, in 1993; Duncan Smith's development of the *NoveList* readers' advisory database in 1994; the establishment of the Readers' Advisory Committee as part of the American Library Association's Reference and User Services division in 1994; the debut of the Fiction_L discussion list by readers' service staff of the Morton Grove Public Library in 1995; and the publication of Ken Shearer's *Guiding the Reader to the Next Book* in 1996.[7] Smith's *NoveList,* which provided readers' advisors with the first online tool to assist in their work, continues to play an important role in shaping readers' advisory services. The Fiction_L list has become a center for readers' advisors to share information and discuss tools, techniques, and the practice of readers' advisory. Books like McCook's and Shearer's continued to build on the discussion of readers' advisory theory and practice, pointing out new directions and making suggestions for the future of the practice.

Where We Are Now

The firm foundation laid for readers' advisory services in the 1980s and early 1990s has undoubtedly led to their current success in the library world. It is generally accepted within the public library profession, at both the administrative and public service levels, that readers' advisory services add value to the library experience. This value comes in a variety of areas:

Although use of reference services has changed and often decreased as a result of the growth of the Internet, users are still coming to the library for leisure reading. A strong readers' advisory program provides these users with support for their reading interests and gives them a reason to continue to use the library.

Stories are essential to people's lives. Wayne Wiegand notes that cultures have always used stories "to validate their experiences, make sense of their worlds, and pass on to future generations what they regard as the culture's collective wisdom."[8] Through an active readers' advisory service, libraries support and promote the role of story in their community.

Readers' advisory services reinforce the human touch in the library. In contemporary society, libraries are one of the few institutions that still place a high value on the direct interaction between staff and users. Readers' advisory service offers a mechanism for establishing and promoting this personal contact.

Readers' advisory services bring the library the opportunity to build a community of readers based around the library and to tap into the existing community of readers who already use the library. The library becomes vital to its community and increasingly connected with community members.

Readers' advisory services can also build support in the community for the library. As Green noted in 1876, "The more freely a librarian mingles with readers, and the greater the amount of assistance he renders them, the more intense does the conviction of citizens, also, become, that the library is a useful institution, and the more willing do they grow to grant money in larger and larger sums to be used in buying books and employing additional assistants."[9]

In slower budget times, readers' advisory services can be a useful tool to keep circulation figures up and to reinforce the high level of service given to users. Readers' advisory services allow the library to promote older and mid-list titles and build an awareness of authors whom readers would otherwise miss. Because of fiscal constraints, libraries are often faced with buying fewer copies of current popular titles. This means longer hold lists for patrons waiting for new titles. Instead of sending these patrons off with just a reserve on a title, a well-trained advisor can suggest other titles the patron may want to read while waiting for the reserved book to come in.

For all of these reasons, readers' advisory should be seen as an important piece of the services offered by libraries to their community.

The past decade of work in readers' advisory services has resulted in a great expansion of the tools and training opportunities available to librarians who wish to develop their skills as readers' advisors. One of the clearest signs of the importance of readers' advisory services and of the success of the renaissance in readers' advisory is the wide range of resources that have become available to librarians.

The publication of *Genreflecting* and of Saricks and Brown's *Readers' Advisory Service in the Public Library* began an avalanche in publishing of readers' advisory titles that continues today. Worth special consideration are the large number of print resources offered by Libraries Unlimited, ALA Editions, and Thomson Gale. Each of these publishing houses has developed a variety of essential tools for readers' advisors. Under the guidance of Diana Tixier Herald, Libraries Unlimited expanded the Genreflecting series to offer titles on specific genres. It also offers various other series, including readers' guides to specific genres, guides to specific reading interests, and the Read On series on genre titles. ALA Editions is noted for its series focusing on specific genres and for its annual guides to best reading. Both houses also publish stand-alone titles on a range of readers' advisory topics. Thomson Gale is best known for its ongoing What Do I Read Next? series of titles on genre fiction. Contemporary readers' advisors have access to a vast array of materials that list important titles and authors and offer practical advice for working with readers.

As a complement to the wealth of print resources available to readers' advisors, the world of online fee-based tools for working with readers has also expanded exponentially in the past decade. In addition to EBSCO's *NoveList*, which has continued to develop and add new resources for librarians and readers, librarians now have a variety of other online tools available for purchase, including Thomson Gale's *What Do I Read Next?* Bowker's *Fiction Connection* and *Non-Fiction Connection*, Libraries

Unlimited's *Reader's Advisor Online*, and ALA's *Booklist Online*.[10] These tools offer readers' advisors various ways to locate authors and titles, to search reviews, to match readers with authors they might enjoy, and to build knowledge of genres.

The growth of the Internet has also provided readers' advisors with a wealth of free online resources. Libraries across the country have developed reader-focused web pages that offer local content, book lists, reading suggestion services, book group information, and reviews. As new technologies become available, readers' advisors have been quick to see how blogs and wikis can become part of the readers' services package in libraries. The interactivity between the library and its users these tools offer seems to match up well with the concept of the readers' advisory encounter being a conversation between the librarian and the reader. Lists of online resources can be found on many readers' advisory websites, including Morton Grove Public Library's Web Sites for Book Lovers (http://www.webrary.org/rs/rslinks.html), Ann Theis's Overbooked (http://www.overbooked.org/ra/index.html), and others. The many tools and resources available to advisors is the focus of chapter 9, "Tools for Readers' Advisors."

As the availability of tools for readers' advisors has expanded over the past decade, so have the training opportunities for librarians interested in working with readers. Unlike the early 1980s when the ARRT was established out of frustration with a lack of readers' advisory training opportunities, the late 1990s and early years of this century have seen a boom in readers' advisory programming at national conferences. The Public Library Association conference has featured a well-attended readers' advisory preconference at every conference since 1988. The Reference and User Services Association Collection Developments and Evaluation Section Readers' Advisory Committee has consistently offered high-quality readers' advisory programming at every ALA annual conference since 1995. Additionally, interested readers' advisors can find a host of relevant programs available at national conferences. The boom in readers' advisory conference sessions has trickled down to the state and regional levels as well, and it is a rare state library association conference that does not feature several programs on working with readers. The readers' advisory renaissance has created a professional milieu where almost anyone can build their skills as a readers' advisor.

It is only in the area of library education that readers' advisory still lags behind the curve. Wiegand has been an active critic of the lack of preparation library schools offer their graduates in the area of working with readers. Jessica Moyer and Terry Weech's article "The Education of Public Librarians to Serve Leisure Readers" uses a case study approach to review library and information science school offerings of readers' advisory courses in Europe and North America.[11] Although there are library schools that offer courses on reading theory and the elements of working with readers, and these classes are increasingly popular with students, other schools have yet to address readers' advisory services beyond a mention in an introductory reference class.

Finally, the past decade has also seen an increase in the development of the theory of readers' advisory as well as its practice. With the publication of works such as *The Readers' Advisor's Companion, Nonfiction Reader's Advisory, Reading Matters,* and *Readers' Advisory Service in North American Public Libraries, 1870–2005: A History and Critical Analysis,* among others, there has been an attempt not only to discuss the practice of readers' advisory work but also to analyze what is being done and to explore new directions in serving readers in the library.[12]

In his 1996 essay in *Guiding the Reader to the Next Book,* Robert Burgin notes that, compared to reference services, there is a lack of empirical evidence regarding the extent to which various readers' advisory practices are employed in libraries and to the relative effectiveness of these practices.[13] This failure to blend theory and practice adequately becomes a stumbling block for librarians who wish to become readers' advisors or to build readers' services at their library. As Burgin points out, in the face of a lack of empirical evidence, our decisions regarding directions and services for working with readers can be based only on anecdotal evidence. Without the same level of research and understanding of other library services (i.e., reference), readers' advisory will always be considered a less professional service. It is essential to the success of readers' advisory services that we consider not only the "how" of what we are doing but also the "why."

This book is the first compilation of essays to combine readers' advisory theory and practice. Here, librarians will find ideas and tools to support and justify the importance of readers' advisory services to users and to the library as well as expand their readers' advisory services. The essays that follow offer librarians the opportunity to reflect on their practice of readers' advisory, with the goal of becoming what Donald Schon calls a "reflective practitioner." A reflective practitioner

> allows himself to experience surprise, puzzlement, or confusion in a situation which he finds uncertain or unique. He reflects on

> the phenomenon before him, and on the prior understandings which have been implicit in his behaviour. He carries out an experiment which serves to generate both a new understanding of the phenomenon and a change in the situation. . . . When someone reflects-in-action, he becomes a researcher in the practice context.[14]

As readers' advisors, we are challenged to become reflective practitioners, using our experiences as professionals to inform the theory behind our work and modifying that theory in light of our reflection.

A great example of reflecting-in-action in the readers' advisory world can be seen in Neal Wyatt's article "An RA Big Think." Wyatt brings together a panel of librarians who are active readers' advisors to analyze how the concept of appeal is changing in the practice of serving readers. In Wyatt's article, a group of reflective readers' advisors look at the way their practice of working with readers has caused them to rethink how they use appeal. As Wyatt points out, "There's a common thread in these new takes on defining and applying appeal: they come through listening to and analyzing reader reaction and conversation."[15] The panelists blend their years of practice of readers' advisory with a careful assessment of reader responses to books and use the resulting knowledge to make connections between books and readers. Wyatt notes that the traditional definitions of appeal are expanding as two decades of practice yield new understandings of how readers approach books and respond to their reading. This case demonstrates the value of merging reading theory and readers' advisory practice to shape new directions for readers' advisory services and can serve as a model for readers' advisors.

Where Are We Going?

What's next for libraries and readers' advisory? That's not so easy to predict. More than twenty years ago a revolution began at public service desks in libraries around the country. Driven by staff who were dissatisfied with their ability to help readers find something "good" to read and readers who yearned for reading assistance, readers' advisory service was reborn, has flourished, and shows no sign of abating. Practices grew out of necessity, and successful strategies were shared with fellow librarians around the country and the world. With this book we enter a new phase, as research into what we do allows us to see where we might improve and good practice offers a forum for further research.

Providing readers' advisory has empowered librarians to employ all their skills. Not only has it created a fertile field for intellectual exploration into reading tastes and the development of tools to aid in providing the best service, it has also promoted the best possible customer service and extensive networking, as librarians share questions and discoveries with librarians and with fellow readers at all levels. What the past and the present indicate is that the future is wide open—that readers' advisory can continue to expand in all the directions we can imagine.

Guided by a better blending of theory and practice, the current generation of readers' advisors will continue to build on the foundations established for readers' advisory over the past 125 years. The thought and opinion offered here is a fine place to begin this process.

NOTES

1. Samuel Swett Green, "Personal Relations between Libraries and Readers," *Library Journal* 1 (October 1876): 78–79.

2. Bill Crowley, "A History of Readers' Advisory Service in the Public Library," in *Nonfiction Reader's Advisory,* ed. Robert Burgin (Westport, Conn.: Libraries Unlimited, 2004), 3–29; Juris Dilevko and Candice F. C. Magowan, *Readers' Advisory Service in North American Public Libraries, 1870–2005: A History and Critical Analysis* (Jefferson, N.C.: McFarland, 2007).

3. Betty Rosenberg, *Genreflecting: A Guide to Reading Interests in Genre Fiction* (Littleton, Colo.: Libraries Unlimited, 1982).

4. Joyce Saricks, *Readers' Advisory Service in the Public Library,* 3rd ed. (Chicago: American Library Association, 2005), 22–23.

5. Mary K. Chelton and Ted Balcom, "The Adult Reading Round Table: Chicken Soup for the Readers' Advisors," *Reference and User Services Quarterly* 41, no. 3 (2002): 238–43.

6. Saricks, *Readers' Advisory Service,* 11.

7. Kathleen de la Peña McCook and Gary O. Rolstad, *Developing Readers' Advisory Services: Concepts and Commitments* (New York: Neal-Schuman, 1993); American Library Association, Reference and User Services Association Collection Development and Evaluation Section Readers' Advisory Committee, 2007, http://www.ala.org/ala/rusa/rusaourassoc/rusasections/codes/codessection/codescomm/codesreadadv/readersadvisory.htm; Morton Grove Public Library's Webrary, Reader's Corner, Fiction_L welcome page, 2007, http://www.webrary.org/rs/FLmenu.html; Kenneth D. Shearer, ed., *Guiding the Reader to the Next Book* (New York: Neal-Schuman, 1996).

8. Wayne Wiegand, "Missing the Real Story: Where Library and Information Science Fails the Profession," in *The Readers' Advisor's Companion,* ed. Kenneth D. Shearer and Robert Burgin (Englewood, Colo.: Libraries Unlimited, 2001), 8.

9. Green, "Personal Relations," 81.

10. Thomson Gale Catalog, *What Do I Read Next?* http://www.gale.com/servlet/ItemDetailServlet?region=9&imprint=000&titleCode=GAL10&type=4&id=111002; Bowker Library Support, *Fiction Connection,* 2007, http://bowkersupport.com/library/products/fc.htm; *Reader's Advisor Online,* product info page, 2007, http://rainfo.lu.com/product.aspx; American Library Association, *Booklist Online,* 2007, http://www.ala.org/ala/booklist/booklistonlinecom/booklistonline.htm.

11. Wayne A. Wiegand, "Librarians Ignore the Value of Stories," *Chronicle of Higher Education* 47, no. 9 (2002): B20; Jessica E. Moyer and Terry L. Weech, "The Education of Public Librarians to Serve Leisure Readers," *New Library World* 106, no. 1 (2005): 67–79.

12. Shearer and Burgin, *Readers' Advisor's Companion;* Burgin, *Nonfiction Reader's Advisory;* Catherine Sheldrick Ross, Lynne E. F. McKechnie, and Paulette M. Rothbauer, *Reading Matters: What the Research Reveals about Reading, Libraries, and Community* (Westport, Conn.: Libraries Unlimited, 2006); Dilevko and Macgowan, *Readers' Advisory Service.*

13. Robert Burgin, "Readers' Advisory in Public Libraries: An Overview of the Current Practice," in Shearer, *Guiding the Reader,* 71.

14. Donald Schon, *The Reflective Practitioner: How Professionals Think in Action* (New York: Basic Books, 1983), 68.

15. Neal Wyatt, "An RA Big Think," *Library Journal* 132, no. 12 (2007): 40–43.

2

ADULT READERS

Readers form the basis of everything we, as advisors, do. Without readers there could be no readers' advisory services. To best serve readers, we need to know about them and understand their needs and interests. Who are public library readers? What do we know about them? What do they want from libraries and advisory services? Above all, how can we best serve them? In this chapter, we focus on answering these questions.

RESEARCH REVIEW   BY JESSICA E. MOYER

Adult readers, reading habits, and reading interests form the basis of all the research reviewed in this chapter. Because this is such a broad area, there is a large amount of research. Also, adult readers in general have been studied for many years, in North America and in Europe, in and outside of library and information science. For the most part the studies included here are from fields of library and information science, since that research is likely to have the most useful information for readers' advisors. Additionally, most of the studies discussed below are fairly recent.

There are three excellent published literature reviews in this area. In 1996, L. Yu and A. O'Brien wrote on adult fiction librarianship for *Advances in Librarianship.* In 2005, I built on their work with a review of studies of readers and readers' advisory services from 1995 to 2003. In 2006, prominent reading researcher and library science faculty member Catherine Ross coauthored *Reading Matters,* a review of reading research as well as a summation of all her work on leisure readers.[1] All three of these works are reviewed below, along with other recent studies not otherwise included. Not reviewed here are publications about specific groups reviewed elsewhere in this book: nonfiction readers in chapter 3, youth and teen readers in chapter 5, adult book group readers in chapter 6, and romance and other genre readers in chapter 7.

"Domain of Adult Fiction Librarianship" and User Studies

User studies can be defined as any research project that attempts to define the members of a specific user community, their information needs, and the ways they meet their information needs. In this case, the user group is any group of adult fiction readers. Each of the studies described below attempts to define the group and to understand their information needs and ways they attempt to meet their needs, as well as the barriers that prevent them from satisfying their information needs.

Yu and O'Brien cover these types of studies published before 1996 in depth in section 4 of "Domain of Adult Fiction Librarianship: Understanding Fiction Readers." As they so aptly point out, "Although fiction dominates what people read for pleasure, the fiction reader . . . ha[s] remained a humble and fairly marginal topic in general reading studies up to the early 1980s. . . . The lack of understanding of fiction readers has hampered the development of fiction services in libraries." Although this situation had been somewhat remedied by 1996, with several important studies by David Spiller, Peter Mann, Barbara Jennings and Lyn Sear, and Deborah Goodall, Yu and O'Brien observe that the research is still a great deal more exploratory than explanatory (particularly a problem in the North American library and information science research) and that much of what has been done has flawed designs. They also note that there is a lack of theories in this area and that much of the research is not theoretically based.[2]

"One Reader Reading" and "Valuing Fiction," by Duncan Smith

Since 1996, several important user studies have been published. Duncan Smith's chapter in *Guiding the Reader to the Next Book* is a case study of a reader whom Smith studied for ten years during various research projects.[3] Smith's essay provides researchers with a personal look at a single reader who embodies many of the theories and research summarized in Yu and O'Brien's review. This is a valuable case study because it provides an ethnographic look at many of the conclusions from previous research. The reader prefers to read books by authors she knows, she frequently browses to choose new materials, specific books have had a lot of meaning for her, reading is a critical part of her life, and she derives a great deal of meaning from reading.

In 1998, Smith published a short article in *Booklist* in which he summarized the results of his research in training readers' advisors. For the past several years he had been videotaping readers talking about books they have enjoyed and responding to suggestions of specific titles. He found that a "deep and complex relationship exists between readers and their stories." "All readers rewrite every story they read . . . in other words, the reading of a novel is as much a creative act as the writing of it."[4]

"Value and Impact of Reading Imaginative Literature," by Bob Usherwood and Jackie Toyne

Usherwood and Toyne completed a study similar to Smith's for which they interviewed readers and conducted focus groups to determine the value of fiction reading in people's lives. Their "aim was to establish the significance of the reading experience and to uncover the common reasons which prompt people to spend time reading imaginative literature."[5] They found that the main reasons respondents cited for reading imaginative literature were escapism, which they found to be the most conscious perception of their need to read; relaxation, to relax as part of a relaxing time (vacation); escape from the present situation; escape into other worlds, which meant either becoming fully immersed into the other world or time in the text or actually becoming actively involved with the text (readers reported "becoming characters"); escape through association, in which readers read about something close to their current life; escape through aesthetic pleasure, that is, enjoying fiction, particularly literary fiction, as an art form; reading for instruction, where readers describe imaginative literature contributing to their learning and practical knowledge;[6] literacy skills; insight into other ways of life and other individuals; and reading as essential "food" for the imagination. Their final conclusion is that reading was a critical part of their readers' lives; no longer being able to read would be a crisis because reading is an important part of readers' identity and reading "forms and informs the developing self."[7]

"Finding without Seeking," by Catherine Ross

In "Finding without Seeking," Catherine Ross reports on a research project in which readers were interviewed about the ways reading affected their lives.[8] Although she reports many of the same results as Usherwood and Toyne and Smith, what makes her research interesting is that she centers her article around the theory of "incidental information acquisition" and sees fiction reading as an important source for this type of information. Ross's results come from 194 open-ended interviews conducted by herself and students in her classes. Students were instructed to pick a "heavy reader" of their choice and given interview instructions. Ross found that readers obtained valued information from the text, either in the form of the narrative speaking to their current situation in some way or by using texts to obtain understanding of an unknown situation. Ross also discusses the process of readers rewriting texts, which was also observed by Usherwood and Toyne. Readers described focusing on certain characters or events that were meaningful for them at that time. Other readers felt that wide and frequent reading would provide the needed information without active seeking.

Ross's readers also talked about books that changed their lives. Some could name a single book or books that really made a difference, and others felt that all the books they had read had affected them in some way. This agrees with Usherwood and Toyne's result that reading forms and informs personal identity. When readers did talk about a specific book, helpful responses were elicited as the conversation became focused on a single event. In the context of the transformative book, readers mentioned that the book opened them up to new experiences or perspectives. Other books reinforced the familiar and emphasized their own experiences. Another common response was about books from childhood that provided comfort and reassurance. Ross sets these results in seven categories and illustrates with examples from the interviews. More information about Ross's work can be found in an upcoming section of this Research Review, which reviews Ross's *Reading Matters* and her lengthy chapter on adult readers.

"Out on Loan," by Mark Norman

Mark Norman's "Out on Loan: A Survey of the Information Needs of Users of the Lesbian, Gay and Bisexual Collection of Brighton and Hove Libraries"[9] explores the information needs of this special group of users and finds that libraries are important to the users of the lesbian, gay, bisexual community. That community supports having separate collections, and it is possible that this centralized collection with focused reference sources and bibliographies was seeing increased use. Many of the users were using the library for recreational use, particularly for fiction. More than 90 percent of respondents reported using the library for pleasure reading, and gay and lesbian novels made up 68 percent and 38 percent, respectively, of items borrowed by users. This further validates the genrefication theories: users are able to find and borrow fiction items of interest because they are shelved together in a collection.

"A Practical Typology of Adult Fiction Borrowers Based on Their Reading Habits," by L. Yu and A. O'Brien

In this most theoretical study of readers, Yu and O'Brien develop a typology for fiction users based on short interviews with three hundred English readers over two months.[10] After mapping readers, Yu and O'Brien are able to reduce their results to seven types of readers: *Readers of particularism* are readers "whose reading scope was almost exclusively confined to books by a very small number of particular authors and whose reading tastes would change very little over time." *Readers of frequent literary pluralism* are those who "preferred literary fiction to recreational fiction and whose reading tastes could be fairly easily defined by the authors of types of books usually read." *Readers of infrequent literary pluralism* do not regularly select fiction, and when they do it tends to be literary fiction, usually of a specific author or type. *Readers of frequent recreational pluralism* generally prefer recreational fiction and generally read specific authors or types. *Readers of infrequent recreational pluralism* borrow rarely, but when they do they tend to read recreational books and "books by authors they knew or books of their type." *Readers of frequent universalism* read all types of books by many authors and borrow regularly, and *readers of infrequent universalism* read all types but borrow less often. Yu and O'Brien hope that their typology can be used by readers' advisors to better understand their patrons and provide better service.

International Studies

In recent years there have been several published studies of reading from all over the world, including a series undertaken by librarians in Russia and other former Soviet countries.[11] These studies provide a fascinating look into reading cultures quite different from those described above for North America and Western Europe. Instead of interviews or focus groups, most of the Eastern European articles are based on national user surveys and statistics collected from national library systems and booksellers, and so they provide particularly national views. For considerations of length and the general North American focus of this book, I do not review the international reading studies in depth here. To read about these articles, see my complete literature review in *Reference and User Services Quarterly*.[12]

"Adult Readers," by Catherine Ross

In this section we look in depth at chapter 4 of *Reading Matters*, "Adult Readers."[13] *Reading Matters* is both a compilation of Ross's own work and a thorough review of the research on reading and readers. Though *Reading Matters* focuses on library and information science research, Ross also includes relevant work from other fields, notably education and literacy. This inclusion of other research is just one of many reasons *Reading Matters* is the most important publication about adult readers. The reason for its heavy emphasis in this research review is that Ross has been and continues to be one of the most outstanding researchers of adult readers, and this book represents all her work on adult readers over her career. Ross's work in reading research has consistently been of great importance to readers' advisors, and this book is no exception.

"Adult Readers" is a complete review of reading and reader research through 2004. At the end of each of its nine substantial sections, Ross includes a recommended reading list in addition to her extensive notes and references, guiding the novice researcher to the best and most comprehensive works in each area. Below I discuss the sections that deal most directly with understanding readers and would be of most benefit to advisors.

"THE WHO, WHAT, WHY, WHERE, WHEN OF READING"

Section 4.1 of Ross's book focuses on large-scale surveys of readers in the United States and Europe, ranging from the early twentieth century to the early twenty-first. Over time, these surveys have consistently found that around 50 percent or more of the population reads regularly and 10–15 percent are avid readers. Women consistently read more than men, occupation is more important than age when it comes to predicting reading habits, and education is the most robust indicator. Interestingly, people in the U.S. West read more than those in the East, and northern Europeans read more than southern Europeans. Ross not only reports these results but discusses their various sources and the issues related to each study.

Ross goes on to discuss several early reading research studies by Waples, Strang, and Ennis, making this section a valuable resource for librarians interested in understanding the history of reading research and the way it relates to current studies, such as those by the Book Industry Study Group. The most recent and international study Ross reports on is the "Reading the Situation" study commissioned by the Library and Information Commission in the United Kingdom in 2000. Ross emphasizes the shallow and limited nature of survey data (few get at the question of why) and concludes with a case study of readers from a book group, three points of "Research Tells Us," and the extremely useful "What Libraries Can Do." In this case, Ross concludes that accessibility of all types of materials (not just books) is one of the most important things libraries can provide to encourage reading.

"THE READING EXPERIENCE"

To get at the real reasons people read, beyond the limited data of survey results, Ross's section 4.2 focuses on case studies of real readers reading. She begins by reviewing books about reading, such as *Ruined by Reading*, by Lynne Schwartz.[14] Ross extracts seven themes from these studies of readers: Effortlessness, Joy, Surrendering to the Book, Emotional Dimension of Reading, Living in a Chosen World, Places for Reading, and Delight in Language. In addition, she includes a section on frustrated readers. This single case study does an excellent job of enumerating the difficulties less fluent readers face, difficulties that may be nearly incomprehensible to regular readers (and librarians). Ross recommends that libraries make a special effort to match readers with books at their reading level—noting that, unlike schools, libraries are not required to make judgments about reading abilities and can give frustrated readers the experience of success.

"WHAT ROLE DOES READING PLAY IN THE LIFE OF THE READER?"

For many readers, reading provides something they cannot get any other way, and reading becomes an essential part of their lives. The idea of losing the ability to read is terrifying to most avid readers, because it is such a critical part of their identity. Reading is also the preferred way for avid readers to learn new information. Reading is also very personal; the connection between the book and the reader can be difficult to predict and can change over time. Yet that connection is how many readers create an identity from reading. "Readers use the text to create a story about themselves," Ross writes in section 4.3. "They read themselves into the story and then read the story into their lives, which then becomes a part of them." For many, reading is a gateway into new perspectives and eventually into a discovery of their own identity: "Readers make sense of the text in terms of their own identity themes."[15] Most important for readers' advisors, Ross concludes that each reader's experience is personal and changeable, based on his or her current situation and mood. Each reader experiences a book uniquely on the basis of personal experience, current mood, and identity—all factors that should be considered by advisors.

Delving further into the issue of reading and identity, Ross comments that "books provide models, examples to follow or rules to live by. Readers report that reading changes their beliefs, attitudes, or pictures of the world, which in turn alters the way they choose to live their lives after the book is closed." Ross finds that most readers, regardless of what they choose to read, have this type of experience at some point in their reading lives. Readers also read to connect with others and alleviate feelings of being alone in the world. Most readers are able to find characters in books with whom they can identify, especially when those kinds of people are not available in their daily lives. Readers relate no longer feeling like "an ugly duckling" after connecting with a character in a book.[16] Reading can also serve as reassurance, comfort, or consolation in times of stress or illness. Readers seek out favorite books that will provide a familiar, comforting reading experience, often choosing books from childhood or a book such as a series romance or other formulaic genre fiction that is both predictable and has a known ending. Again, Ross concludes this section with an excerpt from an interview, this time with one of the most committed readers in her study.

"BETTER THAN LIFE"

Ross takes her section 4.4 title from the 1992 French book *Better Than Life*, by Daniel Pennac, and this section discusses negative aspects of reading. Many readers report feeling guilt about reading too much, especially that it is keeping them from other things they should be doing, such as housework or "real life." Many readers feel resentment from nonreaders, especially when close friends or family members are the nonreaders and are jealous of the time their loved one spends reading, which they consider a solitary activity. Ross notes that Radway found this same result in her studies of romance readers. Reading can take up precious resources of time, money, attention, and even space for book collections that can cause rifts between readers and nonreaders. Ross concludes with a case study of an avid reader discussing her feelings about reading: "I think it is something that can set up barriers between people . . . an intentional barrier. And sometimes, even when you don't intend it to be [others] don't understand that you can be just relaxing and it's okay to interrupt. . . . And so it becomes a barrier." This reader concludes by saying, "It's a double edged sword. . . . [I] read to avoid being lonely. And yet, again, perhaps that's keeping me from forcing myself to go out and meet people."[17]

"READING HIGH AND LOW"

In section 4.5, Ross covers the "quality versus trash" reading debate along with lamentations over the decline of modern literature. She shows that this debate has been going on as long as there has been leisure reading and that the arguments made in the nineteenth century against popular novels are much the same as they are in the modern age. Most important for librarians in this section is that some readers feel anxiety about reading the "best books" and have a strong desire to own or know about them. Both the Oprah Book Club and the Book of the Month Club (studied by Radway) fed this "middlebrow anxiety" to read important literature. And now, as it has been in the past, most of what people read is popular and a product of popular culture. Libraries and advisors need to make sure they are not conveying to their readers any messages about the relative importance or value of some library collections over others. We consider this issue in chapter 7 in the context of romance and genre readers (the popular fiction most often derided as trash) and in chapter 11 in terms of collection development.

"BESTSELLERS, PRIZES, LISTS, AND THE MANUFACTURE OF TASTE"

Section 4.6 is closely related to section 4.5 with its focus on best sellers and best-seller lists. Ross discusses the development of best-seller lists and the role they play in modern society. Most important for better understanding readers is that most readers read best sellers, whether purchased at the bookstore or borrowed in the library. Advisors need to be prepared to work with readers who enjoy reading best sellers. Ross suggests having prepared lists of read-alikes for best sellers with long hold lists as well as lists for readers who have read everything by their favorite author and do not know what else to read. Ross suggests that advisors create lists or displays of "great books" or classics with known appeal for readers who have a desire to read "the right books."

"HOW DO ADULT READERS CHOOSE BOOKS TO READ?"

In section 4.7, Ross focuses on the critical moment in reading, the selection of the next book. Other than using best sellers and other lists, how do readers select books? Few readers actually read "just anything"; many have quite a few limitations on the books they enjoy. In reviewing the literature and her own work with avid readers, Ross proposes several themes and strategies that make up the book selection process.

For some readers, this process is more difficult, particularly those new to reading. "This is the 'difficulty-getting-into-it' problem. As with any learned skill, a task that an old hand finds easy can be daunting for a novice."[18] Newer readers know less about authors, titles, and genres and thus are worse at predicting whether they will enjoy a book. Many experience repeated failures and utilize browsing as their most common strategy (see more on browsing in chapter 10 of this book).

As is no surprise, Ross finds that "success breeds success." Readers who find books they enjoy can more easily locate more books that fit their criteria. Readers who experience repeated failures in book selection may be entirely put off from leisure reading, thinking that there is nothing out there they will enjoy. Readers can get frustrated with spending time to pick and start reading a book they end up not enjoying.

What strategies do successful readers employ? Confident readers have many successful strategies. Mood is key to many readers and is the initial influence in the reading selection process. For avid and confident readers the selection process is complicated, but it includes three main factors: previous experience and knowledge of books and authors (e.g., interpreting cover art), information from reviews or other mentions in popular media, and trusted sources of recommendations. Additionally, readers prefer known and trusted authors and favorite genres. Ease of access is the final step in the selection process: "The likelihood of a reader's choosing a particular book can be regarded as a ratio of the degree of pleasure expected from the book divided by the degree of work needed to appropriate, physically and mentally, the book."[19]

New Publications

READING AND READER DEVELOPMENT, BY JUDITH ELKIN, BRIONY TRAIN, AND DEBBIE DENHAM

Several other recent publications not included in *Reading Matters* or my *Reference and User Services Quarterly* literature review deserve discussion.

This recent U.K. publication by Elkin, Train, and Denham seems to have slipped under the radar of many North American librarians and researchers. Similar to the books edited by Shearer and Ross, *Reading and Reader Development* is an important contribution to readers' advisory studies. Chapter 1, "The Reader," provides an introduction to the book and an overview of the world of reading research as it was in 2003.[20] Elkin draws in a wide variety of research, from Ross to Radway, as well as venturing into popular culture and the literary world for more views on readers and reading. Because of the lack of emphasis on research grounded in library and information science, this chapter is of limited interest to readers' advisors, and its most important conclusions are included in Ross and elsewhere. It is, however, worth checking out for its European view of reading, since too rarely do North American librarians consider research and publications from across the Atlantic.

READING AND THE REFERENCE LIBRARIAN, BY JURIS DILEVKO AND LISA GOTTLIEB

Reading and the Reference Librarian was published in 2004, and because most of the book studies academic librarians it is usually not included in reviews or discussions of readers' advisory research.[21] Its results are, however, still very relevant to readers' advisory services and say something important about the role of reading in our daily lives. One of the tenets of readers' advisory is that to be a good advisor one must be well read in a variety of genres of popular fiction. Dilevko and Gottlieb conclude that those who consider themselves the best librarians, whether public or academic, are the ones who are well read. Most librarians who read regularly and from a variety of sources feel not only that they are more successful in their jobs but that without reading they would be unable to do their jobs well. Interestingly, the type of reading material does not matter; librarians who read popular fiction respond in much the same way as librarians who read other types of materials such as newspapers, popular culture magazines, or web pages. If it is so important that librarians read, then it is even more important that we understand the role leisure reading plays in our lives and the lives of our patrons.

"LEARNING FROM LEISURE READING," BY JESSICA E. MOYER

This most recent study of readers was published in *Reference and User Services Quarterly* in summer 2007.[22] "Learning from Leisure Reading" is a study of educational and recreational outcomes of leisure reading of adult public library patrons. The purpose of this study was to look further at what, in terms of education, readers get from leisure reading materials, by asking the readers themselves about educational outcomes during leisure reading experiences. One of the ideas investigated in this project is the concept of a single book or reading experience serving multiple purposes. Keeping books that are traditionally marketed as leisure reading materials in mind, it appears that, although a book may serve the primary purpose of leisure reading material, it may also serve a secondary purpose as an educational tool. For some people this secondary role may be of great significance. This is important for librarians to understand because to be able to suggest leisure reading materials they must understand the potential multiple purposes a leisure book may serve.

One contribution of this article is its inclusion of incidental information acquisition theory, which had previously been used to study leisure readers only by Ross in "Finding without Seeking." There are a limited number of theories related to education and leisure reading, and most of those relevant to this study come from studies of information-seeking behavior. The most applicable concept for this research is incidental information acquisition. In this study, incidental information acquisition is defined as information gathered from leisure reading material that at some point becomes useful to the reader and results in some type of learning experience (educational outcome). The gathering of information is not done purposefully, nor does the reader generally have an immediate need for the information; instead, he or she sees it as something that may become useful at some later point in life. In this study, readers were asked only about information seeking as an aspect of leisure reading. In this way they talked about an activity with a specific purpose (leisure reading) whose primary goal was not purposeful information seeking.

Four categories of educational outcomes became apparent in this study:

1. *People and relationships.* This category was important to many of the respondents. It includes learning more about yourself, learning about others, learning how to understand/empathize/interact with other people, gaining insight into your and others' relationships, and generally helping with personal problems. It also includes learning more about your own faith/religion as well as that of other people. Results showed that readers could learn about themselves and others from any type of reading experience.

2. *Other countries, cultures, and time periods.* Along with countries, cultures, and time periods, this category included relating what had been read to news stories. This was a popular outcome, and historical fiction was the genre most associated with this area. Titles mentioned by respondents

included the Flashman series by George McDonald Fraser for learning
about Victorian England and the various parts of the British empire and
Tony Hillerman's mysteries for learning about the Four Corners area in
the modern-day American Southwest.

3. *Enriches life.* This category encompasses the more abstract aspects of
the reading experience and was largely created from the interview results
as respondents talked in general about the value of reading. Aspects of
value include reading leading to having a livelier mind, increasing "literary IQ," sparking the imagination, making one want to learn more about
something read, leading to other reading, and increasing learning in general. Many participants talked about reading a fiction book that then led
them to read nonfiction books on a similar subject. Respondents spoke
of feeling that reading just made them smarter, better people. A common
example was increasing vocabulary and familiarity with certain words,
just by reading them over and over in different books. Reading, they felt,
is essential for personal growth and development; without reading, their
minds would stagnate. One subject thought that reading was necessary
to her development as a writer, that without reading regularly she could
never really become a good writer. Overall, reading, even reading books
that could be categorized as "fluff" or "escapist," was thought to have
some educational value and to fill readers' needs for lifelong learning and
education.

4. *Different perspectives.* This was a frequently mentioned category
that crossed through all respondents and all genres. It includes learning
about different perspectives, whether understanding people of a different race, class, or culture within the United States or getting a different
perspective on a political problem or world event by reading about the
people involved in it. Also mentioned among responses in this category
were having assumptions challenged and being moved to think in a different way or think about something that respondents had not previously
considered. This category is closely related to both people and other countries and cultures, and many of the examples given from those categories
also crossed over into this area, but it is distinct because it was repeatedly
emphasized by all respondents. Ross also uses this category in "Finding
without Seeking"; it seems to be of universal importance to readers.

Clearly, readers value educational outcomes from a leisure reading
experience, even though the educational outcome is not likely to be the
primary reason for choosing a particular book. It was important enough
to the respondents in this study to have a fairly large influence on their
reading experience. In terms of readers' advisory services, these results

should affect the way librarians interact with readers. With educational outcomes most often serving a secondary role in the leisure reading experience, readers may not be able to describe their significance to staff, but they are still a factor to be taken into account. Advisors will likely need to ask readers about the importance and type of educational outcomes they value in their reading experiences. The four categories described above can serve as conversation starters.

The importance of educational outcomes is not limited to the one-on-one readers' advisory interview; they should be taken into account for other types of readers' advisory situations. Staff conducting booktalks or writing reviews could highlight some of the educational outcomes in specific books. New read-alike lists could be oriented to support different outcomes. Most important, we need to remember that the more we can talk to our readers and learn about them, the better we can suggest titles.

LIBRARIAN'S VIEW   BY JANE JORGENSON

Public libraries in the twenty-first century have to be a lot of things to a lot of people. We are the last outpost for those who don't have access to the digital universe, an educational resource for reference and research purposes, a community gathering place and the providers of mass media entertainment, and a whole host of other things. As we spread ourselves ever thinner to meet the varied demands of an ever-changing public, one of the things that moves further down the list is our basic role of providing leisure reading material. Whether because of shrinking budgets or the distraction of technology, we are in danger of losing sight of books—our name brand item.[23]

In *Reading Matters,* Catherine Ross lays out several points about reading and readers that are essential for librarians to consider. First and foremost is the radical idea that reading for leisure purposes is not only a luxury, it is a necessity. "To lack literacy skills means being shut out of jobs and opportunities, conversely, being able to read and write is a ticket to ride."[24] Ross argues that to be proficient at anything takes practice. If you accept that premise, then you can agree that the only way to become proficient at

Jane Jorgenson is the home services coordinator at Madison (Wisconsin) Public Library, where she also edits the book review blog MADreads *and leads the team that created a paper and online readers' advisory service. She also teaches for the distance education program at the University of Wisconsin–SLIS.*

reading is to read. And, as any reading instructor will tell you, people learning to read practice far more often if they enjoy what they are reading.

The theory seems stunning for its simple common sense, and yet it is
something libraries have always struggled with. For as long as there have
been public libraries, librarians have debated about which materials to collect. On one side of the debate is the argument that the library is a type of
continuing education facility for people and thus should stock its shelves
with "good" books. On the other side it is argued that we should listen to
our customers and meet the demand. The problem with the debate is not
in determining which side is correct, it is in giving both sides equal support for their defense so that the debate can be honestly joined.

What the research does is even the sides. Traditionally librarians arguing for the inclusion of reading materials that are meant to be leisure or
entertainment vehicles had to rely solely on the theory that they were giving people what they want. Ross's research changes that. Valuing reading
for its own sake not only provides avid readers with more scope, it also
helps frustrated or reluctant or out-of-practice customers with the literary
proficiency they need to make it in a highly literate world. So the most
important thing we can do for readers is to inform ourselves by studying
the research.

In library school and on the job in a public library, the first thing they
tell us about helping readers is to be readers. We are instructed to read,
read, read. Read books across genres, read the reference books about the
genres, read the reviews about all those books, and when we have a little
extra time read some more. All perfectly valid. What is missing in all that
reading is the analysis and research about readers and reading (or nonreaders). Can we truly understand our patrons without being aware of
reading research? With reading research most often published in scholarly periodicals and as serious-looking library school texts, our study of
research is too often finished the minute we leave library school (if we even
do it there), and we miss out, especially on some of the new and exciting
research like *Reading Matters*. Research into readers and reading generally
offers three aspects: interesting or useful data, a measure of common sense
(as illustrated by Ross's argument), and, if we're lucky, a whole new way
of looking at our constituencies and how we are serving them. All of these
are important for us if we are truly to become better and more professional
readers' advisors.

This is not to suggest that what we already do read is less meaningful.
In fact, in day-to-day library service and on busy frontline desks, genre
guides and readers' advisory tools of all kinds are practical and irreplace-

able. Without these tools, many librarians would be lost when trying to help the customer standing in front of them asking for a recommendation of a "good book" or for more books like the *No. 1 Ladies Detective Agency*, by Alexander McCall Smith. What these sources don't do is inform our behavior when it comes to the bigger issues: Where will the library be in five or ten years? What could we be doing in broader terms to satisfy our common mission and, should the digital age completely overtake us, thrive or even survive? Reader research does not answer these questions directly. But it can demonstrate broader patterns of reading behavior that will help us refine our service right now and decide where we should spend our energy and dollars for the future. It will also help us understand our patrons and ourselves as readers.

Much of what we know about our customers and the usage of public libraries across the country is based on circulation numbers. We know how much has been checked out and from where. We can tell if people are using our catalogs to place holds on materials and if they pick those holds up. From year to year we have concrete numbers that can tell us if people are using our services more or less. And those numbers are used in communities to convince the powers that be to maintain their library budget or, in some lucky cases, to increase their budget.

What those numbers do not tell us is anything about what our users are reading, or why they are reading it, or where else they might be getting leisure reading materials, or what our collections might be lacking. All of these are important questions. We do not want to violate anyone's privacy by keeping track of what they check out. That being said, the data we do have are not always synthesized as fully as they could be. As Yu and O'Brien point out, "A wealth of information exists, based on demographic and other quantitative data, as well as a lot of professional experience, but often the outcomes have been understood and applied in a fairly shallow way."[25] This is where the research comes in. The wealth of data and anecdotal evidence we can get from the research can be incorporated into the broader backdrop of what libraries do. If we are aware of what the research is telling us at an organizational level, we are much more prepared when it comes to the day-to-day work of helping readers. Research can be put to use in marketing, collection development, or even dealing with boards and the other organizations with whom we work. What city council doesn't like data?

So what does the research tell us? Whether we accept the seven typologies of readers as proposed by Yu and O'Brien, or merely study the range of personal interviews ranging from frustrated to avid readers in Ross's book, or learn how reading patterns changed in Russia after the fall of communism, we can't help but understand the importance of reading in our customers' lives. Once we have gotten that point, the next step is to put the knowledge to concrete use in our libraries.

If we accept what the research shows and the idea that reading is a good thing in and of itself, our next step is to examine how that fact will play into our patterns of behavior as advisors. In her discussion of adult readers, Ross examines the role of hierarchies put in place by any number of learned people (including librarians) on books and reading.[26] We all know the thought processes here—in fact, they have been around as long as books have. There are books that constitute worthy reading and there are those that don't. Literature versus trash. Even readers make these distinctions when describing what they read. How often have you had a customer ask for the latest Nora Roberts and then defensively explain that he is just looking for a little escapist reading or, conversely, had someone tell you she doesn't read trash—she wants "good" books? These hierarchies are so pervasive as to be almost inescapable.

As public librarians our job is to serve readers of all levels and tastes at all times. The first step in avoiding the hierarchy trap is to examine our collection development policies. Only library staff (and to some extent the public) decide what goes on library shelves. Only after books arrive on the shelves can they attract readers. Bearing in mind what the reading research has shown, we should think about what we are collecting and how accessible it is for our customers. Leaving aside different formats (addressed a little later), what is the best way to serve a reading population that ranges from nonreading to avid readers? That's a pretty wide range, and none of them can be discounted. We cannot forget the avid readers because they are our core, our bread and butter, our primary constituents—nor can we neglect the nonreaders or reluctant/frustrated readers, because they may be the ones who need us most. The choices made in selecting, cataloging, and shelving have concrete consequences. And only in reading and understanding reading and reader research can we be sure that our collections are serving the full range of readers.

Ross suggests that we "take a good look at how popular materials are being treated in public libraries, especially types of books that historically have been denigrated. Is there anything about the way romance books or westerns are catalogued or shelved that could give readers the message that these genres are considered second-class citizens, barely tolerated?"[27] But let's take a step further and examine the allocation of funds for these collections. Can we do a better job budgeting money for collecting and cataloging items that would be ranked at the lower end of the reading hierarchy? What is now at the bottom? Is it westerns and romances, or has the ranking changed to place manga and graphic novels in the bottom tier? Budget allocations should match the actual popularity of collections, not what some library staff think should be circulating. Frustrated readers may seek out the "lower" texts on the hierarchical scale because those are the books that are accessible to them. Our decisions about these collections before the books even make it to the shelves can make or break the library in these readers' minds. This is not just a case of "give 'em what they want"; more accurately, it is giving them what they need. If we don't do it, then they will go elsewhere. And if we do provide materials for frustrated readers or nonreaders, they may end up becoming lifelong readers and library supporters.

The next big question is format: hardcover, paperback, tape, CD, VHS, DVD, MP3—which do libraries provide? I would certainly agree that public libraries have been willing to provide a variety of formats. We have offered everything from braille to MP3s, with recent expansions into digital and downloadable options. But too often libraries find themselves either playing catch-up (e-book readers, anyone?) or jumping in because it's the newest, coolest gadget (Library 2.0's many incarnations). Neither option is all bad or all good. What rushing in or the slow dipping of a toe in the already cooling water have in common is that they are both reactive. And what public libraries need falls somewhere in between the two extremes. Our budgets will always be tight, so reactive purchasing of different formats is the last thing we should be doing. Someone has to do the groundbreaking with any format, but just because something comes in a new format doesn't make it an automatic purchase for your library. Conversely, just because it's a new format doesn't make it something to pass up until it has been time-tested.

Where between those two extremes does the answer lie? I don't have the answer. What I do suggest is that, first and foremost, libraries spend more time, and money, working on the answer in an ongoing way. How often does your library update its collection development policy? Most of us are busy, I know that. But given the fact that formats are changing so rapidly, can we really afford to look at the policy once every five years or so? What if, instead, libraries had teams established to keep track of the new formats, web applications, and the like? Though budgets are shrinking, the money spent to give staff a little time to study in a proactive way new formats and possibilities would pay off in the long run by making sure your collection money was well spent.

Most recently much of the debate has focused on electronic formats. How do libraries decide? The research can help. A recent trend in our everyday, practice-oriented library literature is about a current generation of readers who won't read anything not in a digital format. Not so, according to Ziming Liu's research. Although Liu did find that online reading behavior is different than print—more skimming and scanning rather then in-depth reading—he also found that the overwhelming majority of readers in the study preferred print to digital in certain cases. Readers in an online environment tend to read only the first screen of text unless they want to read a full article or text. If they want to read in depth, they print it out.[28] Liu's research proves wrong our assumptions about who our readers are and what their preferences are. In the end, being aware of research like Liu's may be more important than relying on anecdotal feedback or assumptions about your patrons.

Once we have collected the materials (and formats), the next step for our customers is being able to find books they want to read. When I was just out of high school, I got a job in a local shoe store selling shoes. Though having the willingness to talk shoes with the customers was key, the best sales tip I learned was to limit the number of pairs I showed a customer. If I could keep their choices to five pairs or less, I was much more likely to make the sale. The same has held true in my bookstore job and at the library. Customers who are given too many choices become overwhelmed or, as Ross's research has found, overloaded.[29]

To a novice reader, a library can be an overwhelming prospect. And though we do what we can with the Dewey Decimal System and genre sections, readers' success is still dependent on their ability to browse these still large collections or find ways to eliminate large sections easily. Think about how well displays generally do or what happens when you put a cart of recently returned materials in a public space. Readers, especially those who visit the library less frequently, gravitate to these smaller, more manageable collections when looking for leisure reading materials. How might the collection be divided even further? And how can we make those who may be intimidated by the scope of our collections more successful in their quest? Sharon Baker did pioneering work in this area in the 1980s, and the integration of her research into current library practice is seen in the increasing presence of displays and small collections, but we still have a ways to go. Without Baker's work we would never even know this was a problem for readers.

According to Ross,

> Inexperienced book selectors who don't have a store of books and authors in their heads and don't know much about genres are also the least likely, when browsing, to find books that interest them. This is a problem because, while practiced readers are willing to tolerate the occasional dud, novice readers give up, not just on the particular book but on reading in general. The successful choosers become more successful and the unsuccessful stop trying.[30]

Displays are one way to help readers make choices. Others include annotated book lists and something we have shied away from that is an invaluable help to readers, recommendations. Imposing our taste on readers who are seeking advice has been discouraged by the profession, with the frequent admonition to suggest, not recommend. But when it comes to reading, one of the most commonly cited resources for readers is personal recommendations.[31] Among those whom readers trust to provide recommendations are librarians. Use that to your customers' advantage and as a way to break out more of the collection for browsing. Just like in bookstores, staff picks can be one of your best long-term displays.

In recent years more experienced users and librarians have had access to book databases like *NoveList* or the *Reader's Advisor Online*. These databases have made it easier for staff and readers to find new books and make more informed reading choices. Increasing remote access to these tools and to library OPACs has made it easier for avid patrons to have more access to library collections and resources. If, for example, a book is mentioned on *The Daily Show*, think how many holds are already in the system when the library opens in the morning. For the avid reader in particular, these resources have been of particular benefit. Looking up a favorite author and getting other reading suggestions within seconds can't be beat. And as technology improves, these databases can only get better. And that is wonderful.

What is not so wonderful are the readers left behind when we rely on these resources. If readers are intimidated by the overwhelming size of the collections in the library, how much more overwhelmed will they be by a database? And as great as some of these tools are, many of them have a learning curve that is too much for less technologically inclined readers. Keeping this in mind helps us temper some of our excitement.

So, although these tools are incredibly helpful, they cannot replace a book in the hand or an in-person interaction with a knowledgeable staff person. Most important, we cannot forget that sometimes talking about books with another person can be what a reader really needs. One of the greatest joys of reading a great book can be the chance to talk about that experience with another person. Librarians need to remember that sometimes we just need to listen.

How important are staff to the library experience? Usherwood and Toyne's study of reading on individuals and communities explored this and some other important questions. They found that leisure reading contributed to "a greater general awareness, language acquisition . . . and also personal self-development." But their study also showed that library staff could sometimes be a barrier to readers hunting for the imaginative literature they wanted to read. Not only did they find libraries intimidating, but in some cases staff attitudes put them off the library. Once again, staff can be both a barrier and a facilitator between readers and books.[32]

Though some of those surveyed by Usherwood and Toyne found staff to be intimidating, others thought that libraries needed "to offer more guidance to users to ensure that inexperienced readers secured a good read."[33] Enter the knowledgeable staff person. For all the money we might put into our collections and facilities and our databases or other readers' advisory resources, the most useful, powerful thing the public library has going for it is the staff.

Training staff to deal with the broad range of readers they will meet is often a neglected facet of staff development in readers' advisory services. A recent discussion on the PUBLIB reading list explored the idea of core competencies for staff helping people with basic computer questions. The same concept could be put to use as part of a reader development plan. Knowing that your library subscribes to *NoveList* or being able to point *Genreflecting* out on the shelf is not sufficient training. Libraries need to invest in their staff and their product by better preparing them to utilize these tools. Most of us have to learn our way around new resources on the fly because many libraries do not have training budgets—which is in fact counterintuitive. If libraries are spending thousands of dollars for a database (or hundreds of dollars on readers' advisory texts) that does not get used because of a lack of staff knowledge and experience, then what is the point of having it? We make those tools more cost-effective if we provide training at the front end rather than leave it to the librarians to make their way. Training sessions with knowledgeable instructors are key. With the advent of OPAL and other online instruction software, training can happen as and when the staff needs it. Additionally, management should keep abreast of what library schools are doing. Many are now offering continuing education courses online and allow students to do the work when it fits into their schedules. As research demonstrates, readers come in different stages. Being able to find the newest book by Grisham for the avid seeker is not going to help the inexperienced reader when they ask for help. By fully training staff, libraries can better meet the needs of all readers.

Elkin, Train, and Denham explain that the skills needed in readers' advisory "are a mixture of professional and personal skills, including self-confidence and respect for individuals—whatever their background or reading needs; communications skills; book knowledge; promotional skills; enthusiasm and commitment."[34] Training staff with the ability to be flexible and having an arsenal of tools that is diverse are crucial to helping the broad spectrum of readers who walk through our door—and these resources take time and planning.

Trained staff, varied collections, and good resources will be parts of any reader development plan your library creates to address the customers who walk through the door. But keep in mind the idea that the plan should also consider those readers who don't walk through the door and the ways the library can reach them. Though tight budgets make outreach difficult, libraries can partner with other agencies to stretch their dollars and spread the reading wealth. Local literacy groups are a way to reach inexperienced readers, and booktalks for local book groups are a way to reach others.

Traditionally we have thought of outreach as requiring staff to leave the building or having groups come in to work with us. Both of those are still valid and, in fact, desired. But public libraries should also explore using digital means to reach readers. The *BookLetters* newsletter service, Cincinnati Public Library's *Turning the Page,* or Madison Public Library's *MADreads* review blogs provide those all-important recommendations readers crave.[35] Williamsburg Regional Library is reaching out to readers electronically with their new web-based readers' advisory service, *Looking for a Good Book?* Readers complete the online questionnaire, and library staff make reading suggestions based on the answers provided.[36] The Williamsburg website also has a blog with daily librarian suggestions, taking the staff picks concept to the Web. As technology continues to make leaps forward, the electronic possibilities for outreach will increase. Though we don't have to jump at every wiki and podcast, being aware of the possibilities can only improve our chances of reaching those who might not otherwise use their public library.

In the summary of their book, Elkin, Train, and Denham explain the value of reading to readers.

> Readers of all kinds feel that reading has made a difference to their individual lives. . . . Reading can educate, inform, help to develop language and vocabulary, and enrich the imagination. Reading can be life enhancing, health enhancing, stress relieving and therapeutic. Reading can bring freedom, empowerment and personal development.[37]

Pretty powerful statements. And almost all of them could be applied to the power of the research into reading and how it can affect our views and abilities as public librarians.

NOTES

1. L. Yu and A. O'Brien, "Domain of Adult Fiction Librarianship: Understanding Fiction Readers," *Advances in Librarianship* 20 (1996): 151–89; Jessica E. Moyer, "Adult Fiction Reading: A Literature Review of Readers' Advisory Services, Adult Fiction Librarianship, and Fiction Readers," *Reference and User Services Quarterly* 44, no. 3 (2005): 220–31; Catherine Sheldrick Ross, Lynne E. F. McKechnie, and Paulette M. Rothbauer, *Reading Matters: What the Research Reveals about Reading, Libraries, and Community* (Westport, Conn.: Libraries Unlimited, 2006).

2. Yu and O'Brien, "Domain," 157–62.

3. Duncan Smith, "One Reader Reading," in *Guiding the Reader to the Next Book*, ed. Kenneth D. Shearer (New York: Neal-Schuman, 1996), 45–70.

4. Duncan Smith, "Valuing Fiction," *Booklist* 94, no. 13 (1998): 1094–95.

5. Bob Usherwood and Jackie Toyne, "The Value and Impact of Reading Imaginative Literature," *Journal of Librarianship and Information Science* 34, no. 1 (2002): 33–41, quote from 34; see also Usherwood and Toyne, "Reading the Warning Signs: Library Book Reading Research," *Public Library Journal* 15, no. 4 (2000): 112–14.

6. This idea is elaborated in Catherine Sheldrick Ross, "Finding without Seeking: What Readers Say about the Role of Pleasure Reading as a Source of Information," *Australasian Public Libraries and Information Services* 13, no. 2 (2000): 72–80.

7. Usherwood and Toyne, "Value and Impact," 34–40.

8. Ross, "Finding without Seeking," 72–80. Incidental information acquisition theory is also described in Kristy Williamson, "Discovered by Chance: The Role of Incidental Information Acquisition in an Ecological Model of Information Use," *Library and Information Science Research* 20, no. 1 (1998): 23–40; and Sandra Erdelez, "Information Encountering: A Conceptual Framework for Accidental Information Discovery," in *Information Seeking in Context: Proceedings of an International Conference on Research in Information Needs, Seeking and Use in Different Contexts*, ed. P. Vakkari et al. (London: Taylor Graham, 1997), 412–21.

9. Mark Norman, "Out on Loan: A Survey of the Information Needs of Users of the Lesbian, Gay and Bisexual Collection of the Brighton and Hove Libraries," *Journal of Librarianship and Information Science* 31, no. 4 (1999): 188–96.

10. L. Yu and A. O'Brien, "A Practical Typology of Adult Fiction Borrowers Based on Their Reading Habits," *Journal of Information Science* 25, no. 1 (1999): 35–49.

11. Ales Haman, "Reading in Czechoslovakia 1989–1991: A Survey of the Public's Reception of Works of Fiction," *International Information and Library Review* 27, no. 1 (1995): 75–87; Jadwiga Kolodziejska, "Reading and Libraries in Poland Today: Between Romantic Traditionalism and the Free Market," *International Information and Library Review* 27, no. 1 (1995): 47–57; Aira Lepik, "Readers and Reading in Changing Estonia," *International Information and Library Review* 27, no. 1 (1995): 25–36; Zhanat Abaevna Beisembaeva, "Reading in Kazakhstan," *International Information and Library Review* 27, no. 1 (1995): 37–46; V. D. Stelmakh, "Russian Reading in a Period of Social and Cultural Change," *International Information and Library Review* 27, no. 1 (1995): 7–23; Lucy Charlewood, "Book Preferences, Conceptions of Books and Reading Practices among Urban Adults with a Basic Level of Literacy," *African Research and Documentation* 83 (2000): 61–73; N. J. Opoku-Agyemang, "Reading Love Stories by Women from Ghana," *African Research and Documentation* 83 (2000): 49–60.

12. Moyer, "Adult Fiction Reading."

13. Catherine Sheldrick Ross, "Adult Readers," in Ross, McKechnie, and Rothbauer, *Reading Matters*, 133–221.

14. Lynne Schwartz, *Ruined by Reading: A Life in Books* (New York: Houghton Mifflin, 1996).

15. Ross, "Adult Readers," 165–67.

16. Ibid., 167–68.

17. Ibid., 173, 177–79.

18. Ibid., 198.

19. Ibid., 204.

20. Judith Elkin, "The Reader," in *Reading and Reader Development: The Pleasure of Reading,* by Judith Elkin, Briony Train, and Debbie Denham (London: Facet, 2003), 1–29.

21. Juris Dilevko and Lisa Gottlieb, *Reading and the Reference Librarian: The Importance to Library Service of Staff Reading Habits* (Jefferson, N.C.: McFarland, 2004).

22. Jessica E. Moyer, "Learning from Leisure Reading: A Study of Adult Public Library Patrons," *Reference and User Services Quarterly* 46, no. 4 (2007): 69–82.

23. Cathy De Rosa et al., *Perceptions of Libraries and Information Resources* (Dublin, Ohio: OCLC, 2005). Available online at http://www.oclc.org/reports/2005perceptions.htm.

24. Ross, "The Company of Readers," in Ross, McKechnie, and Rothbauer, *Reading Matters*, 3–4.

25. Yu and O'Brien, "Practical Typology," 35.

26. Ross, "Adult Readers," 181.

27. Ibid., 187.

28. Ziming Liu, "Reading Behavior in the Digital Environment: Changes in Reading Behavior over the Past Ten Years," *Journal of Documentation* 61, no. 1 (2005): 700–12.

29. Ross, "Adult Readers," 200.

30. Ibid., 201.

31. Ibid., 202.

32. Usherwood and Toyne, "Reading the Warning Signs," 112.

33. Ibid.

34. Elkin, Train, and Denham, *Reading and Reader Development*, 228.

35. *BookLetters*, 2007, http://www.bookletters.com; Public Library of Cincinnati and Hamilton County, *Turning the Page . . .* , 2007, http://www2.cincinnatilibrary.org/blog/; Madison Public Library, *MADreads: Book News and Reviews from Madison Public Library*, 2007, http://www.madisonpubliclibrary.org/madreads/.

36. Williamsburg Regional Library, *Looking for a Good Book?* 2007, http://www.wrl.org/bookweb/RA/index.html.

37. Elkin, Train, and Denham, *Reading and Reader Development*, 226.

3

NONFICTION READERS AND
NONFICTION ADVISORY

The past few years have seen a marked expansion of readers' advisory services, most notably in the area of nonfiction, and a resulting influx of new research. Fortunately for readers' advisory, nearly all the best research and publications on nonfiction and readers' advisory were gathered by Robert Burgin and published as *Nonfiction Reader's Advisory* in 2004. This was followed in 2006 by a readers' advisory guide to nonfiction in the Genreflecting series, *The Real Story*, by Sarah Statz Cords. Nonfiction is now a firmly accepted field of readers' advisory services, yet because of its newness and many librarians' lack of familiarity with it, nonfiction is still one that can be challenging to many readers' advisors.

RESEARCH REVIEW   BY JESSICA E. MOYER

The research review for this chapter was both easy and difficult. Easy because I really needed to consult only one source, Burgin's *Nonfiction Reader's Advisory*.[1] Difficult because I had to sum up an entire book's worth of research in one short section. Burgin, coeditor of *The Readers' Advisor's Companion* discussed in previous chapters, is the sole editor of the first readers' advisory research compilation to focus on a specific area of readers' advisory, in this case the newly emerging area of nonfiction advisory. With many similarities to the earlier research compilations, *The Readers' Advisor's Companion* and *Guiding the Reader to the Next Book*, *Nonfiction Reader's Advisory* is an equally important contribution to the field.

Here I focus on *Nonfiction Reader's Advisory* chapters that provide the best and most useful information for readers' advisors working with nonfiction readers. Notably, I do not discuss Bill Crowley's excellent chapter, "A History of Readers' Advisory Services in the Public Library," other than to note that this is one of the best overviews of the history of readers' advisory services currently available.

Nonfiction Readers and the Appeal of Nonfiction Reading

"MANY KINDS OF CRAFTED TRUTH," BY DAVID CARR

"Many Kinds of Crafted Truth: An Introduction to Nonfiction" is the first of several *Nonfiction Reader's Advisory* chapters about understanding why some people enjoy reading nonfiction and the role nonfiction reading can play for readers. Carr's chapter is especially important for the many readers' advisors who do not themselves enjoy reading nonfiction. Carr helps us understand why others consistently choose and enjoy nonfiction, just as we consistently choose and enjoy fiction. Understanding where the reader is coming from is an important first step in readers' advisory.

> Nonfiction isn't fiction; it is "true" and it is "real." It isn't "made up." And when the fit is right between our self the reader and itself the text, nonfiction addresses our memories, our curiosities and unfinished questions, and our hopes to learn about something remarkable and real, something transforming and true, something lost and something discovered.[2]

Why do readers choose nonfiction? What is the appeal? For many readers it is the very fact that it is real.

Carr discusses what makes something nonfiction and then moves on to a useful discussion of the variations of nonfiction. He analyzes "notable" titles from 2002 and 2003 that were reviewed in sources such as the *New York Times Book Review* and *Publishers Weekly*. Carr clusters like titles together, creating rather conventional groupings of nonfiction, such as biography, history, and memoir. In some ways these can be seen as the "genres" of nonfiction, a classification readily understood by librarians, but as Carr points out "the broad categories are deceptive; they communicate little or nothing about the nature of their constituents."[3] Carr explores the diversity of subjects within the broad categories of biography, memoir, history, contemporary issues, and other (which includes science, food, travel, sport, and crime), using many examples to illustrate his new classifications.

Next Carr looks more deeply at nonfiction and why it appeals to readers. He investigates popular nonfiction themes such as moral choices, thinking at the edge of change, and understanding how civilizations and cultures are formed. He concludes: "We read nonfiction to feed our desire to experience fresh truths." Carr proposes another way of looking at types of nonfiction, the deep dimensions. For some readers, these may get closest to appeal factors. Carr's categories are deep tellings, inside encounters, rescued histories, lives in context, journeys and places, losses and understandings, and growing through narratives.[4]

In his last section Carr returns to understanding why readers read nonfiction:

> They will read nonfiction to have mysteries explained, experiences recollected, questions answered, histories retold, and extraordinary experiences brought into the light of the text. They will read to gather information, to make up, literally construct their own minds. By pursuing unfinished questions and unending curiosities of one life, a person makes sense of the personal conflict, the private observation, and the problematic crisis. Our lives are nonfiction; we want them to hold the qualities we seek as we read: authenticity, confirmation, integrity, discipline, veracity, and insight. . . . They are crafted truths that expand our understanding of the possible, shaped by both lived and understood experiences.[5]

"THE APPEAL OF NONFICTION," BY KENNETH SHEARER

Kenneth Shearer's chapter expands on Carr's understanding with his explorations of the appeal factors of nonfiction.[6] "The Appeal of Nonfiction: A Tale of Many Tastes" was one of Shearer's last publications but still as worthy a contribution as his previous groundbreaking work in readers' advisory research. He uses the wonderfully evocative metaphor of Planet Bookscape to illustrate the differences between fiction and nonfiction and the appeal factors of reading nonfiction. He helps North Pole (pure fantasy fiction) readers understand those people who live in the Southern Hemisphere, the home of nonfiction readers. This will be an especially helpful chapter for advisors who rarely venture off the North Pole in their personal reading habits, for Shearer's writing is clear and engaging and his poles metaphor is remarkably easy to visualize and understand.

"READING NONFICTION FOR PLEASURE," BY CATHERINE ROSS

Catherine Ross makes a critical research contribution with "Reading Nonfiction for Pleasure: What Motivates Readers?" Her research data come from 194 lengthy interviews with avid leisure readers. Many of Ross's previous contributions to our understanding of readers and reading come from prior analysis of these interviews. She returns to the transcripts and looks in depth at nonfiction readers, including those who read both fiction and nonfiction as well as a few who read only nonfiction for pleasure. Ross focuses on understanding the following questions:

> Do [readers] distinguish between fact and fiction? Do they experience the two kinds of reading very differently, for example, by turning to fiction when they want a pleasurable experience, but choosing nonfiction when they want to find out facts about the real world? Are there special qualities about the nonfiction reading experience that attract readers? What is known about nonfiction readers' experiences with books that can be applied in the readers' advisory transaction?[7]

Ross answers these questions and more with thirteen points about nonfiction readers:

- Many readers read both fiction and nonfiction for pleasure.
- An interest in a particular subject often trumps the distinction between fiction and nonfiction.
- Exclusive nonfiction readers say they want to read about things that are "real."
- Some readers report that nonfiction is easier than fiction to read when one is likely to be interrupted.
- Some readers feel they "should" read nonfiction to increase their knowledge.
- Readers distinguish between two types of reading: reading for pleasure and reading to take something away.
- The stance taken by the reader is not determined by the text.
- Readers read nonfiction to follow up on their interests in and engagement with the world.
- For some readers, a passion for a single topic is the impetus for reading.
- Sometimes readers don't want to do something, they just want to read about it.
- Part of the joy of reading is serendipitous discovery.

- Readers read biographies in areas related to their interests or their own lives.
- Story is a key element in the appeal of many nonfiction books.

The importance of Ross's findings about nonfiction readers cannot be overstated. This short chapter reveals more about nonfiction readers than any other single source and should form the basis of advisors' understanding of nonfiction reading patrons. To emphasize this, Ross outlines five implications for readers' advisors. She repeats what others have said before: the readers' advisory interview is key. For example, readers can be very particular about biographies, and Ross suggests asking readers additional questions about the type of biography they enjoy reading. Ross advocates the creation of displays to reduce overload and facilitate browsing. She suggests that displays include both fiction and nonfiction selections, based around similar appeal factors. Think more about nonfiction in terms of appeal factors, not just subjects. Echoed by other authors, this particularly important point indicates that appeal factors are a key part of the nonfiction reading experience. Then think about nonfiction in terms of genres and learn about the differences the same way you studied the differences between fiction genres. Finally, Ross advises us to be aware of the nonfiction counterparts to popular genres of fiction—mystery/true crime, horror/occult, westerns/historical accounts of the Old West, action-adventure/survival stories, war stories/history and biography centered in warfare—because, as she noted earlier, many readers enjoy reading both fiction and nonfiction, and advisors should not be afraid to cross the divide.

"TRUE STORIES," BY DUNCAN SMITH

In "True Stories: Portraits of Four Nonfiction Readers," Duncan Smith provides the results of four case studies of nonfiction readers. "These personal journeys will show the relationships that exist between the lives of readers and the stories that call to them."[8] Smith's in-depth analysis of these four readers and their relationships to story makes a good counterpoint to Ross's broader study, and the personal focus of these stories may work particularly well for some librarians. Because of the personal and detailed nature of Smith's studies, it is impossible to do justice to them in a brief summary. Instead, I recommend that anyone interested in reading case studies of nonfiction readers consider Smith's chapter.

Nonfiction Advisory Services and Programs

"BEYOND BOUNDARIES," BY KATHLEEN DE LA PEÑA MCCOOK

Kathleen de la Peña McCook's chapter in *Nonfiction Reader's Advisory* explores the general nature and rationale for readers' advisory services for nonfiction readers as well as the role of nonfiction in library programs and connections to cultural heritage groups. McCook begins with a discussion of the two "types" of nonfiction: fact-based nonfiction, such as that used by the local business community; and creative nonfiction, or "nonfiction literature." With two examples, McCook illustrates the challenges inherent in using traditional library classification or subject schemes for accessing nonfiction. This use of specific titles (especially ones well known to many readers' advisors) is extremely helpful in making an otherwise somewhat confusing point. McCook also emphasizes the importance of the reader: "Readers bring their own knowledge and understanding to the nonfiction they read much in the same way they do to fiction, and these responses to the same text can be very different at different stages in a reader's life."[9] Clearly, for some readers, nonfiction reading plays the same role that fiction reading plays for others, and reader-response theory is just as applicable to nonfiction as to fiction.

On the basis of discussions with the Adult Reading Round Table of Illinois, McCook addresses library programming based on nonfiction and related it to the *New Planning for Results* guidelines used by many public libraries in the United States. She then looks specifically at those programs that involve literary or creative nonfiction and discusses five ways libraries can provide programs or support that involve creative nonfiction. This list will be useful for librarians looking to do more with nonfiction programming as well as for understanding how much nonfiction programming they already do. McCook discusses several national library programs that involve nonfiction, including video series and exhibits, many of which are provided by the ALA Public Programs Office. She expands on this growing area in her final section, which encourages librarians to partner with cultural institutions to provide more nonfiction-based adult programming.

An easily overlooked but extremely important idea McCook raises near the end of her piece is the connection between books and other media. As she points out, people who love watching the Food Network are quite likely to also enjoy reading books about food and cooking. Understanding the relationship between other leisure media and books is an important step for readers' advisors.

"BOOKS THAT INSPIRE," BY ALMA DAWSON AND CONNIE VAN FLEET

Alma Dawson and Connie Van Fleet's unique contribution to the volume, "Books That Inspire: Nonfiction for a Multicultural Society," showcases the Books That Inspire project of the University of Oklahoma Libraries, which displays books that have inspired faculty and staff. More than half of the books cited in this project are nonfiction, which clearly demonstrates the important role of nonfiction in the lives of readers. Dawson and Van Fleet note that

> both fiction and nonfiction by authors of color and about mul-
> ticultural themes are included. . . . Such selections demonstrate
> that authors of multicultural literature inspire others who are
> part of their society but may or may not share their ethnocul-
> tural origins. . . . Their words empower, mirror actions, affirm
> self, impact history, and show the common elements of cultures
> and of humanity.[10]

Librarians may be interested in replicating the Books That Inspire project described by Dawson and Van Fleet, and their chapter will help librarians and administrators understand the project and the powerful impact it can have on a community. Dawson and Van Fleet also show that fiction and nonfiction can be equally inspiring to readers, an important finding for librarians to consider.

"READERS' ADVISORY IN THE REAL WORLD," BY STACY ALESI, AND "THE STORY'S THE THING," BY VICKI NOVAK

In a turn away from research-focused chapters, Stacy Alesi contributes an eminently practical, utterly useful, and much appreciated chapter, "Readers' Advisory in the Real World." Alesi brings years of experiences as a bookseller and readers' advisor and focuses her chapter on communication, noting in her introduction that "even the most well-read person will not be able to assist a patron unless he or she can communicate clearly." Less research oriented than most of the other chapters in *Nonfiction Reader's Advisory*, Alesi's chapter may also prove one of the more accessible to readers' advisors. With sections on body language, listening, and appearing confident, Alesi discusses traditional readers' advisory practices that apply equally well to working with nonfiction and fiction readers. Her section on listening is particularly important in reminding readers' advisors that there is much more in terms of appeal than subject matches and that advisors must listen carefully to readers to understand fully what type of nonfiction reading experience they are looking for. On the topic of appearing confident, Alesi offers some slightly controversial but probably quite useful advice:

> Self assurance is a real plus in helping patrons find reading materials. If you're sure that the patron will like the book, she or he will generally be more willing to try it with an open mind. Conversely, if you appear to be indifferent or unsure about what you are recommending, the patron will also be unsure about accepting your suggestion.[11]

She does note that this tactic will not work with everyone but may be just the thing with certain readers.

Alesi also includes two sections on resources for nonfiction readers' advisory. Primarily web based, her lists are good starting points for any advisor wanting to find more nonfiction choices.

"The Story's the Thing: Narrative Nonfiction for Recreational Reading," by Vicki Novak, also includes a source list.[12] Novak provides many examples of narrative nonfiction titles as she discusses her concept of nonfiction genres. Both Alesi's and Novak's chapters will provide any advisor plenty of tools, resources, and potential titles for working with nonfiction readers.

LIBRARIAN'S VIEW   BY SARAH STATZ CORDS

A few years back I found myself trying to read a novel and thinking, "You know—I really don't like reading anymore." Because reading was pretty much my main pastime, you can imagine how disconcerting that thought was. For years I had been frustrated by the fiction reading I was doing, finding perhaps one novel in ten that I wanted to finish or that didn't leave me feeling that the world was a dreary, dark place. I was lost, casting about for a reading lifeline and worrying that I would have to find a new hobby. But then a wonderful thing happened. I brought home a book from

---

Sarah Statz Cords is the author of The Real Story: A Guide to Nonfiction Reading Interests *and* Public Speaking Handbook for Librarians and Information Professionals. *She works at the Madison (Wisconsin) Public Library. She has taught at UW-Madison's School of Library and Information Studies and is an associate editor for* Reader's Advisor Online.

the library titled *Diamond: A Journey to the Heart of an Obsession*, by Matthew Hart, and before I had finished the first chapter I knew a new chapter in my own life was opening: a nonfiction reader had been born.

Reaction to the Research

I first came to nonfiction readers' advisory research, bibliographies, book lists, and resources (or the lack thereof) not as a readers' advisor in a public library but as a new and zealous nonfiction reader. For my own personal reading interests, the lack of professional research (that I had the time to find) seemed not as egregious as the lack of any helpful and friendly resources like those so readily available for any type of fiction reader. Additionally, I had difficulty finding good nonfiction book review sites and resources, and literary blogs were few and far between at that time. So I simply muddled through, bringing home any nonfiction title that looked intriguing (regardless of subject, author, or "type" or "genre") and assuming I was the only one out there reading nonfiction for fun.

It was with great relief, then, personally and professionally, that I secured a copy of *Nonfiction Reader's Advisory,* edited by Robert Burgin, several of the essays in which (and, by extension, their authors) have helped me in providing better readers' advisory service to nonfiction readers.

When trying to move beyond thoughts of my own personal nonfiction tastes and into the realm of discovering what it is that others enjoy about nonfiction, I found Catherine Ross's findings in "Reading Nonfiction for Pleasure" extremely helpful. I was particularly interested in three of her conclusions: "many readers read both fiction and nonfiction for pleasure," "an interest in a particular subject can trump the distinction between fiction and nonfiction," and "readers read biographies in areas related to their interests or their own lives."[13] In addition to being interesting conclusions, those seem to be custom-made rules of thumb for working with all types of readers. In a short chapter Ross offers several tenets that I have found to be true in my own interactions with readers. Readers often (although not always) consider books of interest across the infamous fiction/nonfiction divide if they are interested enough in the subject area, and readers often consider biographies in subjects they often read about purely for informational purposes. For example, in my own work I have found that readers who check out cookbooks often seem to serendipitously find and check out memoirs like Ruth Reichl's *Tender at the Bone* or Anthony Bourdain's *Kitchen Confidential.*

For me, Ross's research also raised several questions about readers' behaviors: When and why do people read only fiction, or only nonfiction? Why do readers often want libraries to group all of their biographies together rather than interfile them with other nonfiction books by subject (a regular reader comment in my library)? There are so many questions left about nonfiction reading and readers.

Chapters by Kenneth Shearer ("The Appeal of Nonfiction") and David Carr ("Many Kinds of Crafted Truth") are equally valuable for recognizing that nonfiction, like fiction, comes in many forms and appeals to readers for many different reasons. Gone are the days (I hope) when readers believe that all nonfiction is to be read for informational or educational purposes only; the huge popularity of memoirs and other types of "creative" (or narrative, or literary, or really whatever you want to call it) nonfiction indicates that readers have left that belief behind, which is a compelling argument for readers' advisors to ditch the antiquated notion too.

Although readers do not often (okay, probably never) ask for nonfiction titles by the classification of "deep tellings," "inside encounters," or "growing-through narratives" (all of which are "dimensions" of nonfiction discussed by Carr), it is important for library staff to recognize that those terms come as close as any to elucidating what it really is about different nonfiction titles and styles that appeals to readers. You may not have read *The Perfect Storm*, by Sebastian Junger (and frankly, why haven't you?), but you may want to at least open your mind to the possibility that readers who enjoyed it might have enjoyed it because it was a "true adventure" narrative that included such stock elements of adventure writing as heroic and courageous characters, a storyline building toward a disastrous but thrilling climax, and quickly paced writing that keeps readers on the edge of their seats. Yes, its subject matter was the dangers inherent in commercial fishing and a huge storm off the New England coast. But woe be to the advisor who simply tries to offer readers who enjoyed it other works with the subject heading "Northeast Storms—New England." This is the only title in my library with that particular subject heading! But we do have plenty of other titles that could be considered true adventure narratives.

In all, I found *Nonfiction Reader's Advisory* to be a helpful volume and what I consider to be the very best sort of library research and writing: highly readable, concise, practical, and immediately applicable to my professional charge to try to the best of my ability to face all comers to our service desks. In addition to being helpful in its own right, its clarion call to other researchers and writers to venture into the seemingly unexplored

waters of providing readers' advisory services to nonfiction readers is
something I greatly appreciate.

Some Nuts and Bolts of Nonfiction Readers' Advisory

Although as both a reader of and self-appointed cheerleader for nonfiction
I am relieved that such scholarly and practical works are being written on
readers' advisory services for nonfiction titles, I often find myself chafing
at the notion that nonfiction must still be "incorporated" into fiction services. Why haven't we been doing that all along?

My experience, however, has been that initiating the readers' advisory
interview with my standard opening gambits—"Well, what do you usually enjoy?" or "What are you in the mood for today?"—works equally
well for nonfiction and fiction encounters. I cannot tell you that my heart
doesn't jump a little bit with excitement when the reader mentions a nonfiction title; nor am I proud to relate the fear with which I am nearly struck
speechless if they mention instead a science fiction title. Instead I think on
the accepted tenet of readers' advisory, that we are having a conversation
to find the right book for the patron. Joyce Saricks summed this up bril-
liantly: "When we work with readers in a library, we talk with them about
what they might enjoy reading."[14] Of course, there are differences between
nonfiction and fiction books, as well as between fiction readers and nonfiction readers. But there are differences between all readers with whom we
interact, and we have the readers' advisory conversation to interpret and
serve all those unique differences.

I find the new variety of nonfiction reading reference sources to be a
valuable reminder of both the usefulness of categorization and the ever-
present risk of undue rigidity in one's approach to subject and genre classification. What David Carr refers to as "growing-through narratives"[15]
I refer to as "overcoming adversity" and think of them as part of the
broader nonfiction genre of memoirs, which are themselves part of the
"life stories" grouping. Neal Wyatt takes a different approach in *The Readers' Advisory Guide to Nonfiction,* with a chapter dedicated to memoirs and
memoir sections in other chapters, such as on sports or science.[16] In *The
Real Story* I was reluctant to use the label "narrative nonfiction," feeling
strongly that a book such as Steven Levitt and Stephen Dubner's *Freakonomics: A Rogue Economist Explores the Hidden Side of Everything* offered
informational anecdotes but no overarching storyline.[17] Abby Alpert, on
the other hand, includes *Freakonomics* on her list of narrative nonfiction,

which she defines as any nonfiction "which uses literary devices of fiction writing to take nonfiction beyond the summarization of a series of facts and into the realm of storytelling."[18] I make note of these differences not to encourage despair but to highlight the true flexibility of the nonfiction collection as well as the variety of views in this still emerging area.

On the bright side, readers, readers' advisors, and librarians and information professionals of all types have long dealt with such inconsistencies and challenges in the fiction world; what one reader considers "mainstream fiction" might by another be considered "literary fiction." One of the main things to remember, then, in nonfiction as well as in fiction, is that these labels, categories, genres, types, or whatever you want to call them are most useful as mnemonics in our own minds and as a shared jargon in our profession. Most of our patrons are (blissfully) unaware of these definitions and classifications or have their own system, which can be revealed only through a readers' advisory conversation.

What Do Nonfiction Readers Want?

Although picking and choosing where books should go, both on our shelves and in such research and reference works, can be a lot of fun, the larger share of our job in the readers' advisory encounter remains, as ever, translating what readers tell us they like into the vocabularies that allow us to make connections between books of different subjects, types, lengths, genres, appeals, styles, tones, and, yes, even across the dreaded fiction/nonfiction divide. Very few fiction readers say things to me like, "What I need is a cozy mystery featuring an amateur detective, and yes, I'll consider classics." What they *do* say is, "I've read all your Agatha Christie mysteries. Who else writes like her?" Likewise, to expect readers to seek me out and tell me that they want an "adventures-in-science book, please, with an emphasis on thrilling writing" would be a bit much to ask. I have, however, been asked, "My mother just read Richard Preston's *The Hot Zone* and loved it; got anything else like that?" It seems once again that, at least in the case of fiction versus nonfiction readers' advisory, the more things change, the more they stay the same.

There are, however, two issues important to nonfiction readers' advisory that deserve discussion, and both are mentioned by Wyatt: "Many of us do not read as widely in nonfiction as we do in fiction," and "We have trained our readers to think of us as a fiction resource."[19]

There are two primary responses to the first problem. For one, an advisor who wants to feel more at ease and truly become more proficient with nonfiction must start to read some nonfiction titles. Just as advisors read selected titles to become familiar with a new or unread genre of fiction, they can do the same with nonfiction (by perusing best-seller lists, the ALA Notable Nonfiction lists,[20] the "Key Authors" sections in Wyatt's *Readers' Advisory Guide to Nonfiction,* or the "Consider Starting with . . ." lists in *The Real Story*). This sort of thing is easy for me, since I tend to enjoy most of the nonfiction books I read, but rest assured that the onerous duty works both ways. I am not particularly fond of either Elizabeth Berg or Jodi Picoult, but I try to at least skim their new titles as they are published. To each his own, except where readers' advisors are concerned; we must become familiar with a bit of everyone else's own as well.

The second half of the solution is to accept that we cannot read everything, but that we can make a sincere effort to be familiar with enough types of nonfiction books and their appeals to make our best educated guess as to what a reader might enjoy. It is in this educational capacity that the forthcoming nonfiction genre and reading interest reference tools should become particularly valuable. I may not have time to read all the history books that I should, but I can read a section of well-written annotations of such popular works as Nathaniel Philbrick's *Mayflower,* John Barry's *The Great Influenza,* and Mark Kurlansky's *Salt: A World History* on my lunch hour. Likewise, with the availability of Wikipedia and other Internet sources, there can be no excuse for not doing some quick research to round out one's generalist knowledge; if a reader asks for books about Whittaker Chambers, a few minutes spent reading about him online might suggest future related reading interests on the subjects of communism, espionage, or the cold war.

The second issue is that we have trained our readers and patrons to think of us primarily as a fiction resource. Whether we have been completely successful in even that task is still a matter of some debate, but I think there can be no question that the prevailing attitude for some time has been that nonfiction readers can be adequately served by showing them how to use our catalogs and follow up related subject headings in their quests for recreational reading. Has blithely sending nonfiction readers away to the catalog or the correct area of the stacks for so many years made them more self-sufficient browsers who are less likely to approach us? Wouldn't it be great to see some studies of how primarily nonfiction readers (meaning we would most likely have to move away from self-selecting survey participation at the "fiction desk") do their browsing and searching, and of how likely (or not) they are to approach library staff with such questions? I don't really know if helping a nonfiction reader is all that different from helping a fiction reader, but I certainly hope to start to find out, in my own job, as well as through conferences, continuing education programs, and more research studies.

Suggestions for Learning about Nonfiction

As noted previously, knowing one's stuff in nonfiction can be a bit tricky if you don't enjoy nonfiction reading or simply don't have the time to do much of it. Nonfiction books are often denser reads than fiction books and can take longer to read; those that don't employ a strong narrative or story arc may also prove slow going to advisors who prefer strong storylines in their recreational reading. To overcome this difficulty I suggest reading nonfiction books the way some people did to get through college (not me, certainly): read the introduction, the first chapter, the final paragraphs of each subsequent chapter, and the conclusion or last chapter. You'd be surprised how much you can learn about a nonfiction book's subject and tone simply by perusing the introduction, particularly since many authors take the further helpful step of outlining the subsequent chapters of the book for you. In fact, simply getting your hands on some nonfiction books (physically—get out there and check some out and don't be afraid to wander over to the circulation desk and see what people are returning as well) can be extremely helpful: What does the introduction say? What kind of references are in the back? Who blurbed the book on the jacket? What else has the author written, or what does the author do? These clues, even more so than with fiction, may provide valuable information about a book's content.

For example, an author whose political book is blurbed by *The Nation, The Progressive,* or *The New Republic* has probably written a book on the left of the political spectrum; likewise, those authors who garner glowing reviews from *National Review* and *The Weekly Standard* are most likely on the right side of the spectrum. Give the book in your hand a good heft—is it an exhaustive and weighty history or biography with more than a hundred pages of notes and references? Or is it a lighter biography (both in weight and tone), most likely about a celebrity currently in the news, with bigger text, tons of color photographs, and no references to be seen?

Another one of my favorite "getting to know nonfiction" tricks is to be a reader of magazines and a watcher of television (it's a tough life, but someone's got to do it). Many of today's well-known but not often best-selling nonfiction authors also frequently publish pieces in such magazines as *Atlantic Monthly, Business Week, Esquire, Harper's, The Nation, National Review, Vanity Fair,* and *Vogue,* not to mention "literary magazines" such as *The Believer, Orion,* or *American Scholar,* all of which contain nonfiction articles and essays as well as book excerpts and reviews. Keeping an eye on national newspapers doesn't hurt either: the *Washington Post,* the *Wall Street Journal;* many of my favorite nonfiction authors are journalists (Mark Bowden of the *Philadelphia Inquirer;* Pete Dexter of the *Philadelphia Daily News*). Likewise, television programs can be a vital source of nonfiction information and reader queries; whenever a book is highlighted on *The Daily Show with Jon Stewart* or *The Colbert Report* (not to mention PBS or NPR), I guarantee you that a waiting list develops overnight for those titles (Nassim Nicholas Taleb's esoteric *The Black Swan: The Impact of the Highly Improbable,* a possible read-alike for Malcolm Gladwell's hugely popular *The Tipping Point,* is one such title).

Talking with Nonfiction Readers

Many advisors now talk about the value of coming out from behind the reference or advisory desk and approaching readers throughout the library, offering assistance; and although I struggle to develop my skills in that area, I am quite happy to try some "gentle prodding" once a patron has requested my help or suggestions. One of my favorite phrases (only offered after making a few of my best guesses) is, "Well, would you consider some nonfiction (or fiction)?" Phrased in a nonconfrontational manner, I have found many readers who lean their head to the side, think about it, and respond, "Sure, whaddya got?" Of course, it's not a perfect world, so I get a lot of readers who also say, "No, that's not for me," or "No, not today," but at least I can feel like I explored all our options.

I also try to make the connections I'm making visible to patrons: "Well, all my David Sedarises are checked out, but would you consider some travel nonfiction? There's this *Round Ireland with a Fridge* book by a guy named Tony Hawk, who can be quite funny . . . ," or "Reading about ancient Rome? Would you consider fiction? This author Conn Iggulden has a series about Julius Caesar, starting with *The Gates of Rome*—any interest?"

Although it is tempting simply to follow up readers' subject interests, likely appeal factors, genre loyalty, and mood when making suggestions, I think there is also a place for keeping an open mind about what they might consider. If I have the time, and the patron seems amenable, I often try to suggest just one title that I consider more of a stretch, based on the patron's verbal cues. This is not because I feel it is our place to provide "good" or "educational" reading but rather because I am a huge believer in serendipity—which happily dovetails with another of Ross's findings: "Part of the joy of reading is serendipitous discovery."[21]

Much of the time I find myself playing the percentages, or following the common knowledge (and even myths) of our profession, when making suggestions. You all know them: More women tend to read romances, and romance readers tend to want happy endings. More men tend to read nonfiction, particularly history. Older readers want gentle books; graphic novels appeal only to younger readers. I am not advocating that we discard these ideas but rather that we try to understand them better and to push against their boundaries ever so slightly. This has been borne out in my own experience. I am one of those strange people who just walks around Barnes and Noble to see who's browsing where (and where, not surprisingly, I often see more men in the history and business sections and more women in the fiction aisles). But I am also a woman who reads almost exclusively nonfiction, history included, for pleasure, and happy endings tend to annoy me. I never cared much for graphic novels even when I was young, and as I age I don't have any more interest in gentle narratives. I share this information because I firmly believe that we will be better equipped to understand patrons and readers when we better understand ourselves and our own reading habits and proclivities. To that end I would love to see much more research on everyone in our field, including colleagues across all ages, library types, professional classifications, and locations.

My Readers' Advisory Research Wish List

One area in which I'd love to see more research or at least a conversation among publishers, booksellers, and library staff is how booksellers "handsell" titles. Which of their techniques can we adapt for use in our libraries? How can we work with publishers and authors to increase interest in reading in general or offer specific displays or programs that might make reading more of an "event" for adults? (I think many libraries already do this admirably with children and summer reading programs.) How can we encourage adult readers to be as open and trusting with us as many of our younger patrons? How can we foster an atmosphere in which readers can join us for book conversations, and how can we quantify or collect statistics or evidence on the value of that service to our administrators and library boards? Yes, it does take time to foster relationships with individual readers, but I would argue that spending a bit of time with one patron (when the time is available) is as valid a part of our job as answering as many phone calls and reference queries as possible.

I would also like to see more systematic and open studies of training and professional development programs for all staff members. Keeping an open mind is not important only when working with patrons; it starts at least one full step back in working with one's colleagues. When I work the circulation desk, I make sure to discuss BBC DVDs with one of our circulation clerks who has seen everything we own; when I work the reference desk with the librarian who runs our anime club, I try and make an effort to hear about what graphic novels she's been reading. I hope that I can be used as a resource when it comes to nonfiction titles; I still call a former colleague when I'm stumped on romance and mystery titles.

For such a collegial and outgoing group, I think there is a serious dearth of real conversation not only about how we provide readers' advisory services, and how we train each other to provide them, but also about how titles are selected for purchase and what resources are used by library staff who are not on the public service "front lines." I admit that my desire to have a meeting or roundtable discussion among technical services staff, acquisitions staff, and public services staff (including circulation staff) might be simply to go around the room and hear what everybody else is reading. And what would be so wrong about that? I'm sure we have all spent time at work meetings that provided fewer tangible benefits than that.

Luckily, there is now a burgeoning effort to fill this particular communication gap, with such conversational meeting places as the *Reader's Advisor Online Blog* from Libraries Unlimited (to which many "advisors in the field" are contributing) and the RUSA CODES Readers' Advisory Committee Wiki.[22] I would also like to read more about the processes and outcomes of many local groups, such as the Illinois Adult Reading Round Table, where library staff members meet monthly to discuss different genres and books and what about them might appeal to readers, as well as how they personally reacted to the books being studied.[23]

Conclusion

I personally try very hard to view all readers as just that: readers (as opposed to "fiction readers" or "nonfiction readers"). This is one of the reasons I was relieved by Catherine Ross's finding that many readers in fact read both; I also know from my own experience that one can love reading fiction but also be open to nonfiction that tackles a subject in which a reader is interested, is well written, might be something the reader is in the mood for, or any combination thereof. The few small techniques I tend to employ when working with any reader have proved to be just as useful in nonfiction as in fiction: endeavoring to know as much of my stuff as possible, what I think of as "gentle prodding," and keeping an open mind, especially where displays and book groups are concerned.

After rereading my portion of this chapter to provide some sort of summary, I worry that I may not have sufficiently provided an image for how nonfiction readers' advisory services differ from those of fiction readers' advisory. This is most likely because I tend to be all over the map whenever trying to match readers with books they might enjoy; the more the merrier, I always think, and that goes for broad types of writing (fiction vs. nonfiction) as well as more specific genre and subgenre types. I also feel that it is, as yet, difficult to gain an accurate picture of the many ways nonfiction service might well differ from fiction service, hampered as we are by the small amount of available research and resources.

The differences between fiction and nonfiction might be exacerbated by our own habits. Our hesitation in suggesting books we have not read might also be discouraging us from mixing and matching nonfiction titles into book displays, or even creating displays that highlight only nonfiction and seek to make connections also across genre, style, and mood. More research and more resources will soon help us become more familiar with nonfiction genres and reading interests; in the meantime, the quickest way to become familiar enough with nonfiction titles to suggest and merchandise them, as well as to add them to book group rotations, is to read some of the most often requested of them in our libraries. Don't be afraid: bring home a book about diamonds (*Diamond: A Journey to the Heart of an Obsession*). Or economics (*Freakonomics: A Rogue Economist Explores the Hidden Side of Everything*). Or a writer's beloved pet (*Marley and Me*). You may be surprised to find a nonfiction reader within yourself—and once you do, it will be a lot easier to find one in someone else.

NOTES

1. Robert Burgin, ed., *Nonfiction Reader's Advisory* (Westport, Conn.: Libraries Unlimited, 2004).
2. David Carr, "Many Kinds of Crafted Truth: An Introduction to Nonfiction," in ibid., 47–65, quote from 48.
3. Ibid., 52.

4. Ibid., 61–63.

5. Ibid., 63–64.

6. Kenneth Shearer, "The Appeal of Nonfiction: A Tale of Many Tastes," in Burgin, *Nonfiction Reader's Advisory*, 67–83.

7. Catherine Ross, "Reading Nonfiction for Pleasure: What Motivates Readers?" in Burgin, *Nonfiction Reader's Advisory*, 105–20, quote from 105.

8. Duncan Smith, "True Stories: Portraits of Four Nonfiction Readers," in Burgin, *Nonfiction Reader's Advisory*, 121–42, quote from 122.

9. Kathleen de la Peña McCook, "Beyond Boundaries," in Burgin, *Nonfiction Reader's Advisory*, 31–43, quote from 34.

10. Alma Dawson and Connie Van Fleet, "Books That Inspire: Nonfiction for a Multicultural Society," in Burgin, *Nonfiction Reader's Advisory*, 175–96, quote from 176.

11. Stacy Alesi, "Readers' Advisory in the Real World," in Burgin, *Nonfiction Reader's Advisory*, 199–212, quotes from 199, 211–12.

12. Vicki Novak, "The Story's the Thing: Narrative Nonfiction for Recreational Reading," in Burgin, *Nonfiction Reader's Advisory*, 213–27.

13. Ross, "Reading Nonfiction for Pleasure," 107, 116.

14. Joyce Saricks, *Readers' Advisory Service in the Public Library*, 3rd ed. (Chicago: American Library Association, 2005), 76.

15. Carr, "Many Kinds of Crafted Truth," 63.

16. Neal Wyatt, *The Readers' Advisory Guide to Nonfiction* (Chicago: American Library Association, 2007).

17. Sarah Statz Cords, *The Real Story: A Guide to Nonfiction Reading Interests* (Westport, Conn.: Libraries Unlimited, 2006).

18. Abby Alpert, "Incorporating Nonfiction into Readers' Advisory Services," *Reference and User Services Quarterly* 46, no. 1 (2006): 25–32.

19. Wyatt, *Readers' Advisory Guide to Nonfiction*, 26, 29.

20. American Library Association Reference and User Services Association, Notable Books: The Current List, 2007, http://www.ala.org/ala/rusa/protools/notablebooks/thelists/notablebooks.cfm.

21. Ross, "Reading Nonfiction for Pleasure," 115.

22. *Reader's Advisor Online Blog*, 2007, http://www.readersadvisoronline.com/blog/; RUSA CODES Readers' Advisory Committee Wiki, 2007, http://wikis.ala.org/rusa/readersadvisory/index.php/Main_Page.

23. ARRT: Adult Reading Round Table, 2007, http://www.arrtreads.org.

4

AUDIOVISUAL ADVISORY

Readers' advisory isn't just about print books anymore. Readers' advisors need to think beyond print books to audiobooks (a pretty easy jump) to music (many libraries have extensive tape and CD music collections) to movies, because, yes, as much as some may not like it, audiovisual materials in general, and movies in particular, are a large, popular, and growing part of most library collections.

RESEARCH REVIEW   BY JESSICA E. MOYER

Library and Information Science Research Publications

There is a limited amount of library-based research on audiovisual (AV) advisory, and all the articles included in this research review were published after 2001, an indication of the new and growing nature of this area.

"VIEWERS' ADVISORY," BY RANDY PITMAN

Chronologically, the first AV advisory publication appeared in the widely cited *Readers' Advisor's Companion:* Randy Pitman's "Viewers' Advisory."[1] This may be the single most disappointing chapter in *The Readers' Advisor's Companion,* an otherwise excellent collection of research-based chapters on readers' advisory. Pitman's subtitle, "Handling Audiovisual Advisory Questions," leads readers to believe that this chapter is either a how-to for or research about AV readers' advisory, either of which would be important and worthwhile contributions. The first few paragraphs describe an AV readers' advisory question received by e-mail, keeping the reader hopeful. But hopes are quickly dashed as the chapter turns out to be a mishmash of suggested places to look for AV information any reference librarian should know, with altogether too much personal opinion and a nearly complete lack of analysis. Only the last section, "Nontheatrical Video," is worth reading. Librarians working with AV are given a list of sources for reading about and finding videos. But even this section is interrupted by an apparently meaningless rant on the useless information that can be found on the Web, which once again shouldn't be news to any librarian. Most of the other chapters in this book have excellent reference lists that can lead a reader to many interesting and important books and articles about readers' advisory. Pitman's reference list is as disappointing as the rest of his chapter. Librarians looking to become better readers' advisors for AV materials or AV librarians wanting to learn more about doing advisory for their patrons should look elsewhere.

"HEARING AND SEEING," BY MICHAEL VOLLMAR-GRONE

Fortunately for eager AV advisors, there are useful publications. *Nonfiction Reader's Advisory* includes an excellent chapter by Michael Vollmar-Grone, "Hearing and Seeing: The Case for Audiovisual Materials."[2] Though having a practical rather than research focus, this chapter is still an important contribution to AV readers' advisory. Vollmar-Grone starts his chapter with a review of AV materials over time, from the first time a presidential election was broadcast over radio (1920) to the increasingly prominent role of mass media in today's popular culture. This is an excellent background and a nice introduction to this solid chapter. A nice touch is Vollmar-Grone's use of terms and definitions: *AV materials* instead of the utterly generic *nonprint materials,* and *information materials* instead of *nonfiction.* He also includes a brief section on the historical role of AV in public libraries, which is important for understanding the role of AV in today's public libraries, as well as a brief discussion of changing formats. This leads into a discussion of reasons AV is underutilized by librarians; Vollmar-Grone cites primarily unfamiliarity with formats, lack of reference sources, and the difficulty in accessing materials in linear formats. It is useful for librarians to think about these reasons and how they might overcome them in their own work. It is clear that Vollmar-Grone has both experienced AV readers' advisory and thought a great deal about the difficulties other librarians face in handling AV questions and collections, both of which make this chapter worthwhile for librarians facing AV readers' advisory queries.

Vollmar-Grone's section on media literacy is one of the longer ones but also important and relevant in today's media-saturated world. This chapter may be a few years old, but media literacy is still a big issue, maybe even more important today than it was in 2003. Vollmar-Grone does an excellent job of addressing the tension between media as entertainer and media as informer. Librarians working with teachers (and administrators in some libraries) may need to work hard to overcome this tension, and Vollmar-Grone's clear discussion of these issues will certainly help.

In his final section Vollmar-Grone moves into the practical challenges affecting readers' advisors. First, he points out that all readers' advisors should also be viewers' advisors and listeners' advisors—the goals are the same: helping people find what interests them. This is such an important point, and it is heartening to see Vollmar-Grone make it right at the beginning of this section. Two pages of guidelines follow for readers' advisors working with listeners and viewers. By relating AV questions to more traditional readers' advisory questions, Vollmar-Grone provides a nice introduction to AV advisory for readers' advisors beginning to work with AV patrons or wanting to brush up on their skills. Because of the practical focus of this article, which concludes with an annotated list of recommended resources, any librarian who works with AV patrons or wants to expand their readers' advisory services to include AV will certainly benefit from this work.

"SPECIAL NEEDS/SPECIAL PLACES," BY JUDITH ELKIN

Judith Elkin's "Special Needs/Special Places," in *Reading and Reader Development,* brings an international orientation to this discussion. Elkin's focus is readers' advisory for patrons with special needs, which she defines broadly: "The range of disabilities is wide and includes motor, visual, aural, intellectual and emotional. Many of us probably have disabilities which are not even acknowledged as such."[3] Many of the readers included in this category are best served with AV materials, in particular, audiobooks.

As in other chapters of *Reading and Reader Development,* Elkin does an excellent job of reviewing the research in this area. She starts with "Value of Reading for People with Special Needs," which supports the premise that reading can be particularly important for people with special needs, since "people find what they need in what they read."[4] By providing this review of research related to the value of reading for patrons with special needs, Elkin gives libraries the knowledge that there is such research and a place to go to find it. In this section Elkin includes an important quote from Beverly Mathias, powerful enough to be worth repeating here in its entirety:

> Books are not just print, they are sound and vision, large print, large format, CD-ROM. Books can be read using eyes, ears, hands and fingers. . . . Reading should be a pleasure not a punishment, and there is joy, satisfaction, and achievement in encouraging any child to read independently, but even more so when the child has special needs.

Elkin then concludes this section:

> In the context of reading for adults with special needs, reading might be defined as being about the right book in the right format for the right adult at the right time and in the right place. Almost inevitably, libraries and librarians play a significant role in ensuring this is a reality.[5]

Elkin makes some important points that advisors need to consider in the discussions of AV advisory. For librarians who do readers' advisory, Elkin's next section, "Reading and People Who Are Visually Impaired," will be useful, since many visually impaired readers who listen to audiobooks often have the same preferences and needs as sighted patrons who enjoy audiobooks. Elkin urges all library programs to be welcoming to listeners as well as to readers. For listeners to make informed choices, they will likely need a variety of information about an audiobook, information that is not always provided in traditional online library catalogs. Elkin makes the additional important point that visually impaired readers may not be able to access online catalogs or other electronic library resources and thus may need even more assistance than sighted patrons. Elkin notes that in the United Kingdom in 2002 there were few resources for helping readers choose new audiobooks. This is also an issue in the United States and one that Kaite Mediatore Stover addresses in the "Librarian's View" section of this chapter.

Elkin describes a new partnership in the United Kingdom. As part of the Branching Out Project, the National Library for the Blind has shown how popular audiobooks can be when marketed in the library to all patrons. The National Library for the Blind has also partnered with Branching Out on other projects to make libraries generally more inclusive and welcoming to visually impaired patrons, leading one patron to say, "You are engaging us all to take more part not just be passively waiting at the end of the delivery"—an interesting and thought-provoking comment, especially for librarians who provide outreach and delivery services to homebound patrons.

"READING WITH YOUR EARS," BY KAITE MEDIATORE

This next article is more practical than research oriented. From the Readers' Advisory column of *Reference and User Services Quarterly* comes one of the most important recent additions to AV readers' advisory: "Reading with Your Ears," by guest columnist Kaite Mediatore[6]—who also updates and extends the discussion of audiobooks in this chapter's "Librarian's View."

As commutes become longer and readers' lives busier, more and more readers' advisory patrons are turning to audiobooks. They have a perfectly justified desire to have readers' advisors help them find good listens just like they help them find good reads. Mediatore's article starts with an introduction of the increasing appeal of audiobooks and moves into a brief review of the scanty research in this area (as available in 2002). Most of the research has been done by the audiobook industry or published in *AudioFile* magazine and may not be familiar or accessible to many librarians. She reveals that, like leisure readers, audiobook listeners are everywhere and everyone. There is no age group or demographic that does not listen to audiobooks. And most audiobook readers are also avid readers (and already likely patrons of readers' advisory services).

Using many of the aspects of a traditional print readers' advisory interview, Mediatore gives plenty of practical yet research-based suggestions on readers' advisory for listening patrons. In her section on appeal, she hits on one of the most unusual aspects of listeners' advisory, the narrator. Regardless of the plot, the narrator can make or break a listening experience. For some listeners, Mediatore points out, the narrator trumps genre or other preferences. Some listeners will give anything Barbara Rosenblat or George Guidall narrates a try, regardless of the type of story. Mediatore also writes about books that just don't translate well to audio, because of the style of the writing or the special effects of the print. One recent example is Mark Haddon's popular *Curious Incident of the Dog in the Nighttime.* The text includes many puzzles and other visual effects, which just cannot be conveyed in an audio version. So readers' advisors need to remember that not all print makes good audio.

Mediatore mentions the difficult format question, which has become even more complicated since 2003. Audiobooks today can come in tapes, CDs, and a multitude of digital formats. Librarians must be familiar with all the available formats so they can discuss preferences with listeners. And then there is the perpetual question of abridged versus unabridged. Mediatore cites research conducted by Harriet Stow and the Collection Development Committee of the Arlington (Texas) Public Library that indicates that more than 80 percent of readers prefer unabridged, whether it is nonfiction or fiction. Even nonfiction readers, traditionally thought to prefer abridged, are found to prefer the unabridged so they can control the reading experiences and listen to the sections they want, not the sections someone else has deemed the best. Still, some readers do like abridgements. As Mediatore points out, they can be good for sampling or an introduction to a topic, so librarians must be prepared to discuss both formats with listeners.

Next Mediatore considers where librarians can go for assistance with audio readers' advisory questions. Her annotated list of tools is thorough, practical, and useful; it points librarians to better-known sources such as *AudioFile* magazine and more obscure but extremely useful gems like *AudioBooks on the Go.*

Mediatore also adapts the ever-popular readers' advisory tactic of reading a book in ten minutes to "Listen to a Book in Fifteen Minutes." Using this clearly outlined strategy, readers' advisory librarians can quickly and painlessly make themselves familiar with a variety of audiobooks. This may be the most useful part of the article, for it provides a step-by-step method for librarians who are not audiobook listeners to get to know enough about audiobooks to advise listeners, which is of course the ultimate goal.

"A WORD IN YOUR EAR," BY GREG MORGAN

Greg Morgan provides an international view of audiobooks and services for print-disabled readers in this *Electronic Library* article.[7] He describes the Royal New Zealand Foundation for the Blind (RNZFB) and its upcoming initiative to transition from cassette tapes to the DAISY digital talking books for print-disabled readers in New Zealand. This article is valuable mostly for librarians interested in how other countries serve print-disabled readers, but it also discusses the DAISY format for digital audio, which has been adopted internationally. DAISY audiobooks, unlike tapes, are designed so that print-disabled readers can navigate the text with the same facility as a sighted person with a printed book. The RNZFB program could serve as an excellent, well-considered model for programs for print-disabled readers everywhere.

"PERSPECTIVES: 'THAT ALL MAY READ,'" EDITED BY HAMPTON AULD

Hampton (Skip) Auld has edited one of the few articles published in an American library and information science journal that addresses the same topics as Elkin and Morgan.[8] As the first part of the Perspectives column in *Public Libraries,* Auld discusses the Talking Books Program, established by Congress in 1931 and administered by the National Library Service for the Blind and Physically Handicapped (NLS) at the Library of Congress.

The first essay in Auld's collection, by Jim Scheppke, is worth reading for its information on how libraries in other countries are providing digital audio to library patrons—such as in the Netherlands, where in 2005, patrons had access to 30,000 digital audiobooks. Print-disabled readers in the United States will have to wait until at least 2008, when NLS plans to replace its current format of cassette tapes with digital audio. Scheppke argues that this is far too long to wait. If NLS waits until 2008 to start with digital audio, there may not be enough patrons left to keep the program alive. Scheppke also provides valuable research on the Talking Book Program in Oregon and five other states, which makes his column more than just his own opinion and thus an important contribution to the library literature.

In the same collection, Marc Maurer offers a personal view of a lifetime Talking Books patron, but he does little to contribute to the research in this area.

"AUDIOVIDEO 2006," BY ANN KIM

In a 2006 issue of *Library Journal,* Ann Kim provides a completely positive view of audio downloading programs, particularly the Recorded Books/ NetLibrary program from OCLC.[9] What this article fails to mention is that none of these programs support iPods, the dominant device in the digital audio market. It misses the most critical question: should libraries spend money and staff time on a program that will miss 80 percent of potential listeners? The failure to even mention the iPod compatibility problem is a serious oversight.

Research Outside Library and Information Science

The only other research or related publications for AV readers' advisory comes from the bookselling and AV industries.

"AUDIOBOOKS DESERVE MARKETING, TOO," BY EILEEN HUTTON

Aimed at booksellers, Hutton's short (and opinionated) piece in *Publishers Weekly* has both good advice for librarians and some great facts: "More than 97 million people drive to work solo each day and the average delay due to traffic congestion has tripled in the last 20 years."[10] Hutton thinks bookstores are prejudiced against audio, frequently hiding it in the back of the store and giving it little advertising space. There are probably a few libraries that also make this mistake. Hutton offers some excellent suggestions for increasing awareness of audio among staff and patrons, many of which have also been suggested by Kaite Mediatore (see above). For example, "When a customer asks for a new book by Nora Roberts the best response is 'Do you want the hardcover, cassettes, or CD?'" (and now we should add "or download it to your digital audio player"). Such a query gets both staff and patrons thinking about the different formats available and could decrease some of the discrimination against audio. Hutton also suggests the tried-and-true readers' advisory training strategy of getting staff to start a listening program: "When sales people become audiobook addicts, they pass on the addiction to customers." Hutton provides some Shay Baker–style suggestions for increasing visibility of audiobooks, including making the audio version available at every book signing and always shelving the audio alongside the print in displays. And her final suggestion is one of particular importance to libraries: "Stop losing sales to Internet downloads. Carry a selection of titles on MP3 CD and promote them as iPod ready."

"THE GROWTH OF THE AUDIOBOOK INDUSTRY," BY ROBIN WHITTEN, AND THE AUDIO PUBLISHERS ASSOCIATION 2006 ANNUAL SURVEY

Robin Whitten provides one source of data on the audiobook publishing industry in "The Growth of the Audiobook Industry," from 2005.[11] Additional and more recent information can be found in 2006 press releases from the Audio Publishers Association.[12] In terms of formats, downloadable audio continues to grow, increasing from 6 percent of the market in the 2004 survey to 9 percent in 2006. A significant portion of listeners have MP3 players and have downloaded digital audio, making digital audio the fastest-growing area. CDs also continue to grow, up from 63 percent to 74 percent, while sales of cassettes continue to decline, from 30 percent to 16 percent. Fiction continues to dominate, at 58 percent of the market, but nonfiction makes up a healthy 32 percent, marking the trend of popular nonfiction noticed in recent years by many readers' advisors. In general, publishers report publishing more unabridged titles and fewer cassettes, in some areas eliminating cassettes entirely from production.

The publishers' data on audiobook readers tell librarians a lot about the listening patrons they are most likely to serve in the library. Nearly 84 percent of respondents had attended college, making audiobook listeners a well-educated group. They have higher incomes and many have children. They also read printed books, with more than 94 percent indicating that they have read a print book within the previous twelve months. Listeners are readers too.

Listeners still greatly prefer unabridged listening to abridged, which they choose only 17.4 percent of the time. Most listeners who purchase their audio do so at physical stores. The percentage of titles borrowed from libraries has also increased, from 38 percent in 2001 to nearly 52 percent for 2005. "The most important factors for consumers when selecting audiobooks are price, availability on CD, author, description and narrator."

How do consumers actually select audiobooks? More than 40 percent use websites and recommendations from friends, and more than 30 percent use information provided at the bookstore or on best-seller lists. Librarians barely break 30 percent, even though more than half of audiobooks are borrowed from libraries. One good note, according to the publishers: the more titles a listener listens to in a year, the more likely he or she is to ask a librarian for a suggestion. And that is all we know about audiobooks, audiobook listeners, and audiovisual readers' advisory.

LIBRARIAN'S VIEW   BY KAITE MEDIATORE STOVER

All Ears on You: Audiobooks

Earlier this week I encountered a patron at the new shelves in our audiobook section. He was browsing the books on cassette and when I asked if he needed assistance he revealed himself to be The World's Most Perfect Readers' Advisory Patron. He and his family were going to be driving five hours to St. Louis; their car has a cassette AND compact disc player; there would be five listeners in the car, parents and three

Kaite Mediatore Stover is head of reader services at Kansas City (Missouri) Public Library and an audiobook reviewer for Booklist.

children, one a teen, all a family of readers. Mom and teen liked to listen to mysteries, Dad would prefer something else, and yes, they'd listened to all of the Harry Potter audiobooks.

In 2003, when I offered to write an article on readers' advisory and audiobooks, I wrote what I needed at the time.[13] As a readers' services librarian, I had patrons who regularly needed readers' advisory assistance with audiobooks, and I wrote "Reading with Your Ears" to help both myself and other librarians. Since 2003, audiobooks have been increasingly popular, making this a growing area for advisory services. So here I discuss the areas I think are important to advisors, in addition to some of the changes and new challenges to audiobook advisory.

Formats (and thus technologies) are an important concern in working with listeners, even more so now with the growth of digital audio. Traditionally libraries have adopted the stance of waiting for the hi-tech dust to settle and then choosing wisely. It may be time to move away from this position and adopt a more proactive one. Carve out a portion of the budget dedicated to the acquisition and circulation of emerging technologies. Some of these acquisitions may fall by the wayside, and some may find a niche audience among library users, particularly the younger, techno-savvy users. Libraries hate to do them, but user surveys of "favorite gadgets" employed when listening to books on audio are necessary. To best serve our patrons, we need to provide the formats they want to use.[14] As readers' advisors, we need to be aware of format issues when working with listeners.

One new development in audiobook technologies that should be addressed is the Playaway, a preloaded, self-contained portable playback device, self-described as the "ready-to-go audio " (http://store.playaway digital.com). The Playaway is one of the most user- *and* library-friendly devices to come along. With improved production quality, close-to-simultaneous release with the print title, and affordability for consumers and libraries, this little gadget is set to become the latest technology for digital audiobooks. Playaways are as small and easy to manipulate as an iPod and even easier to purchase, since they are completely self-contained. Their packaging and size will have libraries taking a second look. No longer will libraries have to hold an item behind the circulation counter waiting for the last cassette or compact disc to be coughed up from the car's player or a scratched disc to be repaired. All the patron needs to return is the "book," which is then easily readied for the next listeners. Readers' advisors beware: this is a technology to watch for.

The appeal factors laid out by Joyce Saricks and Nancy Brown in *Readers' Advisory Service in the Public Library* are applicable to audiobooks and were a major focus of "Reading with Your Ears." There is one additional appeal element unique to audiobooks, and that is what I call "listenability," or the quality of the narrator's reading. Narration has an impact on each of the appeal elements—story, pacing, character, and frame—and in addition the narrator's own effect on the audio must be considered. For many listeners, the quality of the narrator's performance can make or break a title, and many readers have told me they have ceased to listen to a particular book they were sure they would have loved because of the narrator. Conversely, many other listeners have said that only a narrator's dulcet tones kept them listening to the end of a book that had long ago lost all appeal in other aspects.

Doing readers' advisory with audiobooks requires a little more knowledge of the content at hand. In the stacks, an advisor can pull a book off the shelf, flip through and skim a few pages, and make reasonable evaluations of the writing style, subject matter, and subgenre. This is not as simple with audiobooks. You either know the content or you don't, and you can't flip through the cassettes or CDs to catch up. This is why in my 2003 article I cannibalized one of the most useful tools in the land of readers' advisors, the "How to Read a Book in Five Minutes" technique. I adapted those instructions by upping the time from five to fifteen minutes and including audible qualities in the evaluation process. I still think this is one of the most useful skills an audiobook advisor can develop.

To keep abreast of new audio and especially titles not owned by your library, read the audiobook reviews in professional journals such as *Library Journal, Booklist,* or *AudioFile.* Most of these reviews are also available in subscription databases. Amazon.com and Audible allow users to post reviews, critiques, and evaluations of audio titles on the websites. Often patron comments can be of use to the library staffer looking for evaluative information. Avid listeners may also appreciate being pointed to these resources for independent audio selection.

In this last section about audiobook advisory, I want to emphasize the most important points in conducting audiobook advisory and the differences from print advisory. Audio readers' advisory requires taking format and multiple listeners into account. If the reader/listener is taking a trip with others, then the title must appeal to everyone in the car. Audio advisors must always have a ready cache of family-friendly listening available, in addition to selections for solo listeners.

To conclude, here are what I consider the most important points for audio advisors to clarify with patrons looking for their next good listen:

- What device do you use to listen to your audiobooks?
- Will you be listening to this audiobook with anyone else?
- Is length of the audiobook a concern for you?
- Some audiobooks might have strong language or scenes with graphic violence or adult content. How would you rate your tolerance for listening to this type of material?

Listeners' Advisory: Music

Not long ago, a library patron approached the audiovisual department in my library and asked for "good" classical music and couldn't be much more specific than that. Further investigation revealed the music was NOT for a wedding, a retirement party or romantic dinner music. The patron was merely interested in learning about classical composers and their works.

This query shouldn't sound as alarming as it does. Having music collections is not a new thing in most public libraries. Music collections of the past may have been heavier on classical titles and available on records, but libraries today are spending more money and using less shelf space to provide collections of rock, hip-hop, gospel, country, jazz, alternative, world music, and sound effects in compact disc and other formats. For many listeners, libraries are the last place to experiment with new music at no charge. Avid and casual listeners alike may need assistance in choosing a new CD, and they should be able to get that help at the readers' advisory desk.

Evaluating listening material is radically different from evaluating print material. The descriptors are diverse terms, and the perceptions lie within the ear of the listener. One person's heavy metal is another person's church music. To find music for an inquiring library patron, listeners' advisors should take a page (or a scale) from the experts over at Pandora Media.

Pandora Media employs more than forty "music analysts" to listen to songs and attach characteristics that describe a singer's voice, the bleat of a trumpet, or the word worthiness of lyrics, all part of the Music Genome project (http://pandora.com/mgp.shtml). Unlike Amazon.com, Pandora isn't creating links based on popularity. Its "innovation is to focus on the formal elements of songs, rather than their popular appeal." Thus, listeners who enjoy "Respect" as recorded by Aretha Franklin may be pointed toward a Solomon Burke tune for the similarities in "classic soul qualities, blues influences, acoustic rhythm piano, call and answer vocal harmony and extensive vamping."[15] Pandora Media is poised to become the *NoveList* of the music world with its list-making capabilities, contributions of ratings from users, and use of "music experts" to contribute to the website's content.

A good music advisor must also be aware of current trends in music. As unusual as this may sound, library staff interested in increasing their musical knowledge should spend some time on MySpace in the MySpace Music category. Most bands today have recognized the power of this social networking tool and have created pages with tour schedules, snippets from current and past releases, and descriptions of their music, influences, and own favorite bands and songs. A patron with a current fondness for The Fray may not find much "listen-alike" potential from perusing The Fray's website and may not want to attach descriptors to The Fray's music and search Pandora, but The Fray's MySpace page will reveal other bands who are listed as "friends" of The Fray. Music hounds can click on new bands, get a cursory earful of that band's music, and either stick around for more or easily move on to the next musical "friend."

Viewers' Advisory

The first recorded viewers' advisory transaction took place between video store clerk Jack Lucas and a Crazed Video Customer who asked, in all seriousness, for "something zany, a Katharine Hepburn-y, Cary Grant-y kind of thing" or "something modern, a Goldy Hawn-y and Chevy Chase-y kind of thing" with an emphasis on "something funny, nothing heavy" because she "wanted to laugh, *needed* to laugh." Fans of the cult hit *The Fisher King* will recall Jeff Bridges giving Kathy Najimy the hairy eyeball as he tosses a video titled *Ordinary Peepholes* on the counter and describes the movie's appeal factors in language that cannot be reprinted here.

Although Jack Lucas exhibits poor viewers' advisory behavior by giving the patron what he thinks she needs and not what she states she wants, this is a scenario with all the elements of a typical readers' advisory transaction—one of the more frustrating ones but also one of the more realistic. This exchange also demonstrates what is needed for successful viewers' advisors, in libraries or Blockbuster—a common vocabulary of terms, an understanding of genres that goes beyond those created by Hollywood, and training.

The idea of doing advisory with visual materials such as DVDs may seem almost ludicrous to many readers' advisors. Our collection is already garnering great circulation statistics; what further help could the collection and its users possibly need? The best and most popular movies and documentaries are always checked out, and many items already possess long hold lists. Why would library staff want to do viewers' advisory for a collection that is already thinned and invites easy browsing? How would staff even begin to do advisory for nonprint collections, particularly film?

As stated in this chapter's Research Review, there is very little useful research available on viewers' advisory. Both the Pitman and Vollmar-Grone articles discuss media literacy and the use of AV materials in a reference/information setting. Staff have always known that the majority of circulations for AV materials are for leisure purposes. This is where research with an interest in AV advisory should be placing primary focus. Possibly the authors of the articles felt this use of AV items was a given. Maybe so, but that reason wasn't enough to stop Saricks and Brown from doing an examination of Danielle Steel, John Grisham, Tom Clancy, and Mary Higgins Clark to determine what made those authors appealing for the reader of best sellers. This reason is all library staff need to start looking closely at the AV collections and asking, What do viewers *see* in some of these movies?

Vollmar-Grone touched on those very topics toward the end of his extremely useful article. Now it's time for that subject to be front and center, and here are only a few reasons why. Most libraries, particularly small libraries, have busy AV collections that are not large enough to satisfy the average library user. The most popular "best-selling" items are either constantly checked out, getting snatched up off the "just returned" cart by eager patrons, or won't darken a DVD shelf for nine months or more thanks to the hold list. If this scenario sounds familiar, it should. The last installment in the Harry Potter series prompted many readers to stop by their local library and ask if the book was in. With a perfectly straight face, the public services staffer politely placed a hold (something like no. 376 for thirty books) and then offered something else for the patron to read while she waited for her name to reach the top of the list a presidential term later. This is the same type of service libraries should consider offering for audiovisual materials.

Just as many libraries create "what to read while you are waiting for the next Harry Potter" displays and reading lists, we should be doing the same for popular movies with long hold lists. What about this: "Waiting for the next Pirates of the Caribbean movie? Try these while you wait."

Increase the circulation and awareness of some of those little-known gems that aren't getting the attention they deserve. Library staff go out of their way to give second life to a novel in danger of weeding by featuring it in a display. Consider doing the same with those less flashy movies that viewers don't know they *should* be clamoring for. That tried-and-true display in all the best independent bookstores, "Staff Picks," is always an attention getter, but it is only as good as the content and effort put into creating the display. Since the goal of the display is to draw attention to films of high quality that received little media play, make it a guideline that blockbuster films not receive coveted space on this display. Include neatly handwritten "shelf talkers" that include a description of the film, suitability for certain viewers, and cinematic appeals. Encourage staff to write their own blurbs about the films and not recopy what is on the back of the DVD or VHS case. Potential viewers appreciate the informed opinions of other viewers. Save all the "shelf talkers" at the readers' advisory desk to start a list of "sure bets" for movies. If Joyce Saricks can make it work for books, then it can work for movies too.

ALL EYES ON YOU: THE KNOWLEDGE

Saricks must have felt just as daunted staring at her fiction collection and wondering, "How can all of these books be categorized in ways that will be useful to both library staff *and* readers?" as staff feel looking at the DVD shelves. The Crazed Video Customer in the introductory example probably needed only to be pointed to the romantic comedy section in the video rental store. However, as patrons are wont to complain, libraries (and online catalogs) are not arranged in the same way as bookstores and movie rental stores. Library staff need to listen to the patron, identify the necessary appeals that need matching, and then suggest accordingly. Before that process can begin, though, appeal characteristics must be applied to AV materials.

Library staff have a place to start. The fundamentals are in place. Saricks and Brown gave them to the library world back in 1987. Just as we read new books, we need to start viewing movies and thinking about how patrons ask for leisure materials, apply the language of appeal, and identify other characteristics that might intrigue viewers. This is more important than someone might believe at first glance. It is easy to help the patron who wants only action-adventure or romantic comedy movies; that's the equivalent of the reader who wants nothing but mysteries— cozy, noir, procedural, anything. Most of the characteristics applied to books translate well to film—character, frame, storyline, pacing. No doubt other characteristics will emerge once advisors start thinking and talking about viewers' advisory. Just as readers' advisors know there is more to a book than its title, author, and genre, there is more to a film than its director, stars, and genre. This is where we use our experience in identifying the appeal characteristics of library material and making connections we can then suggest to our users.

VIEWERS' ADVISORY: HOW DO I DO IT?

Since viewers' advisory is a relatively new concept, this section details and analyzes a real viewers' advisory transaction. Most library AV desks do most of their business during the "pre-date" hours, 4:00–6:00 p.m. on Friday and Saturday afternoons. I observed the AV desk at our library and saw the following transaction unfold; thankfully, it did not resemble the one from *The Fisher King*.

> A library patron was browsing aimlessly among the DVD cases when she was approached by a staff member who asked if he could assist in selecting a movie. The staff member asked the patron what she thought she was in the mood to see. She talked about the wild week she'd had at work and that she wanted something to relieve the stress. She anticipated the staff member's next round of questions by saying she didn't find sex scenes too uncomfortable, wasn't offended by language, but refused to watch anything with gratuitous violence or torture and didn't want to see anything in which a child or animal died. She also said she didn't mind reading subtitles but didn't want any "heavy" drama and then added that she didn't like "sophomoric" comedies either. She ended her laundry list of cinematic qualities with "no Meg Ryan or Adam Sandler, I want to feel I spent a worthwhile two hours." The staff member asked what films she had taken home recently and she replied, *Amélie* and *Pulp Fiction*. Further conversation with the patron gave the library staff member enough information to make the following suggestions: *Jet Lag*, *Memento*, and *Diva*.

Later I asked the staff member why he had suggested those films, and he told me that from what the patron had described it seemed she would enjoy *Jet Lag*, a subtitled French film, for the mature yet fanciful romance between the two lead characters, who are both tentative about the possibility of falling in love and the unusual situation that brings them together.

He suggested *Memento* as a match for *Pulp Fiction,* even though the patron had said she didn't care for violence. When prompted, the patron didn't talk about the violence in *Pulp Fiction;* she talked about the unique story-telling structure of the film, the many different views of the characters, and the intriguing storyline, characteristics that are also strengths of *Memento.* The staff member said he tossed in *Diva,* another subtitled French film, because it seemed to be a combination of both *Amélie* and *Pulp Fiction*—quirky and mysterious characters, dark humor, some great chase scenes, and a happy ending.

The key variable in this situation is an extremely knowledgeable staff member with good customer service skills. Like the best readers' advisors, he wasn't trying to get the patron to take home his own favorite film, and unlike the worst video store clerks, he didn't denigrate the patron's taste in movies. Since there are no plans to clone this valuable Kansas City Public Library staffer, viewers' advisors must look for the tools that will help them provide advisory services like our library.

VIEWERS' ADVISORY TOOLS

The "read-alike" started simply. Several library patrons clamored for the same title or author, and a harried librarian put together a list of "other books and/or authors you might enjoy if you enjoyed XYZ." The "view-alike" can have just as humble a beginning and serve the same purpose. We can start with the appeal factors we've been given by Saricks and Brown and go from there. Once we have the same appeal factors attached to several film titles, we will have the list of "view-alikes" we've been searching for. These lists will become the tools we turn to for those hard-to-answer queries from patrons. The easy questions already have sources we can consult: *Video Hound's Golden Movie Retriever, Halliwell's Film, Video, and DVD Guide,* or the Internet Movie Database, to name a few.[16] The latter is a valuable but mixed Internet source. Descriptive content is contributed by eager filmgoers and can vary widely. The "memorable quotes" section gives interested viewers an idea of the dialogue, but there are few mentions of violence, gore, child/animal deaths, or amount or kind of sex and rough language. Vollmar-Grone refers to the above trade publications in his article as useful resources that can assist the library staffer in being more "format literate" and "more closely match[ing] customers' wants on a particular topic or works by specific writers, producers, directors."[17] These references are best used when a viewer wants a Julia Roberts/Akira Kurasawa/Bollywood movie or an answer to a factual question that can be treated as a reference transaction. If only all readers' advisory transactions were this simple. A viewer asking for a Miramax film is the equivalent of a reader asking for a book published by Hachette, and probably just as unlikely.

Library staff might also consider casual and unorthodox tools such as *Cinematherapy; He Rents, She Rents;* or *1001 Movies You Must See before You Die* as more useful starting points for film suggestions, since these titles are aimed at the leisure viewer.[18]

We can teach ourselves to read film reviews the way we read book reviews; looking for phrases and words that identify the item's appeal to its audience will help library staff match a particular film to a patron's taste. Film critics will likely never work language of appeal into their reviews, but we can observe the phrases and vocabulary they do use and infer the appeal characteristics from the review.

ALL EYES ON YOU: THE TRAINING

Now, how do you, a readers' advisor, prepare to answer movie advisory questions? You've probably already done it. One of the most failsafe questions to ask in uncomfortable social situations involving lots of strangers is, "What's the last movie you saw and liked?" Everyone's favorite cocktail party conversation starter is a viewers' advisory question.

As Vollmar-Grone points out, the same rules apply to discussing film and discussing books. Listen carefully. A few more probing questions may be needed than the all-purpose "What do you like to watch?" We have all been in conversations regarding movies that become plot-driven descriptions or gushings over a particular performer. We may need to create a small list of other questions to elicit the information needed to send the customer home with the desired item. For starters:

- Did you like/dislike any characters, and why?
- What did the plot or story make you think about?
- How would you describe the mood or atmosphere of this movie?
- Was it easy to follow or did you have to pay attention in order not to miss any special scenes?

Another important point to address is the patron's tolerance level for certain subjects such as violence, rough language, and sex. Vollmar-Grone points out that "sexuality, violence and profanity can have greater impact on the senses when viewed or heard rather than read."[19] For many viewers,

Pulp Fiction's two most heart-stopping scenes, "hypodermic to the heart" and "brains in the backseat," were unwatchable. The same questions advisors ask readers looking for "gentle books" can be tweaked for viewers looking for a movie. So ask gently and cautiously, listening closely to the patron's response (verbal and body language both may be important here, since some viewers may be uncomfortable answering the questions).

- How much violence would constitute too much violence in a movie you were watching?
- How much strong language is too much?
- Do you find scenes of a sexual nature objectionable?
- Can you give me an example of a movie that was too much for you?
- Can you rate, on a numerical scale, the amount and kind of material you found unacceptable?

Conclusion

Once library staff make concentrated efforts to provide advisory services for patrons of AV collections, they will realize they have probably been doing this all along with the most dedicated viewers. Staff should begin to make connections with audiobooks and print material as well. The purpose for which a patron wants to use the material will not change—an enjoyable way to pass free time. Public libraries that make advisory of all leisure materials in all formats a customer service priority won't just see an increase in circulation statistics. More knowledgeable staff will make the connections between film and other collections and suggestions in multiple formats and a variety of subjects. When staff make connections across all the library's collections, it shows the patrons that all of the library's materials are equally worth checking out, not just "their" section. It also shows that the library itself values all aspects of its collections equally.

When I need research and tools in certain formats or subject areas in order to provide the best advisory service I can, I create my own if I can't find what I need. An area as vast as AV materials begs for research and resources geared toward library use that already implement our established language of appeal and characteristics. There is talk out there in library research land about an advisory tool for audiobooks, and one for video likely isn't far behind.

We, as advisors, are listening to the library patrons tell a story of *how* they wish to spend their very valuable leisure time (some of it is being spent with *us*). That is the common thread in the advisory work we do and the patrons we serve. We are finding the best entertainment materials to match the story the patron just told us about what kind of time he or she possesses and what he or she wants to do with it. The patrons tell the story, we listen and provide a suitable ending. The story is not in the material. The story is in the connection made between library and patron.

NOTES

1. Randy Pitman, "Viewers' Advisory: Handling Audiovisual Advisory Questions," in *The Readers' Advisor's Companion,* ed. Kenneth D. Shearer and Robert Burgin (Englewood, Colo.: Libraries Unlimited, 2001), 229–37.

2. Michael Vollmar-Grone, "Hearing and Seeing: The Case for Audiovisual Materials," in *Nonfiction Reader's Advisory,* ed. Robert Burgin (Westport, Conn.: Libraries Unlimited, 2004), 85–99.

3. Judith Elkin, "Special Needs/Special Places," in *Reading and Reader Development: The Pleasure of Reading,* by Judith Elkin, Briony Train, and Debbie Denham (London: Facet, 2003), 143–70; Desmond Spiers quote from 143.

4. Ibid., 144.

5. Ibid., 146.

6. Kaite Mediatore, "Reading with Your Ears: Readers' Advisory and Audio Books," *Reference and User Services Quarterly* 42, no. 4 (2003): 318–23.

7. Greg Morgan, "A Word in Your Ear: Library Services for Print Disabled Readers in the Digital Age," *Electronic Library* 21, no. 3 (2003): 234–39.

8. Hampton (Skip) Auld, ed. "Perspectives 'That All May Read . . .': Talking Books for the Blind and Physically Handicapped," *Public Libraries* 44, no. 2 (2005): 69–76.

9. Ann Kim, "AudioVideo 2006: The Future Is Now," *Library Journal* 131, no. 9 (2006): 60–63.

10. Eileen Hutton, "Audiobooks Deserve Marketing, Too: It's Time for Store Promotions to Catch Up with the Growth in Audio Sales," *Publishers Weekly* 252, no. 42 (2005): 66.

11. Robin Whitten, "The Growth of the Audiobook Industry," *Publishing Research Quarterly* 18, no. 3 (2005): 3–11.

12. Audio Publishers Association Press Release, September 12, 2006, "Audio Publishing Industry Continues to Grow; Shows 4.7% Increase in Sales: Audiobook Sales Reach an Estimated $871 Million," 2006, http://www.audiopub.org/files/public/APASalesSurveyResultsFactSheet2006COMPLETE.pdf; Audio Publishers Association, "Audio Publishers Association Releases Major Consumer Survey and Announces Increase in Audiobook Usage: Nearly 25% of US Population Is Listening to Audiobooks," 2006, http://www.audiopub.org/files/public/2006ConsumerSurvey COMPLETEFINAL.pdf.

13. Mediatore, "Reading with Your Ears."

14. For more on format problems and digital issues, see Jessica E. Moyer, "Audiobooks and iPods, Comments and a Call to Action," *Readers' Advisor News,* October 2006, http://lu.com/ranews/sep2006/moyer.cfm; and Thomas A. Peters, "Assessing Audiobook Services for Your Library," *Library Technology Reports* 43, no. 1 (2007).

15. Jeff Leeds, "The New Tastemakers," *New York Times,* September 3, 2006, section 2.

16. Jim Craddock, *Video Hound's Golden Movie Retriever 2007*, rev. ed. (Detroit: Thomson Gale, 2006); John Walker, *Halliwell's Film, Video, and DVD Guide 2007* (London: HarperCollins UK, 2007); Internet Movie Database, 2007, http://www.imdb.com.

17. Vollmar-Grone, "Hearing and Seeing," 93.

18. Richard Roeper and Laurie Viera, *He Rents, She Rents: The Ultimate Guide to the Best Women's Films and Guy Movies* (New York: St. Martin's Griffin, 1999); Steven Jay Schneider, ed., *1001 Movies You Must See before You Die* (Hauppauge, N.Y.: Barron's Educational Series, 2005); Beverly West and Nancy Peske, *Cinematherapy: The Girl's Guide to Movies for Every Mood* (New York: Dell, 1999).

19. Vollmar-Grone, "Hearing and Seeing," 94.

5

CHILDREN AND YOUNG ADULT READERS AND READERS' ADVISORY

Readers' advisory has long been an accepted part of children's services and has more recently become an important part of services to young adults. The few library-related publications on readers' advisory for children and teens are either practice-oriented articles or chapters in scholarly collections. Instead, most of the research on youth and adolescent reading comes from and has been conducted by researchers in the field of education. As a result, only a limited amount of research has been conducted on how youth services and young adult librarians provide readers' advisory for their patrons.

The Research Review section of this chapter provides an overview of readers' advisory services as they pertain to both children and young adults as well as some research on these reading groups. I combine these groups because several of the research publications are either about or applicable to both children and adolescents. In any case, the line between youth and young adult services is often blurry and can vary from library to library; sometimes young adult services are a subsection of the children's department, and other times they are a separate unit or even part of adult services. Two Librarian's View sections address youth and young adult services individually.

RESEARCH REVIEW   BY JESSICA E. MOYER

The Power of Reading, by Stephen Krashen

Despite the numerous publications and constant interest in reading studies in the field of education, there have been few texts that make the jump into required reading in library science. *The Power of Reading* by education professor Stephen Krashen is one of the most notable.[1] Since the first edition was published in 1993, this text has shown up over and over again on the reading lists for young adult and youth services classes in library and information science graduate programs. Heather Booth, author of *Serving Teens through Readers' Advisory*, cites it as her single best source for understanding reading research.

The Power of Reading was one of the first publications from the field of education to address the idea that, when children read for enjoyment, they improve their reading skills. Not only did he explore this idea, Krashen backed it up with the results of many major research projects, including his own research on Free Voluntary Reading (FVR). The second edition is equally powerful and important. It is impossible to distill Krashen's work into a few paragraphs for this book. Instead, I wholeheartedly recommend it as an excellent resource for reviewing reading research from the field of education up to 2003. For school media specialists wanting research to back up readers' advisory programs or a free reading program, this is the best source, especially since Krashen's name is well known to many educators.

Reading Matters, by Catherine Ross, Lynne McKechnie, and Paulette Rothbauer

The Power of Reading is just one of many excellent publications from the field of education on reading. Because there are so many, and almost none relate the findings to library science, I do not review them individually. Instead, I include extensive write-ups on two chapters from *Reading Matters*, by Ross, McKechnie, and Rothbauer.[2] These lengthy chapters include thorough reviews of reading research from both education and library science for children and young adults. Most important, McKechnie and Rothbauer make the essential connections between research and library practice. Published in 2006, *Reading Matters* is also one of the most current sources on reading research.

"BECOMING A READER," BY LYNNE MCKECHNIE

In "Becoming a Reader: Childhood Years," McKechnie covers the current state of reading research, how children become readers, boy readers, and the intersection of children, libraries, and reading. She reviews research published prior to 2005, which also makes this one of the more recent articles in children's readers' advisory. And it is also one of the best.

Section 1 of "Becoming a Reader" reviews research about children and reading; it is a succinct and relatively easy-to-read overview of all the most relevant and landmark research in this area. No other publication brings together library-based research with the work done in the field of education. McKechnie includes important works such as *Voices of Readers*[3] and Krashen's essential *Power of Reading*. She also reviews the results of national reading surveys from the United States, Australia, Canada, and the United Kingdom that are rarely mentioned in other library publications. From library science McKechnie brings in the results of research done on children's reading preferences—namely, that they like to read popular books just as much as adults. Librarians who are trying to justify having popular (i.e., "trashy") books in their library now have a single place to access this research.

Section 2 focuses on how children learn to read and read proficiently and reviews in more depth several important studies on children and the process of learning to read. McKechnie includes a section from Ross's work on adult readers and their reading since early childhood, which serves to emphasize that children who become readers have a greater chance of continuing as readers (and library patrons) for life. In the section on early reading, McKechnie brings up the important concept of emergent literacy. She then goes on to pull together a list of "Factors That Foster Early Reading," a powerful resource that supports many of the programs and goals of children's services: reading aloud, providing space for quiet reading, ready access to materials, choice of materials, a sense of reading as a valuable activity, and, most important, access to an enabling adult. This section will give any children's librarian who wants to start or continue literacy programs for very young patrons plenty of ammunition. The last aspect of the enabling adult is important enough that McKechnie expands on it in the next section, "Children and Adults Reading in the Zone of Proximal Development." The concluding list "What Libraries Can Do" not only makes this section useful for the reviews of relevant research but also ties it directly into library services. Few other works are able to make this direct a connection, which is one reason this is such a valuable contribution to library science and readers' advisory.

Section 3 tackles the ever-troubling series fiction problem. Since 1929 (and probably before) librarians have argued over whether or not to even collect, let along promote, series fiction for younger readers. McKechnie ably brings together all the various viewpoints on this thorny issue, providing readers' advisors once again with one place to find all the research. She relies heavily on Ross's earlier work on series fiction, "If They Read

Nancy Drew—So What?"[4] It was here that Ross first chronicled the impact reading series fiction as children had on avid adult readers. Ross's conclusion: at some point nearly all avid adult readers had read series fiction, and it was a significant part in their development as readers. As much as some librarians may despair spending precious collection dollars on popular fiction series, not only do kids read them and enjoy them, reading series books is crucial in their development as readers. Librarians have a role to play in this beyond just providing the books. They are the best resource for young readers who have read everything in a popular series and need something else enjoyable. This is where a children's librarian well trained in readers' advisory can have a positive and long-term effect on the life of a child.

Reading differences between the sexes is a growing area of research and publication. McKechnie begins section 4 with a literature review, focused on national and international surveys, highlighting the differences between boys and girls reading, from learning disabilities to genre reading preferences. She expands on this, exploring what materials boys prefer and how they interpret them as reading. McKechnie finds that boys prefer magazines, gaming manuals, comics, and newspapers over traditional print novels. What is really important here is that both adults (teachers or parents or librarians) and some boys don't always see this type of reading as valuable as reading printed novels. Instead, they are seen (or think of themselves) as nonreaders, even though they ingest as much print as a more traditional reader. In particular, librarians may want to think about more ways to collect, market, and circulate these types of materials, making sure their collections are as appealing to boys as they are to girls. This can be a challenge for both teachers and librarians, which are female-dominated professions, but one that cannot be ignored. This section is a must-read for anyone working with young male readers.

In a brief section 5, McKechnie brings it all together, making the connections between children, libraries, and reading. She concludes that school *and* public libraries are essential in children's reading development from infancy to the young adult years.

"YOUNG ADULTS AND READING," BY PAULETTE ROTHBAUER

In the next chapter of *Reading Matters*, "Young Adults and Reading," Rothbauer does for young adults and reading what McKechnie does for children. She reviews and sums up the research about young adult reading in a comprehensive and accessible manner, making this chapter an essential read for any librarian working with young adult readers. Although children's reading has been reviewed and discussed in other venues, notably Krashen's *Power of Reading*, less work has been done in regard to teenagers and reading. Many teens report being regular readers as children but dropping the habit as they move into the difficult and busy teen years, making adolescent reading a particularly important area of study. Library services to teens has continued to grow over the past several years and is increasingly recognized as a separate service and population. The establishment in 2001 of the Printz Award, a literary award for young adult books, is just one example of professional recognition of the growing attention to teen library users and readers.

In six sections Rothbauer reviews the literature on young adults and reading, focusing on reading and identity, reading other forms of media, and the relationship between reading and writing for young adults; she concludes with a section on reaching out to young adults. She begins with several headlines lamenting the reading problem among today's young adults and follows with several commonly held assumptions about young adults and reading: young adults don't read; young adults don't like to read; young adults would rather watch television, play with computers, and listen to music than read; and reading means reading certain kinds of books. She goes on to dissect each of these assumptions, showing them to be misconceptions not supported by the research. Rothbauer immediately catches the interest of her readers, since young adult librarians will immediately start thinking about these assumptions in terms of their own personal experiences with teens.

Rothbauer reviews research that shows that young adults both read and like to read for pleasure—their reading choices just might not be those adults think they should be. She finds that for young adults leisure reading frequently ties in with other interests, such as interests in video games, films, and other media; a Belgian study found that newspaper reading, especially of local news, was actually quite high, with nearly 40 percent of teen respondents reporting regular newspaper reading.

In terms of fiction, Rothbauer finds that over the past seventy years of research young adults have consistently reported enjoying similar types of books. Romances and contemporary fiction are and have been consistently popular with girls, and books with action- and suspense-driven plots are popular with male readers. She also highlights the recent work on nonfiction and factual reading, particularly by young men. Most important, she notes that there has been continual and unfortunately ongoing pressure for young adults to select "good" books, which are probably not the ones they actually want to read. Teens are often overly conscious of their "trashier" selections because of pressure from parents, teachers, and sometimes even librarians.

The section on libraries and young adults is essential and compelling reading for any librarian involved with young adult services. Young adults have consistently reported that libraries do not have the kinds of books (or other materials) they actually want to read, that libraries are not cool places to hang out, and that library staff are not welcoming or helpful. The research Rothbauer cites for this section is a few years old, and we can hope that some of these perceptions have changed in recent years. It is clear, though, that libraries that wish to serve young adults well need to provide the books *and other materials* they want for leisure reading, no matter how trashy or worthless librarians might think they are. And these materials need to be displayed and made accessible. If a library subscribes to several popular teen magazines, it might be important to let these items circulate rather than restrict use to the library. If the library is not a particularly welcoming place for young adults, they might be more likely to read the magazines if they can check them out and read them in another space where they are more comfortable.

Young adults also read adult books and may want to ask questions at the adult reference desk. Adult librarians may need to be trained on ways to interact with young adults, and in particular on providing readers' advisory services to them. Young adults who read adult books often need guidance. They may have read only one adult author, such as Stephen King, and not know what other adult authors they might enjoy. An adult services librarian trained in readers' advisory can just as easily help this sort of young adult patron as a teen services specialist. Adult librarians need to be prepared to interact with and assist young adult readers, and reading Rothbauer's chapter is a great place to start.

Rothbauer next focuses on the role of identity in leisure reading. Young adults are still exploring who they are and are busy forming their own identities. We know from Ross's work that identity formation was an important aspect in leisure reading for her adult readers. Many of her readers report reading their most important book (the great book) as a young adult. Rothbauer also reports in depth on her own work with leisure reading of gay, bisexual, and transgender young women. She ends the section by summing up the role leisure reading can play in the development of identity by young adults, providing a strong argument for supporting and encouraging young adult reading of all types.

In "Reading Diverse Media Forms," Rothbauer explores the emergent research area of media beyond print books. Going past the increasingly accepted forms of comics, magazines, and graphic novels, she looks at the very recent research on young adult interaction with video games, especially those played online (massively multiplayer online role-playing games, or MMORPGs), blogs, and the many other Web 2.0 applications popular with teens. She also includes more traditional media such as audio and video, which are becoming increasingly accessible in online, digital formats. Do these constitute reading? How do they affect more traditional reading? Rothbauer raises these and several other interesting questions that have yet to be answered in the existing research. This is an emerging area of research and one that is undoubtedly important to young adult leisure reading and library services.

In a section of particular importance to libraries, Rothbauer explores the relationship between reading and writing for young adults. Libraries have the potential to be one of the best places to support teen writing. They can host poetry slams and other writing-based events, such as teen writing groups. They can bring in popular young adult authors to talk about the writing process. They can get young adults to respond to something they have read. Recently many libraries have started to host blogs. A blog hosted by a young adult section of the library, with contributions from both young adults and library staff, even one based around print reading, could be a successful and ongoing activity. This section will provide librarians the research they need to show that writing events are important to young adults and will promote reading, an always compelling argument for library administrators.

Finally, Rothbauer talks about ways libraries and librarians can reach out to teens where they are and ways they can make reading a social event. In many ways this section ties together all the previous sections. It offers several ways librarians can reach out, from going out to the local community to creating a presence in a virtual community patronized by young adults. Rothbauer also discusses ways to create discussion around books that go beyond the typical after-school book discussion group, which many young adults would like to attend but find difficult to squeeze in. This chapter is important reading for any librarian working with young adult readers, not only for its excellent research reviews but also because of the many suggestions on what libraries can do to improve reader services to young adults.

Reading and Reader Development, by Judith Elkin, Briony Train, and Debbie Denham

Reading and Reader Development has many similarities to *Reading Matters*. Whereas *Reading Matters* takes a North American perspective, *Reading and Reader Development* was written entirely by authors based in the United Kingdom and thus offers a valuable European perspective on reading and readers' advisory, starting with the title.[5] "Reader development," for those not familiar with the term, is the European equivalent of what North American librarians know as "readers' advisory."

"READING: A UK NATIONAL FOCUS," BY DEBBIE DENHAM

In "Reading: A UK National Focus," Denham uses the section "Reading Schools" to address the crucial difference between the teaching of reading in the school setting and leisure reading.[6] Denham believes that it is critical that schools promote reading for pleasure, though in many European schools this activity has recently been dropped in favor of national reading initiatives; her points sound a lot like the critiques of the No Child Left Behind act in U.S. schools. Denham goes on to provide an overview of the National Literacy Strategy and how children are currently being taught to read in the United Kingdom. She neatly sums up the various arguments for and against leisure reading during the school day, mostly with U.K.-based research, and argues for a reintroduction of leisure reading to the curriculum. This makes a nice addition to the work done by Krashen and is especially relevant in the wake of the No Child Left Behind school reforms.

"SPECIAL NEEDS/SPECIAL PLACES," BY JUDITH ELKIN

Also in *Reading and Reader Development* are several sections on working with nontraditional children or in nontraditional locations. The first section of Elkin's "Special Needs/Special Places"[7] is about children who are in the foster care system, orphanages, or other fluid care situations. Elkin describes five programs designed to reach out to these children: The Who Cares? Trust, A Book of My Own Project, The Right to Read Project, The Network and Access to Books, and Reading Projects for Young People in Public Care. All are inspiring projects that have reached out to a traditionally underserved population, and all are great examples for librarians interested in starting outreach projects of their own.

In another section Elkin discusses ways reading can help young victims of abuse, once again highlighting innovative programs for underserved populations. In particular she discusses a research project in which victims talk about being inspired by characters in books, particularly those with strong characteristics of perseverance and resourcefulness. Abuse victims also report using reading (particularly books from public libraries) as a way to escape unhappy situations at home.

Keeping with her theme of readers' advisory in nontraditional settings, Elkin goes on to describe a readers' advisory program at a children's hospital in London. This program reaches children who because of their hospitalization are not able to access school and public libraries and may be in particular need of recreational activities to pass the long hours in bed. In this program, library staff visit the hospital and provide many of the same programs found in public libraries, such as storytelling, booktalks, and author visits. Most important, the library staff also do some training with the regular hospital staff to ensure continuation of services between librarian visits. Elkin concludes with a short review of other research on reading therapy in hospitals, which would provide excellent background for any librarian contemplating such a program.

Reading and the School Library Media Center

"ADVISORY SERVICES IN THE SCHOOL LIBRARY MEDIA CENTER," BY CAROL A. DOLL

Readers' advisory services for youth and young adult patrons are not limited to the public library or outreach programs. In "Advisory Services in the School Library Media Center," a chapter in Shearer and Burgin's *The Readers' Advisor's Companion,* Carol Doll writes about readers' advisory services in the school setting, a location for reader services for children and young adults that is frequently overlooked in the literature.[8] For many children and young adults, the school library media center is their first and easiest (and sometimes only) location for leisure reading materials. Public library visits may require transportation by parents or another adult, and some children do not even live in an area served by a public library. For many children, particularly those with unreliable transportation, overdue fines may be a real barrier to borrowing books from the public library. Thus school library media centers can play an essential role in readers' advisory and leisure reading.

Doll discusses the differences and similarities between doing readers' advisory in a public library and a school media setting. The most important difference is that school media centers are part of the school itself and therefore represent the educational goals of the school. Too often leisure reading's educational impact is either ignored or dismissed, making it difficult for school media specialists to collect and support leisure reading materials and activities. And media specialists who spend time helping students find leisure reading materials may be seen to be wasting time that could be devoted to something educational. Right from the start, school media specialists can encounter difficult barriers.

Doll begins with a discussion of the school culture and the functions the school media specialist may serve, such as working with a teacher to find reading materials to go with a specific lesson plan or to integrate information literacy instruction into the curriculum. For the media specialist who wants to add readers' advisory to an already full schedule, Doll lists several "techniques," many of which draw on traditional children's services training: reading aloud, storytelling, readers' theater, booktalks (possibly in teams with public librarians), author visits (likely teamed with a public library), book clubs, creating bibliographies, and individual guidance. She describes each technique, ways to implement it, and several resources for further information. This is a useful and practical section that will be most helpful for the school media specialist who has the time and support to work on such projects; unfortunately, Doll does not give much detail on how to persuade administrators and other teachers to support these programs.

The final section of Doll's chapter is a discussion of the various tools school media specialists can use for finding specific titles. The first two suggested areas are print-based bibliographies, such as the Wilson catalogs. Although these have traditionally been taught as good tools for readers' advisory, in fact they are expensive and outdated almost as soon as they hit the shelf, especially in terms of popular fiction. The titles aimed at nonfiction are a little better, though again they often point to outdated titles. Doll has a short section on e-resources but dismisses subscription products as too expensive. Since she wrote her chapter in 2000, though, not only have prices on such resources dropped, but consortial agreements and even statewide acquisitions have made these products available to school libraries at very low prices. Contrary to Doll's advice, the school library media center with a limited budget would be best served by purchasing a single electronic product such as *NoveList K–8*, which is both more up to date and more accessible to multiple patrons. The rest of the e-resources category is, however, helpful in emphasizing the use of free Internet sources, an area that has increased only in the past few years. Doll discusses the resources available on the ALA website and suggests that school media specialists sign up for LM-NET, an extremely active electronic discussion list for school librarians and a valuable resource for all topics related to school media specialists, including readers' advisory–related questions.

"FOR THE LOVE OF READING," BY JILL HERITAGE

Readers' advisory services in the school setting have also been addressed by Jill Heritage in "For the Love of Reading," a master's paper written in 2004.[9] This is one of the few publications to study the actual readers' advisory interview with children. Heritage begins with the premise that readers' advisory services are an essential role of the school library media specialist and that the readers' advisory interview is the heart of readers' advisory services. In her literature review Heritage finds that rarely, in all the library and education-based research, is the role of the school library media specialist studied. "Thus, when education literature specifically addresses the act of matching a student with a book to read, the valuable role to be played by the media specialist is rarely acknowledged." Heritage's paper covers many of the same studies as McKechnie but is still a good source for an overview of education and library literature on reading and readers' advisory because of its focus on elementary school–age children.

Heritage conducted ten interviews with currently practicing school library media specialists. Her overarching research question was "What are the steps taken by elementary school media specialists in the readers' advisory interview to help second grade students select reading books for pleasure?" Heritage focused her interviews on readability, leveling, developmental characteristics, student interests, teacher philosophy on recreational reading, parental opinion, use of reference sources, direct instruction, and follow-up. Her "Results" section includes detailed discussions of each interview, including many examples and useful practical information. It also shows the variation among school media specialists within a limited geographic region.

Three themes emerge from the interviews: free choice, just-right books, and saving face. Media specialists placed importance on allowing children to choose the books they are interested in regardless of reading level. All participants were concerned in helping students find the just-right book, but what that was varied greatly among participants, with concerns revolving around reading levels and interest. All media specialists were concerned about helping students maintain image. One librarian made a special effort to include low-level books in whole-class booktalks so readers who needed lower-level titles would not feel stigmatized. Overall, "most [media specialists] saw the classroom as the place for leveled books . . . and the school media center as a place for free choice and reading independent selection." It was noted that this is an area where teachers and school media specialists can have differences of opinion that may need to be negotiated. Heritage's study is an important contribution to readers' advisory services in the school media setting and the readers' advisory interview with children.

Young Adults and Readers' Advisory

A few recent publications not included in the previous sections also focus on readers' advisory services for young adults.

"LEADING THE HORSE TO WATER," BY ANGELA BENEDITTI

In 2001, Angela Beneditti published "Leading the Horse to Water: Keeping Young People Reading in the Information Age" in *The Readers' Advisor's Companion,* which provides a brief overview of readers' advisory services to teens as seen in 2000.[10] Her chapter is a good introduction to young adult readers and services to young adult readers but has since been eclipsed by Rothbauer's and Booth's more recent publications.

In 2003, Elizabeth Spackman wrote a master's paper on recreational reading in high schools.[11] This set of four case studies is a good supplementary resource for understanding how high school library media centers support young adult reading.

"RA FOR YA," BY HEATHER BOOTH

In 2005, Heather Booth published, "RA for YA: Tailoring the Readers' Advisory Interview to the Needs of Young Adult Patrons," one of the first articles to focus solely on readers' advisory for young adults.[12] Published in *Public Libraries,* Booth's article won the 2005 Feature Article Contest. She begins with the assumptions that young adult librarians can and will do readers' advisory and that reading is important to teens. She focuses her article on the ways readers' advisory for teens is different from readers' advisory for adults and suggests how librarians trained to provide readers' advisory services to adults can adapt to best meet the needs of teen readers.

Booth makes the important point that all librarians, whether youth, young adult, or adult services, are seen by teens as authority figures giving unsolicited advice. Readers' advisory for teens is not about recommending a book that is good for them to read (they get enough of that already) but about finding them a book they might enjoy. Librarians working with teens may need to work extra hard to convey the message that they are there to find books (or other media) that are for fun, that nothing they suggest is "required," and that *anything* teens enjoy reading is okay. Booth also emphasizes the importance of making teens feel welcome in the library; many teens have experienced being unwelcome somewhere solely because of their age. And this is an important part of the readers' advisory interview. Using the frame of a typical teen patron who is reluctant to ask for assistance, Booth details the most effective steps and techniques for conducting a readers' advisory interview. She finds a crucial difference between teen and adult readers: questions that frequently work well with adults do not necessarily elicit similar or even useful responses when used with young adult patrons. This makes her inclusion of a variety of possible questions especially valuable.

Booth follows with an excellent description of ways to tailor the book pitch part of the readers' advisory interaction for teens—who need a book description based on their own interests and want to know what it is actually about. This requires some practice and quick thinking on the part of the librarian, especially one accustomed to talking to adult readers.

Booth notes that sometimes, no matter what the librarian tries, the readers' advisory interaction fails. And with teen readers that can be okay—they want to experience "the power of finding their own books." She concludes by reminding librarians that to work with teens they must be approachable and clearly taking the teen's reading interests and requests just as seriously as those of an adult. Even if the first time fails, as long as the librarian does a good job there is a pretty good chance that the teen will be back again. This is one the best practice-oriented articles and the best on using the adult readers' advisory model to provide readers' advisory services to teens.

"READERS' ADVISORY BY PROXY," BY HEATHER BOOTH

Booth has also written "Readers' Advisory by Proxy," in which she focuses on a specific type of readers' advisory interview, one that is generally unique to youth and young adult services.[13] All too often teens are too busy to make it to the library, and parents may be the ones picking up and even picking out books. And these parents not only need help, they usually don't hesitate to ask. This is a tricky but all too common situation librarians need to be prepared for, and Booth's article is a great place to start preparing. There is nothing out there in the library literature that addresses this situation, and readers' advisory librarians may be challenged by many of these requests. Do they try to find something the child will enjoy? Will it have to meet the parents' standards? Do the parents even have a clue as to what their teen actually enjoys reading? Booth reminds us that no matter how challenging this situation becomes it is still positive. The teen has an adult who cares about their leisure reading interests and is involved in their life.

Booth's suggestions are practical, thoughtful, and extremely useful. She suggests starting with a thorough interview with the adult. There is nothing wrong with trying to gather as much information as you can about the child and his or her reading interests and about why the adult is looking for a book. Booth tells librarians to use their reference interview training to get "to the root of the request." Don't hesitate to ask if the teen can be reached by phone—many teens carry cell phones, and a few quick questions can be a big help. This also lets the teen know that you the librarian are genuinely interested in finding something he or she will enjoy reading. For follow-up Booth suggests sending home prepared book lists with further suggestions, including references to the library's website, which may be more accessible to busy teens. Include the department e-mail address so the teen can follow up directly with the librarian. If you provide readers' advisory via a virtual reference service, make sure to send along this information as well. Any way you can get feedback on books you have suggested is helpful; if it goes well, there is good chance you will be working with this parent or teen again. Above all, this will make it clear to teens that the library cares about their reading interests and might even get them to visit the library on their own.

New Directions and Publications

Nearly all the research about children and young adults is about reading—learning to read, reading skills, development of readers, the teaching of reading—and much of that comes from the field of education, not from library science, as can be seen readily in McKechnie's and Rothbauer's reference lists. Clearly readers' advisory services to children and young adults is an area in great need of further research. We need to understand as much about what children say and need in a readers' advisory transaction as we understand about adults. Can you (successfully) ask children about mood? Or pacing? Or tone? Is it okay to question children about their reading levels? How do you find out what they are and are not supposed to be reading (parental and school restrictions)? How can a librarian successfully conduct a readers' advisory interview with a student who has a class assignment to read? How are librarians trained to provide these services (if at all)? None of these questions has yet been adequately addressed in the research literature, though they are clearly important to library services.

SERVING TEENS THROUGH READERS' ADVISORY, BY HEATHER BOOTH

The newest contribution to this area is Booth's *Serving Teens through Readers' Advisory*.[14] Modeled on Saricks's classic *Readers' Advisory Service in the Public Library*, Booth's work offers the first comprehensive introduction to readers' advisory services for young adult patrons, an important contribution to the rapidly growing field of young adult services especially because of the increasing amount of crossover reading interests. Many young adult readers, especially genre fiction fans, read from the adult stacks and want to talk to adult services librarians about their reading interests. And an increasing number of adults are realizing that books published for young adults can be just as interesting, if not better, than a great deal of adult fiction. Librarians who are able to talk knowledgeably about adult and young adult books, and work with adult and young adult patrons, will be going a long way in providing high-quality readers' advisory services for all readers.

YOUTH SERVICES LIBRARIAN'S VIEW   BY AMANDA BLAU

As a youth services librarian, I agree with the Research Review's conclusion that more research on readers' advisory for youth is needed. Though there is much research about children learning the mechanics of reading, there is not enough research into best practices for selecting books for pleasure reading for children or books that will help children grow into lifelong readers. In this section I discuss some of the many challenges to readers' advisory for youth—from readability, to teacher and parent expectations and desires, to the need to serve reluctant readers—and highlight some recent trends I have noticed in my work in a suburban Chicago area library.

Amanda Blau is a children's services librarian at the Downers Grove (Illinois) Public Library.

Readers' Advisory for Children: Challenges and Differences

Readers' advisory for children poses some unique challenges and important differences from adult readers' advisory. One of the biggest differences is the need to gauge not only children's reading taste but also their reading ability. Several leveling systems or readability gauges have been developed and are used in educational circles, but I find it more useful to know what books other children in the grade have liked than to know any readability score for a given book. A common mistake is assuming that a book given a third-grade reading level appeals to most third graders. Readability scores do not to take into account the themes of the book, tone, character appeal, writing style, or genre. The ability to read a text and the desire to read a text are different things. It would be interesting to see a study of how readers' advisory service differs when the advisor does and does not have information on the child's reading level from a test. Because of the increasing significance attached to readability scales, by both schools and parents, I briefly discuss the two readability scales I most often encounter.

The Accelerated Reader (AR) program gives books a grade level and a decimal spot within that grade level (www.renlearn.com/ar/). For example, a book rated 3.5 is rated at a middle of third grade level. AR also gives an interest ranking of lower, middle, or upper grades that is independent of the readability ranking. The AR vendor also sells quizzes on individual books, with the idea that children will read the books and then take brief computer quizzes. AR assigns point values to books, and children in the program can get points for their reading by passing quizzes.

Beyond questions about the concept of reading for points rather than pleasure, a key problem for readers' advisory is the limited books on which children have an available quiz, since schools are required to purchase quizzes individually. Although AR has made an increased effort to have quizzes available for the newest and hottest titles, participating schools may not yet own them. Schools also rarely own quizzes for nonfiction titles, which recent research has shown often resonate strongly with boys. Additionally, in the public library it is necessary to know which school the child is from to determine which quizzes are available. All of this serves to limit the number of books a librarian has available to suggest.

The objection to the practice of reading for points rather than for pleasure should be clear. There are fewer things more frustrating than getting a child excited about reading a book only to have him put it back for a less interesting book that happens to be on his AR list. This along with the limited reading options have brought the AR program criticism from both library science and education. Still, the levels themselves do give an idea of the readability of a book and could help a librarian pick a book at a particular reading level. Also, the assignment of an additional interest level is helpful. A book rated 5.2 with an upper grades interest ranking may be at a fifth-grade reading level, but it probably has themes best suited to older students. This can be especially useful information when working with readers with very high or low reading abilities for their age group.

AR seems to have passed its peak of popularity, at least in the Chicago area schools. Recently I have seen a greater focus on Lexile scores (www .lexile.com), which correspond not to grade levels but to points on a range from 200 for beginning readers to 1700 for advanced texts. *NoveList* now lists Lexiles for the books in its K–8 module and allows users to search by Lexile range. In my community, schools test the Lexile reading score for children, and that information is given to parents. They now come to the library requesting books at their child's Lexile level.

Lexile scores readability, not content or interest level. For example, a Berenstain Bears chapter book may have the same Lexile score as the popular teen Clique novels, but clearly it does not appeal to the same readers.

Lexiles are a useful tool for evaluating the difficulty of a text, but they are not a system for recommending books to readers. I frequently explain to parents that a children's librarian who can provide readers' advisory is much better than a list of books with a given Lexile score. I point out that *Lord of the Flies* has the same Lexile score as *Llama in the Library*, though the themes and contents of these books are appropriate for very different readers. Parents, it seems, can get lost wanting their children to be reading right at their highest Lexile number, if not above. Some children also feel the need to read at their highest level. I like to remind parents that we adults often enjoy reading well below our maximum reading level, and children are the same way. Just because I can read philosophy books by Immanuel Kant (Lexile score 1500–1680) does not mean I will not want a John Grisham novel (Lexile score 680–930) when selecting my pleasure reading. Too often Lexile-based reading selections lead children to read above their comfort levels.

Reading instruction references three levels of reading ability: independent, instructional, and frustrational. *Independent* reading is a comfortable level with limited unfamiliar words or difficult sentences. *Instructional* reading benefits from occasional adult help. In the *frustrational* reading level, the child is not able to read without a great deal of assistance and a subsequent loss of comprehension. The frustration level can easily be reached by children who read only at the highest end of their Lexile range; the independent and instructional levels are much more likely to provide children (and adults) an enjoyable leisure reading experience. Clearly, matching children to books at their independent reading level is critical, and we need more research into methods and questions librarians can use to provide the best matches.

How do advisors discern a child's current reading level? From the practical side, the classic readers' advisory question of asking for a book title the child has read and enjoyed is a good indirect way to start. Sometimes, though, children may mention a book they read in the past that is not indicative of their current abilities; or they may give a title that a parent or teacher read to them that is above their independent reading level. For these reasons, I like to pull a range of books around what I suspect is the child's reading level. When I am unsure of a child's ability, I open a book I am recommending, show a page of text, and see the child's reaction to the number of words on the page and the size of the font. If the child seems hesitant or if I can see uncertainty on his face, I pull a book that is at a lower reading level, shorter in length, or includes pictures. Sometimes I ask if the child is looking for a shorter story or likes stories with pictures. These are indirect ways to determine if a child is looking for something easier without requiring the child to tell you that he is reading below grade level.

One nice thing about the public library is that it costs nothing to take more than one book home. Children are often interested in popular books they do not yet have the skills to read. If a child wants to take a book I suspect is above their independent reading level (a frequent occurrence with popular books), I recommend some easier titles with similar appeals to go home with the harder book. I might also suggest that a parent or other adult read aloud the more challenging titles, for children are often able to comprehend books at a higher level when they are read aloud. For the same reason, I recommend our audiobook collection to readers who may be fascinated by popular books above their independent reading level. In my view, a goal of readers' advisory is to show children that books contain stories and information that match their interests. Once they discover that, their interest in reading should grow. I don't want to stop children from taking a book home that is too hard for them, but I do like them to also have books they can read independently.

A readers' advisory challenge unique to youth is having children or parents come in with assignments that require them to read from a particular list of titles. This means searching for a pleasurable read that also satisfies a teacher's requirements. To help with this, I try to become familiar with books that straddle genres. Within historical fiction, for example, one can find family fiction, romance, mystery, horror, and medieval reads that border on fantasy. By finding out which kinds of books the child has read and enjoyed, it is often possible to find a good match even within the limitations of the assignment. Tools like *NoveList* can also help identify reads within one genre that also hold reading appeals to match a given child and assignment.

Teachers often also stipulate a minimum number of pages to be read, which adds another limitation to the perfect book search. If I find a good book that is just under the page limit, I encourage children to ask the teacher if the book might be okay. I tell them I can send a note recommending the book or pointing out that it is on target for their grade level. With frequent minimums of 100 pages, I find I do this most often when recommending biographies. It can be hard to find a matching biography on a contemporary sports star, for which 80–90 pages seems to be the most popular length. Since some teachers may not bend requirements, I also try to find these students a book that fits the requirements exactly. Again, it is important to provide the children several options. It lets them know that the librarian actually wants them to find and read something they will enjoy, not just something that fits the requirements. It could also bring the child back to the library for more leisure reading materials.

Another challenge for readers' advisory with children is dealing with an adult who is looking for books for a child. The challenges of dealing with proxies in readers' advisory for youth are reviewed in Heather Booth's article "Readers' Advisory by Proxy" (see this chapter's Research Review). In my experience, often these adults know a lot about what their children are reading. If they are not sure, they are usually aware of the child's favorite television programs, movies, and hobbies, which can be valuable input. Again, I like to send proxies away with several books and invite them to let me know which ones their child chose so I can find better targeted books the next time.

One readers' advisory by proxy issue I encounter regularly is adults who want us to find what they think their children should be reading rather than what the children would like to read. This is where it can get tricky. These transactions are most difficult if you have both the adult and child together at the library desk. I had a grandmother swear her sixth-grade grandson was interested in reading classic adventures. After the boy had turned down Jules Verne, *Peter Pan*, *Treasure Island*, and several others, I asked him what he was looking for in an adventure. He said he liked things that were funny with a lot happening. He ended up taking Artemis Fowl, and though his grandmother did not look pleased, he thought a book about an underage supergenius with a farting troll character sounded great.

I tend to err on the side of finding the children what they want, although with specific parental requests it can be a balancing act. Common parent complaints are "All he reads are books with dragons" or "She'll only read Garfield comics." Parents often want me to encourage the child to read something in a new direction. I enjoy these questions, especially if the child has run out of whatever she was reading exclusively. I make sure to validate children's initial reading choices and then present other choices, making sure to show them how these new choices relate to what they had been reading. I find that if I present the new choices as titles popular with other kids who have also read the series of choice, I get more interest from the children trying something new. For the reader who has read all the Junie B. Jones books, I might suggest the Judy Moody books by saying, "Kids I know who liked Junie B. really like Judy Moody books too." Children get a lot of advice from adults, and this frames the new choices as coming from other children. I also say that they do not have to finish a book if they do not like it. If it turns out not to be a fun read, I invite them to come back and tell me what they did not like so we can find them something they will enjoy. This emphasizes to children that I truly do want to help them find a book they like. The advisor may be the first person a child encounters who is concerned with the child's reading enjoyment, so it is especially important to make it clear to young readers that they can tell advisors what they really thought of a book. This type of encouragement to return is important when doing readers' advisory for children.

A readers' advisory challenge particular to working with children is that children are less adept than older readers at explaining what they like about a book. They may not be able to say they like a clever protagonist or even that they like scary stories. I would love to see more research into how children describe and talk about books they enjoy. If I have the title of a book a child likes, I begin by asking about its features. Do you want another animal story? Did you like that it was funny? Did you enjoy the rural setting? Sometimes this sort of questioning gets a response; sometimes it does not. If I can't get much from the child, I begin pulling things similar to the book he read, booktalking those I know and gauging the child's reaction. I make a point to let the child know that, even though I may like a book, it does not hurt my feelings for him to think it sounds dull. I am trying to find a book that he will like, not sell him on a book I like. There are plenty of opportunities for empowering kids in their reading choices at the library.

New Trends in Readers' Advisory for Children

There are some new trends in readers' advisory for children. In the past, readers' advisory was perceived as only for fiction readers. This seems to be changing. For example, more attention is being paid to nonfiction for pleasure. The Siebert Award now honors the best nonfiction book for children. Presentations at library conferences highlight the best new nonfiction. Articles and presentations on encouraging boys to read suggest that building and promoting nonfiction book collections is a prime way to engage boy readers. In both adult and children's services, there are an increasing number of book discussions focusing on nonfiction books and readers' advisory tools for nonfiction leisure readers. When a child comes looking for a book to read for fun, it is good to remember that nonfiction books on weird animals, sports, famous people, historical events, pirates, or aliens may be the perfect match.

There has also been a much larger focus on readers who are not book readers. The traditional view of a reader is someone who reads fiction books, but there is a great amount of reading to be done in other categories. The reading of newspapers, magazines, comics, web pages, and even video games is being talked about more in the library community. Though spending time reading web pages and magazine articles does not build the same literacy skills as reading a novel, there is no doubt that reading skills are being improved to some extent. Many library websites link to fun sites for kids in what could be considered Internet readers' advisory. Summer reading clubs and other library reading incentive programs regularly find ways to reward children for time spent reading, regardless of format, or include rules to permit some number of magazines, comics, or graphic novels. A recent *Booklist* article discussed book recommendations for teens based on what video games they liked to play.[15] Asking about which websites or video games kids enjoy would be another readers' advisory question to consider.

Earlier in this chapter we touched on the persistent debate over "trash" literature and series fiction for children. Graphic novels are probably the latest book form being denigrated as not worth kids' time, with frequent arguments that they could be reading something better. Of course, now that graphic novels have won major national book awards and are increasingly reviewed in standard review journals, they are becoming ever easier to defend as part of a children's collection. For example, three years ago my children's department pulled together all the graphic novels and comics compilations into one section. I have not had any formal parent complaints about this new section. Occasionally I overhear parents saying that they wish their children would read something else. When that happens, I focus on the fact that comics are just part of the collection and offer to help the child find other books of interest. I also highlight the fact that comics hold great appeal for struggling and reluctant readers. Of course, I also have some favorite graphic novels that I feel are high-quality literature for children, and sometimes I recommend these to parents.

Another phenomenon that has affected readers' advisory for children is the popularity of the Harry Potter books. Harry Potter has had as much impact on children's relationship to literature as Oprah has had on adult reading. The Harry Potter series is a children's book series that has become a phenomenon—a series of books at the center of an enormous media event. One need only look at the dozens of bibliographies or displays developed solely to help one find "what to read while you wait for the next Harry Potter," or "what to read after Deathly Hallows," to see the readers' advisory effects. I love Harry—more for the way the series has raised a book release to the same cultural footing as a new Star Wars movie or a new video game console than for Rowling's plot or characters. Though Harry Potter's story may have ended with book seven, the books' effect on parents and children will be long-lasting.

With the profitability of the Harry Potter movies, there has been an increasing look at children's books as big-money possibilities for adaptation to the silver screen. It would be interesting to know how children drawn to a book by its movie adaptation react to the book and whether it leads them to other reading choices. I know children who read everything Louis Sachar wrote after seeing *Holes* or read all the *Chronicles of Narnia* after seeing the first film. We need to see research into the power of movie adaptations on children's reading habits.

Another new trend at my library is parent-led book clubs for increasingly younger children. On our book club shelf early readers by Cynthia Rylant sit next to the latest Jodi Picoult. One dad asked me for recommendations for his child's read-aloud book club for pre-readers. All the parents in this group read the same book aloud to children at home and then get together for a play date and read the same book together again, asking the four-year-olds about their favorite parts. The idea of book clubs for children as an out-of-school leisure activity seems to be growing and has led to a new kind of readers' advisory question. It has meant coming up with books with broad appeal and discussion points for very young children. The level of parent involvement and willingness to translate their enjoyment of book clubs into an activity their children may enjoy is impressive, as well as an exciting new readers' advisory challenge. (For more in this area, see chapter 6 on adult book groups and readers' advisory for book groups.)

A final area that should not be overlooked is passive readers' advisory. The crafting of high-quality bibliographies for print and for the library website is a great way to reach shy children who may not approach an adult for help finding a book. I count as one of my greatest readers' advisory successes a thank-you note from a mother who said that her son, who had not been reading much, was given a bibliography of middle school action-packed fiction I had created and read every title on it. Shy children might not talk to a librarian at a service desk, but we still have the opportunity to reach them. Especially as the Internet becomes a large part of younger children's lives, we need to make sure there are as many passive readers' advisory tools online as there are in the physical library or schoolroom. An area for further research here would be children's reactions to different kinds of book lists. Do they prefer book lists of a genre, books at a grade level, or new popular books of all types? Does it help to have book covers on the book list? What do children need to see in an annotation? Answers to such questions would help librarians make the most of their book list–creating efforts.

Displays are another important passive readers' advisory strategy. They provide an excellent opportunity to pull together and highlight similar books or other media to reach additional readers. In my experience, children are better at browsing a display than facing long rows of books in the stacks. Seasonal, topical, and grade-level displays boost circulation and show patrons just how many great books we have. Children are no different than adults when it comes to browsing: smaller collections are easier to peruse. Additionally, seeing titles that someone else thinks are good may be just as important for children as it is for adults. Browsing is discussed in depth in chapters 9 and 10, but clearly it matters equally to readers of all ages.

Conclusion

To keep current and fresh as a readers' advisor, my suggestions are simple. Read children's books from a variety of genres and age levels; force yourself to read books you would not pick up naturally. Record what you read in a journal, blog, or other format for future reference. Perhaps most important, talk about books with other librarians and with children. These discussions with other readers let me get to know tastes outside my own and let me practice booktalking. The Internet gives me a variety of places to discuss books and to read what others are saying about their reading, from personal and library book blogs, to user comments on bookstore websites, to review journal websites.

This is a great time to be a readers' advisor for children. There has been an increased focus on literacy as a determining factor in children's success in school, and the role of leisure reading in developing literacy skills highlights the need for readers' advisory work. The media attention paid to children's books means they compete strongly with other entertainment options for children. The Internet allows us to discuss books with a widening group of colleagues on blogs, electronic discussion lists, and book websites. Yet still more needs to be done.

In terms of research, I would welcome more research into the readers' advisory interview for children, the ways children describe their pleasure reading, the effects of media on children's pleasure reading, how reading level and methods for gauging children's reading ability play into readers' advisory, best practices for reaching out to reluctant readers, passive readers' advisory, and anything else that might illuminate the best ways to help children become lifelong readers.

YOUNG ADULT LIBRARIAN'S VIEW   BY HEATHER BOOTH

Many of the issues relevant to readers' advisory for children are also applicable to working with teens, such as the need to assess reading level, working with proxies, and the distinction between reading for recreation and reading for school. As mentioned in the research discussion earlier in this chapter, many studies include a broad swath of ages or grade levels.

Heather Booth is the young adult specialist and a literature and audiovisual services librarian at the Downers Grove (Illinois) Public Library and the author of Serving Teens through Readers' Advisory.

Additionally, much of what we know, or assume we know, about readers' advisory for teens comes from extrapolating data and information about readers' advisory for children or adults. There are, however, definite distinctions that must be addressed, and we must hope that as the prevalence of readers' advisory service geared specifically for teenagers gains, so also will the body of research specifically focused on this dynamic age group.

As public librarians seek out information on how to help their teen readers, we encounter a significant block when it comes to backing our theories and practices with research. The vast majority of research on teen reading is either anecdotal or based on reading in a school setting. We understand that there will be a larger body of research related to reading for school—reading ability, reading choice, the impact of various styles of reading instruction, and the like. Educators function within a structure that must justify its methods with measurable outputs. Additionally, studying teen reading within a school setting makes sense because school is simply where the teens often are. But if we are to really motivate teens to read for fun, to pick up a book instead of a remote control, laptop, or game controller, we need to be equipped with knowledge about how and why teens choose to read the material they do. The selections highlighted in the Research Review provide good information about what research currently exists and indicate several areas for further investigation. There are two areas I want to discuss further: specific challenges to readers' advisory for teens, and new directions in readers' advisory for teens.

As shown by Ross's research on the longitudinal reading habits of adults, retaining an interest in reading through the teen years is essential if someone is to grow into a lifelong recreational reader. Also, in *Reading Matters*, Rothbauer points out research to indicate that teens do enjoy reading for pleasure. What, then, can librarians do to combat the decline in reading for pleasure during the teen years? Because teens are more heavily subject to pressure (explicit or implied) that they should avoid reading "trashy" titles, acknowledging, validating, and encouraging the types of material that teens *want* to read is certainly a good first step. Educating librarians on methods by which they can become more familiar and comfortable with high-demand teen reading material would lead to more comfort and competency in high-quality readers' advisory for teens. Is it simply a matter of bulking up graphic novel collections? Or should we place copies of local or national newspapers in the teen area? Would teens respond to suggestions of blogs, message boards, or web-based magazines that read like their favorite series? And just what impact would this type of reading have on teen reading fluency and interest in recreational reading? Reliable research must be conducted to determine the answers to these important questions.

In *Reading and Reader Development*, Denham presents a compelling point about the distinction between reading in a school setting and reading for recreation. As admission to top colleges becomes more and more competitive, and schools are bound by score-based outputs and faced with the decision of whether or not to "teach to the test," recreational reading and its benefits may be losing footing in schools, after the gains made through sustained silent reading programs. Because of this, librarians, in both schools and public libraries, can fill a very important gap in serving the recreational reading needs and interests of teens.

Elkin's chapter in *Reading and Reader Development* offers a good reminder to librarians: if the readers don't come to us, we can make more attempts to go to the readers. Reaching out to teens with readers' advisory in nontraditional settings could make a huge difference to teens in those situations. Elkin mentions hospitals and public care facilities as places where a book can make a difference in a child's or teen's life. News about programs that provide books and readers' advisory to incarcerated teens or teens in crisis shelters appears from time to time. Learning how readers' advisory functions in these settings, and how it differs from traditional readers' advisory for teens, would add an interesting layer to the conversation.

Specific Challenges to Readers' Advisory with Teens

An issue Rothbauer alludes to in her chapter in *Reading Matters* that merits a deeper look is the dynamic that develops between teen readers and adults in a position to suggest books. She notes that the pressure for teens to select "quality" material is felt from all sides—parents, teachers, and librarians. This is a symptom of perhaps one of the biggest blocks to providing good readers' advisory service for teens. Teens are in a developmental phase in which they are realigning themselves with the adult world. They are (and should be) challenging authority in a variety of ways. One of the more significant ways in relation to library service is that an "us versus them" mentality may begin to develop, not specific to librarians but in terms of the general adult population. Still, we are the adults, and as such we have a divide to bridge if we are to assist teens in finding recreational reading. Teens may be suspicious of our motives when we suggest a book. Why should they trust that the novel we are suggesting is something they will want to read in their free time, when their recent history of book suggestions from adults may have been mainly for instructional purposes? What's more, even initiating a conversation with a teen can be difficult because of the same dynamic. They may assume that if we are headed in their direction we are planning on scolding them for misusing equipment, talking too loudly, or having too many people at their table.

Teens are consumers of information and space at the library just as they are consumers of goods in commercial establishments. Most of us have experienced or observed less than gracious service toward teens on the part of many restaurants or stores. If we are to conduct successful readers' advisory interactions with teens, we must look at the way we approach teens and devise strategies to put them at ease and make them feel comfortable in the library. Most important, we must indicate to them that we librarians really and truly do want to help them find recreational reading material that meets *their* interests and *their* needs, not just what they need to read for school, and not just what others may think they *should* be reading. Successful readers' advisory with teens starts with building a trusting relationship between librarian and reader.

But this is just the beginning of the way readers' advisory for teens can differ from readers' advisory for adults or children. In addition to Rothbauer's insight about a perceived or real pressure for teens to select and adults to recommend "quality" reading, the main differences I see are how we approach the teen, variations in the way a readers' advisory interview unfolds, the type of information we present to a teen when making suggestions, a need to deal with sensitive subjects, validating recreational reading and reading selections, and working with proxies.

APPROACH

In my interactions with teens, I have found that approaching them with specific questions or comments, rather than asking if they need help in a general way, leads to more productive conversations. A teen may hear, "Are you finding everything you need?" or "Can I help you?" as just another version of an adult checking in on them. Or they may be unaware of the types of assistance we are able to offer them. Instead, I find that using more specific wording, such as, "I've heard that book is good. Have you read anything else by that author?" or "These shelves can get out of order pretty quickly. Are you looking for a specific title I could help you find?" does more to open the conversation. This is a technique that can work with any age group, but it seems especially effective with teens. Research about adolescent brain development has recently found that the amygdala, the emotional center of the brain, takes over many of the decision-making processes during adolescence, rather than the prefrontal cortex, which typically handles rational thinking and moderating emotional response.[16] It makes sense, then, that interacting in this concrete manner, rather than using more abstract questions or offers of assistance, would be an especially good fit with teen patrons. By wording our offers of help in a straightforward, specific manner, we enable a teen to understand more clearly exactly what we mean and remove the guesswork of interpreting inferences.

INTERVIEW

In the interview phase of a readers' advisory interaction with teens, we need to acknowledge that, as we ask questions about reading preference, teens, like children, may be unaccustomed to articulating their taste. Additionally, at this point in their lives many teens are also unaccustomed to being asked to explain their preferences. Teens are frequently asked, "What's your favorite class?" or "Do you play sports?" or "Do you have any hobbies?" but much more rarely asked, "What is it that you like about biology?" or "What do you think about all the pressure that gets placed on athletes?" or "Where do you get your ideas for your art projects?" Questions that enable teens to express their interests and thoughts, rather than just parrot back information, indicate to teens that their interests and thoughts are valid and important. Asking teen readers what they prefer to read and then inquiring further about why they like those elements, or simply probing deeper and asking clarifying questions about specific elements, are important parts of readers' advisory for teens. It doesn't just help us find the best books to suggest; it also demonstrates to the teens that their views and opinions matter. It shows them that we as librarians are honestly interested in what they have to say and that we will respond to it through our suggestions.

PRESENTATION

When we are presenting selected books to teen patrons, they need more plot description than we typically use with adult patrons. Whereas adults are often happy getting a mainly appeal-based description of a book, teens generally want to know what happens. Surely, knowing that it's action packed, or a really romantic book, or has very tense pacing will help the teen decide whether or not to select the book, but by and large teens do not make this decision without knowing the plot outline. Additionally, teens are often interested in the relative popularity of a book. Saying, "This one has been really big lately" or "I've heard a lot of guys your age say that they really liked this book" validates the choice, just as adults frequently ask us advisors if we have read the book.

SENSITIVE SUBJECTS

The topic that most frequently seems to worry readers' advisors who are pressed into work with teens is what to do about books with sensitive subject matter. Teens are in a phase of life in which pushing boundaries and challenging their values is expected, whether or not it is welcome. It's not just in their active lives that these challenges occur but in their imagined, internal lives as well. Reading materials that challenge their beliefs or press their comfort level can actually serve as safe places in which to experience, contemplate, and make personal decisions about risky behavior or emotionally challenging topics such as sex, violence, religion, or politics. Additionally, reading such "risky" material recreationally, when it is self-selected, has the added benefit of allowing the young reader to put the book down and walk away from it if it becomes too uncomfortable. Almost all of the teens I have spoken with about this topic have indicated that, if they do feel uncomfortable about the content of a self-selected book, they do not continue reading it. Though teens often have a bad reputation for being irrational and impulsive, most of them are quite capable of censoring themselves given the opportunity and choice.

All of this, though, may do little to assuage the nerves of the librarian fearful of a challenge to her collection or personal discretion. The first line of defense in safeguarding against such an event is to be clear about the content of the book when presenting it as a suggestion. This should not, however, be done in a way that puts the teen on the spot or indicates a judgment about the teen that depends on her choosing or rejecting the suggested book. When pitching a book that has content I think bears mentioning, I often say something along the lines of, "There's a lot of romance, and some sex, and it does get a little graphic, just so you know," or "There are really interesting characters who seem totally realistic, and there's quite a bit of swearing, in case that matters to you." By mentioning the topic or content you feel may be controversial in the context of the book, but not emphasizing it, it becomes an element just like any other element you are commenting on.

A technique I have found to be particularly effective is physically putting the book down after giving the description rather than trying to place it in the patron's hands. I place it on a table or at the end of a bookshelf, or just tip the book sideways on the shelf so that the teen can see where it is but does not feel pressured to choose or reject the book in front of me. This allows the teen to make a decision free of any kind of perceived judgment about the selection.

VALIDATING RECREATIONAL READING AND READING SELECTIONS

Another challenge specific to readers' advisory for teens is, again, tied to their main role as students. Teens are busy—with school, with after-school activities, with family obligations, and with developing and maintaining friendships. The time they have to allot to leisure reading is often nearly filled by the time they finish reading for assignments or researching for projects. It is crucial, then, to be encouraging and excited about the material they choose to read in their spare time. The term "trash" gets thrown around frequently when referring to various paperback series, comics, or manga, even brief nonfiction books on subjects of transient popularity such as unauthorized biographies of actors or sports figures. But the research shows that the act of reading itself—regardless of the subject matter or format—has scholastic benefits, and just as important (or perhaps even more important in terms of nurturing lifelong readers), as Ross points out, those who retain their interest in reading through their teen years are significantly more likely to be avid readers as adults. By encouraging teens to read recreationally—whether that means edgy problem novels, light humor, crime capers, series fiction, manga, graphic novels, vignettes in *Chicken Soup for the Soul,* magazines, or how-to books—we enable them to fit recreational reading into their lives on their own terms, and we emphasize the concept that librarians are caring and encouraging of our young patrons' interests and hobbies.

If we consider teens as those age twelve through eighteen, the diversity of interest and reading level is vast. As libraries consider the layout and arrangement of books in teen areas, it is important to consider this diversity. Does the teen area consist mainly of fiction? Are popular genres indicated by spine labels, designated shelving, or another means? Are magazines and newspapers accessible? Are recreational nonfiction books included and, if so, how are they organized? In general, does the library, by its organization and layout, communicate to teens what we believe they should be reading?

PROXIES

Just like children's advisors, readers' advisors who work with teens will undoubtedly work with proxies. What is often different in working with proxies for teens is that the parent is rarely up to date on the material a teen is interested in reading. Reading preferences can change drastically during the teen years as adolescents reach out to form new social connections, are exposed to new activities and hobbies, and challenge their values and interests. It is also a time when teens are pulling away from the family unit and moving toward forming tight social bonds with friends. It is understandable that parents are not always able to keep up with shifting interests. When parents or caregivers come to the library to find books for their teen, it is important to remember that, though the interaction may be frustrating because of a lack of information, the adults are still doing a great thing in trying to keep their teen in touch with recreational reading material. Asking questions about current hobbies or interests, favorite movies or television shows, or topics of conversation that seem to pop up at dinnertime are ways to ascertain the teen's interest if the parents are not aware of the current reading preference.

Helping to find a book when the teen and parent have different ideas of what kind of book the teen should be reading poses an especially touchy situation. When faced with a dueling parent and teen, I always try to continue addressing my questions to the teen. She is the one who will ultimately be reading the book, and she is the one whose preference will determine the enjoyment of the process. Still, if it is clear that the parent has a strong difference of opinion, this must be taken into account. Offering to pull a variety of books, or suggesting that the pair take more than one title home, allows us to do our job in providing a good variety of material but leaves the ultimate decision to the parent and child to make at home.

Training Children's and Adult Services Librarians for Readers' Advisory Service to Teens

In many libraries, even if they have an area designated for teen books and perhaps even a place for teens to lounge and do work, young adult services are still an offshoot of either children's or adult services departments. Relatively few libraries have the space, the resources, and the staff to dedicate an entire department to teen services. Even communities that are fortunate enough to have a dedicated staff member who serves teens typically have just one person tasked with serving this group. Even then the teen librarian can't be at work all library hours, nor is that staff member available on the library floor to work with teens any time a teen comes into the library. This means that the task of serving teens in real time frequently falls to staff members who are not teen librarians.

Such a situation can greatly enrich the diversity of service teen patrons receive, but it works only if the other staff members are adequately trained and motivated to step in and help to provide high-quality readers' advisory service. Teen librarians may often find themselves responsible for providing training materials, pathfinders, and resources for their fellow librarians to use when conducting readers' advisory for teens. It would be interesting to see research on just who it is that serves teens in our libraries. Are these people who specifically trained through their library and information science programs for work with teens, or did they come by this role later in their library career? What kinds of resources do librarians use to educate themselves on teen services? Are there significant gaps that need to be filled by courses, training workshops, print materials, or online collaborations?

Alternate Formats

My last observation about how teens are served in our libraries again ties back to the types of materials we have to offer teens. Once we know what formats, subjects, and genres are most interesting and useful to teen recreational readers, we must take the next step and educate ourselves about how to conduct high-quality readers' advisory with these materials. The emphasis thus far has been on fiction reading, which is still quite valid and popular. But how many libraries that have graphic novel collections also have librarians knowledgeable about these collections—what makes specific titles or artists popular, how to help find a reader move from one book to the next based on appeal elements? Staff training with regard to the materials and methods with which to best serve teens must keep up with the interest. It is, obviously, a moving target, but one at which we must aim nonetheless. Graphic novels are just the beginning. Nonfiction can be popular, but it is an overlooked area of recreational reading for teens. How many young adult areas even have nonfiction leisure reading collections, let alone librarians ready to talk about nonfiction readers' advisory? Teen librarians need to be prepared to learn not just about new authors or genres but about new formats and reading interests as well.

New Directions for Young Adult Readers' Advisory

Where will the research lead next? In what new directions are our teen patrons heading? One significant development I have noticed is the impact of literature circles on the way teen patrons talk about and seek out books for recreational reading. Schools are using literature circles in their English and reading curriculums as a way for students to read widely across topics or genres. Students select a book within a set range of parameters (e.g., historical fiction, nonfiction, contemporary fiction, romance), read their books, and come together during class time to discuss their selections. High schools in my community have been using this model for three school years, starting with each new freshman class. Over the past three years, it has been astounding to see the impact this model has on our readers' advisory interactions with teen patrons. Many of the teens we work with seem significantly more comfortable asking for help with recreational reading suggestions. Many are even using appeal factors in their requests (e.g., "I like character-driven books," "I'm looking for historical fiction, and I really like interesting locations") and seem more comfortable articulating their preferences. I am interested to know what the research will reveal about the long-term impact of such a teaching style on recreational reading habits of young adults.

Literature circles are interesting partly because they encourage teens to interact with one another and discuss books. I see this happening in another venue as well. The Internet provides teens previously unheard-of access to their favorite authors. Authors have websites, blogs, MySpace accounts, and e-mail addresses available for anyone to find and use. Online spaces are ripe with active communities of teens discussing books with one another and with the authors they admire. Will teens who have such easy access to their favorite writers feel more connected to their work over time? Will the vastness of online social networking extend to connecting teens with other authors and reading material? Researchers should not overlook the potential impact of these exciting and dynamic areas of interest.

Finally, I would like to see more scientific research on recreational reading habits of teens. Online surveys provide an interesting glimpse into trends, but the self-selected nature of these surveys prevents us from seeing a true cross section of teens. Research related to school assignment reading and school libraries is illuminating, yet because of the need for the reading to relate to a school assignment, we don't see the breadth of the recreational aspect of teen reading interests. How do teens really find the books they are interested in? Why do they choose them? What genres and formats are waxing and waning in popularity? Most important, what can libraries do to help teens find the material that they want and assist them in maintaining their interest in recreational reading across a lifetime?

NOTES

1. Stephen D. Krashen, *The Power of Reading: Insights from the Research*, 2nd ed. (Westport, Conn.: Libraries Unlimited, 2004); 1st ed. (Englewood, Colo.: Libraries Unlimited, 1993).

2. Lynne E. F. McKechnie, "Becoming a Reader: Childhood Years," in *Reading Matters: What the Research Reveals about Reading, Libraries, and Community*, by Catherine Sheldrick Ross, Lynne E. F. McKechnie, and Paulette M. Rothbauer (Westport, Conn.: Libraries Unlimited, 2006), 63–100; Paulette M. Rothbauer, "Young Adults and Reading," in ibid., 101–31.

3. Robert G. Carlsen and Anne Sherrill, *Voices of Readers: How We Come to Love Books* (Urbana, Ill.: National Council of Teachers of English, 1988).

4. Catherine Ross, "If They Read Nancy Drew—So What? Series Readers Talk Back," *Library and Information Science Research* 17 (1995): 210–26.

5. Judith Elkin, Briony Train, and Debbie Denham, *Reading and Reader Development: The Pleasure of Reading* (London: Facet, 2003).

6. Debbie Denham, "Reading: A UK National Focus: Reading in Schools," in ibid., 77–81.

7. Judith Elkin, "Special Needs/Special Places," in Elkin, Train, and Denham, *Reading and Reader Development*, 150–56.

8. Carol A. Doll, "Advisory Services in the School Library Media Center," in *The Readers' Advisor's Companion*, ed. Kenneth D. Shearer and Robert Burgin (Englewood, Colo.: Libraries Unlimited, 2001), 149–64.

9. Jill Heritage, "For the Love of Reading: The Readers' Advisory Interview in the Elementary School Library Media Center," thesis, University of North Carolina, School of Information and Library Science, 2004, quotes below from 9, 22, 82. Available online at http://hdl.handle.net/1901/46.

10. Angela Beneditti, "Leading the Horse to Water: Keeping Young People Reading in the Information Age," in Shearer and Burgin, *Readers' Advisor's Companion*, 237–48.

11. Elizabeth Spackman, "The Role of Recreational Reading in High School Media Centers: Four Case Studies," thesis, University of North Carolina, School of Information and Library Science, 2003. Available online at http://ils.unc.edu/MSpapers/2853.pdf.

12. Heather Booth, "RA for YA: Tailoring the Readers' Advisory Interview to the Needs of Young Adult Patrons," *Public Libraries* 44, no. 1 (2005): 33–36.

13. Heather Booth, "Readers' Advisory by Proxy: Connecting Teens and Books through Positive Interactions with Parents and Caregivers," *Young Adult Library Services*, Fall 2006, 14–15.

14. Heather Booth, *Serving Teens through Readers' Advisory* (Chicago: American Library Association, 2007).

15. Kelly Czarnecki, "Books for Teen Gamers," *Booklist* 103, no. 13 (2007).

16. Jami Jones, "Teens Will Be Teens," *School Library Journal*, January 2005, 37.

6

BOOK GROUPS

Though it is speculated that reading groups have existed in America since Anne Hutchinson started one aboard a ship bound for the Massachusetts Bay Colony in 1634, it was not until Oprah Winfrey announced the plan for her book club in 1996 that such clubs were commonly acknowledged as forces driving contemporary popular culture and wielding cultural capital.[1] No one knows exactly how many book groups currently exist, but estimates run as high as 500,000 in the United States alone, and it is evident that the number is growing.[2] Clearly a large and growing number of people are voluntarily taking time from their busy schedules to read a work that they might otherwise not and to meet regularly to discuss that work with others who have also read it. This increase in book group participation indicates changes in how people acquire, utilize, and transform literacy and provides a public presence for an activity that has traditionally been viewed as solitary. Service to these groups has become a major dimension of readers' advisory work. But what do we know about them?

RESEARCH REVIEW   BY JOAN BESSMAN TAYLOR

Books about Book Groups

Through surveys of reading groups in the United Kingdom, United States, and Australia, Jenny Hartley in *Reading Groups* and Pat Valentine in *Why*

Joan Bessman Taylor holds a doctorate from the Graduate School of Library and Information Science, University of Illinois at Urbana-Champaign. She is currently an assistant professor in the School of Library and Information Science at the University of Iowa in Iowa City. Her research investigates the leisure reading and writing of adults with particular emphasis on collective contexts.

Book Clubs? provide snapshots of the diversity in types of groups, size of groups, types of works read by members, frequency of meetings, and more.[3] Most of the basic information about book groups comes from these two popular books, which report the findings of surveys distributed to adult book groups and are written to appeal to popular and academic audiences. Published in trade paperback format, they feature less formal reporting and include data in the form of anecdotal excerpts rather than schematic analysis.

READING GROUPS, BY JENNY HARTLEY

Hartley's study of reading groups reports the findings of questionnaires distributed to local and national media outlets such as Orange, *Mail on Sunday*'s YOU magazine, and Radio 4's *Open Book* program and advertisements placed in local and national press such as the *Times Literary Supplement* and *Woman's Weekly*. Defining reading groups as "people who meet on a regular basis to discuss books," the questionnaire focused on recreational/voluntary groups. It asked how long ago each group was started, how it started, how often it meets, what they read, how they choose books, how many members are in the group, among other questions.

The strength of this study is that it introduces the varied landscape of reading groups—they vary in foci, reasons for existence, and structure for discussion. Hartley's results provide good background information about book groups, and that which is likely to be of the most use to readers' advisors is discussed here. Some groups choose books based on genre, author, or theme; others rely on outside cultural arbiters such as newspapers, televised programs, and librarians for their selections. The survey found that about a third of the books men read are written by women, whereas women read about half female and half male authors. The most popular category for group reading "by far" is contemporary fiction. The four factors leading to good discussion were identified as (1) the books themselves (though books do not have to be liked for discussion to go well), (2) the range of opinion in the group (too much agreement can be problematic), (3) the background of context or information that people bring to the book (information on the author, topic, etc.), and (4) the congenial atmosphere of the group.

Hartley's survey found that there are upward of 500,000 book clubs in the United States and 50,000 in Great Britain. She determined that 66 percent of reading groups are all-female groups, 6 percent are all-male groups, and the remainder are mixed-gender groups. The results also indicated that, the older the members of the group, the more likely it is for the group to be mixed-gender. This information is especially important, since nearly all the research exploring contemporary book groups has been on solely female memberships. This points to a gap in the current scholarship and suggests the need for further research into mixed-gender and all-male groups.

WHY BOOK CLUBS? BY PAT VALENTINE

In *Why Book Clubs?* Valentine focuses on the following questions: Why are book clubs such a significant force in the lives of so many Western Australians? Where did these groups have their origins? Valentine began her study in 1995 with a query letter that was subsequently placed in newspapers and forwarded by the Arts Access Bookhire scheme and Bookshops. Beginning with descriptions of clubs from the 1880s, Valentine's study traces the history and development of book groups in Australia with an emphasis on contemporary groups throughout the country. Though much of this study represents information unique to Australia, it also shares many of the findings of Harley's survey. Unfortunately, much of the information contained in the richly detailed responses received by Valentine is not comprehensively analyzed, possibly because it was written for a popular audience. *Why Book Clubs?* features responses from interestingly diverse groups including the Association for the Blind of Western Australia Library Book Clubs, the only mention of blind readers in the discussion of collective reading thus far. The geographic diversity of groups is also unique inasmuch as her respondents represented a more dramatically varied demographic than that documented for the United States.

BOOK CLUBS, BY ELIZABETH LONG

The most extensive and in-depth published research on contemporary reading groups is that of sociologist Elizabeth Long. Long was the first to bring modern book groups to the critical attention of scholars, so her work is exploratory in nature. Using a case study approach, it represents the first mapping of the terrain and is the widest in scope aside from the significant but more taxonomic work of Hartley. Long considers the phenomenon of book clubs from the perspective of the sociology of culture, focusing on the relationship of such groups to the larger social order. She has been publishing research on book groups since 1986, when "Women, Reading and Cultural Authority" appeared in *American Quarterly*. Her work became more widely read through her chapter "Textual Interpretation as Collective Action" in *The Ethnography of Reading*. This chapter was the foundation for her most significant contribution, *Book Clubs: Women and the Uses of Reading in Everyday Life.*[4]

Book Clubs addresses reading as a social process. Having visited approximately thirty white, all-women's groups in Houston, Texas, Long centers her investigations on demonstrating that the act of reading is not the passive, solitary activity it is often depicted to be but rather a social activity that "is in fact integral to the construction of both social identity and the socio-cultural order." The social nature of reading has become something of a given in contemporary reading studies, a situation due largely to Long's work and the work it has inspired. Her primary thesis is that reading represents "a form of behavior that performs complex personal and social functions for those who engage in it. . . . This activity is quite literally productive in that it enables women not merely to reflect on identities they already have but also to bring new aspects of subjectivity into being."[5]

Long presents several observations about what happens during book discussion. The first of these is that reading group members talk with deep engagement about books "but very differently from experts or professionals," sometimes interpreting novels "with marked disregard for learned opinion." This claim seems somewhat problematic in light of the membership of some of the groups she studied, which have a minimum of a college-level education and include former teachers or professors, making the category of "expert" somewhat slippery. Nonetheless, it is intriguing that these women use the group setting as a means for resisting institutionalized approaches to reading. It is apparent that they join leisure groups to hold a different type of conversation about books than they would find in a classroom. "Indeed women often expand on an opinion by discussing their personal reasons for making a certain interpretation, thus using the book for self-understanding and revelation of the self to other participants rather than for discovery of meaning *within* the book." Long's perspective is that these women use literature to achieve personal insight or, borrowing Kenneth Burke's term, as "equipment for living." Through their responses to characters, discussants draw parallels between the characters' situations and those of the people and situations in their own lives in order "to explore the meaning of their own life situations" and to question their own values.[6]

According to Long, book group members "usually approach books as if they were relatively transparent" and "retain a certain humanistic 'innocence' about meaning, and a deep allegiance to the conventions of realism." She elaborates on this adherence to realism:

The assumption that books should represent or imitate reality appears to discourage attention to the crafted nature of the text. When a book is successful, discussions spring outward from it into what people liked or disliked, what it related to in their past or present-day lives, and what they felt they learned from it. Only rarely do women discuss a novel's structure, and usually only when it is problematic. The plot comes up in two circumstances: when it is not "believable," and when members recount the plot to refresh people's memories or fill in for those who haven't finished the book. In like fashion, groups rarely discuss the aesthetic dimension of the writing. If they do, they tend to say they thought a book was "beautifully written" and then they read from the text.[7]

There remains much to unpack in the phrase "when a book is successful," including what it means for a book to be successful, by whom is it viewed as such, and what the consequences are of its being or not being "successful." Long acknowledges that through book group discussions members are "reinterpreting or even reconstituting the book" but claims that groups usually do not "self-consciously acknowledge this process" of reconstitution or view it as part of meaning production.[8]

More Australian Research: CAE

Given how few studies have been conducted on contemporary book groups, it is interesting that there have been four from Australia and that three of these studies focus on the institutionally organized book groups formed through the Council on Adult Education (CAE, more recently known as the Centre of Adult Education).[9] Each of these studies focuses on all-women groups, though there are CAE groups that include men. The CAE services more than 11,000 participants in 988 reading groups and provides reading guides that accompany selections. Originating in the 1930s as the "Box scheme," traveling libraries in the form of pine boxes contained twelve copies of a selected book with accompanying notes and provided correspondence-style education to citizens throughout the country towns of Western Australia. Today these groups still exist but are less academically focused and more concentrated on reading for pleasure.

Among the CAE-related studies, Frances Devlin-Glass analyzes "the aesthetic and educational objectives of the providers and consumers, and the issues of 'taste' which govern collaborative book-selection/discussion," whereas Marilyn Poole examines "the degree of interest in and commitment to feminism among reading group members, the commodification of books as cultural products, the relationship between reading group participants and cultural valuers, and the significance of the book in terms of group cohesion."[10] The data for these studies were compiled from two interviews with CAE staff, ten years of circulation data, responses to thirty-six questionnaires, fourteen interviews with group members, and transcriptions of eight group meetings (two for each of four groups). The four groups selected varied in terms of longevity and age of participants but were all located within metropolitan Melbourne.

"MORE THAN A READER AND LESS THAN A CRITIC," BY FRANCES DEVLIN-GLASS

Devlin-Glass found the readers she studied to be "seriously middlebrow"; they do not fully embrace the practices of the literary establishment but yet do not question the "aesthetic assumptions that underlie their practice." She found them to prefer contemporary fiction, books written by women, and books generated within their own Australian culture. Women take part in the groups because they feel the CAE will assist them in extending their range of reading to items they would not have found or selected on their own, and they appreciate the discipline the structure of a group provides. Their discussion is "rarely analytic textual study," yet at the same time groups are aware of literary prizes and make use of published book reviews. Interestingly, group members take issue with the CAE notes included with book selections and intended to guide discussion. Groups often select a book based on the availability of notes but resist the overly academic language and focus of them. Instead, the notes serve as a source of shared jokes and "a discourse for bonding."[11]

"THE WOMEN'S CHAPTER," BY MARILYN POOLE

Drawing on the same data as Devlin-Glass, Poole found that the CAE discussion groups rejected male membership because they were interested in talking about women's lives, though they did not engage in explicit discussions of feminism, thereby failing to support the author's initial hypothesis that the groups operated from a feminist orientation. Members' reading for the group focused on "good" books, which were defined as books to which readers could relate on a personal level and included vivid portrayals of characters, held relevance for contemporary life, and employed an engaging writing style and an exciting plot. These readers made distinctions between what they read for the group and what they read on their own, which included mass-market romances, formulaic fiction, detective novels, and the like.

"SPEAKING SUBJECTS," BY LYNDSIE HOWIE

Howie, as a student of sociology, explores the value women place on their book group membership. After surveying ninety CAE book groups, she interviewed twenty-one group members and determined that book groups provide women-only spaces in which women can explore and expand their self-identity. Her study focuses on three themes: ritual, journeying, and consideration of subject positions and self-understandings. The "ritual" of book groups provides women escape and opportunity for change within a safe environment while "journeying" through varied environments (fictional and real) in their consideration of new identities. Howie's use of interviewing gives voice and specificity to the motivations and feelings of the readers she studied, readers who appear in the other studies of CAE book groups as statistics and generalized entities. Though this study has been critiqued as "limited by its tendency to take the participants' responses at face value and by the fact that it has not examined what the groups do as distinct from what they say they do,"[12] it is useful in its focus on studying real interactions of particular readers.

Dissertations from the United States and Canada

Since 1996, there have been five dissertations written about reading groups in the United States and Canada with potential for informing readers' advisory practice. Two of these focus on particular types of readers: Sisson on African American women and Griffin on romance readers. Gregory and Rehberg Sedo both studied multiple all-women groups existing in specific contexts, and I examined the ways discussion affects the reading practices of various groups.

"THE ROLE OF READING IN THE LIVES OF AFRICAN AMERICAN WOMEN WHO ARE MEMBERS OF A BOOK DISCUSSION GROUP," BY MICHELLE SISSON

Sisson explores African American women's book clubs as avenues for adult education.[13] This is the only study that has specifically focused on a contemporary African American book group. Sisson's study investigates fourteen group members who are identified as avid, lifelong readers living in a mid-sized southern city. Using semistructured group and individual interviews, she addresses two guiding questions: What role does reading play in the lives of African American women who are members of a book discussion club? How has being a member of a book discussion club been meaningful to the women readers?

Sisson identified eight themes emerging from the women's responses: (1) self-education (using both fiction and nonfiction), (2) monitor own reading processes (explore what they have learned and how they feel about reading), (3) reading as a means of connection in their personal worlds, (4) reading as a comfortable and self-indulging act that is a self-renewing ritual for members, (5) making meaning together, (6) sharing in a comfortable, safe place, (7) sharing ideas and experiences unrelated to the text, and (8) club as motivator. She found that participation in the reading group led to "increased participation in more learning endeavors," that members were empowered to reinvent themselves as a result of being engaged readers, and that African American women readers are empowered to critique their own and others' responses to African American literary selections as a result of being members of a community of readers.

"AN ANALYSIS OF MEANING CREATION THROUGH THE INTEGRATION OF SOCIOLOGY AND LITERATURE," BY LINDA GRIFFIN

In her critical ethnography of a romance reading group, Griffin attempts to "(1) describe the social conditions that may have given rise to the growth of reading groups; (2) discern the ways women readers use romance novels to construct meaning in their lives; and (3) understand the dichotomous relationship between those who represent cultural authority and those who consume mass-marketed literature."[14] The group consisting of twelve women between thirty-five and seventy-four years of age met once a month for two to three hours at a bookstore in suburban Houston, Texas. They were avid readers, reading four to six books a month. Only one member had a college degree, two members were employed outside the home, and all but one member had children. Griffin attended meetings for one year, conducted group and individual interviews, and visited the group several times over the next year. Her inquiry is remarkably self-reflective, providing clear justifications for her methodological choices and manner of approaching data collection and analysis.

Griffin found that the meetings she attended were not focused discussions of a book but rather comprised several conversations going on at once and often about books other than the month's selection. These romance readers were often content to say that the month's selection was "good" and move on to what the researcher identified as the primary activity of the group: exchanging books and sharing book recommendations. This finding conflicts with Long and Ellen Slezak, who claim that the length of discussion about a book indicates a group's feeling about the value of that book; that if the discussion about a book does not fill an hour, it was not viewed as a "good" book.[15] The characteristics Griffin found true of her romance readers are sometimes also true for the mystery discussion group as I reported (see below). It is precisely when a book is "good" that a group has less to say about it. Readers then use the time allotted for discussion to make personal book recommendations—a practice highly valued by their group mates.

Griffin phrases her overarching question in the following way: "How did the women relate the text of romance novels to their experiences in order to create meaning in a collective interpretation not of the text but of life?" She establishes a series of either/or relationships in order to determine how the romance reading group she studied interpreted the texts they read. The first of these is summarized by her question, "Is romance reading playful irreverence or avoiding reality?" and elaborated by her goal "to determine if the readers are avoiding reality or merely attempting to redefine how to cope with the realities of life through discussions in the group meetings."[16] Though perhaps establishing an artificial polarity in that the two motivations are not mutually exclusive, these questions provide insights into the nebulous experience of reading for pleasure. In the case of Griffin's readers, pleasure reading is that which does not deal with pain and which engages positive emotions within the confines of accuracy and believability. According to Griffin's analysis, these romance readers used the group to achieve self-awareness and accomplish self-improvement. These uses of reading were enabled by the ways readers attempted to make sense of *why* they derive pleasure from reading and discussing romance novels. Griffin articulates this through her identification of collective roles within the group's discussions. These roles, sometimes describing the group and sometimes individuals within it, include the "rebel" reader, the "expert" reader, the "teacher" reader, the "student" reader, the "engaged" reader, the "discontented romantic" reader, the "growing" reader, and "the outsider." Griffin's focus on a genre-based group should be of particular interest and use to readers' advisors.

"WOMEN'S EXPERIENCE OF READING IN ST. LOUIS BOOK CLUBS," BY PATRICIA L. GREGORY

Appearing a year after Griffin's study was Gregory's American Studies dissertation in which she compares Progressive Era women's reading groups of St. Louis to contemporary women's reading groups meeting in that same city.[17] Though not spectacularly informative about modern-day groups, the approach confirms that contemporary reading groups did not spring up out of nowhere or come about strictly because celebrities like Oprah Winfrey created them. In actuality, some groups have met continuously since their founding in the 1800s. One strength of Gregory's study is her identification of twelve groups established in St. Louis between 1874 and 1920, groups that because of scattered and minimal documentation are often unrepresented in scholarship. Gregory paints a picture of the continuity of group reading as a cultural practice over time.

"BADGES OF WISDOM, SPACES FOR BEING," BY DENEL REHBERG SEDO

"Badges of Wisdom, Spaces for Being," conducted by Rehberg Sedo in the School of Communication at Simon Fraser University, focuses on groups in Canada.[18] Blending ethnographic and survey methods, the study has two main parts. The first was based on an online survey of forty-one questions, yielding a total of 251 responses. Survey questions covered topics such as the role of reading in a person's life, where readers get their books and how much they spend on them, and queries about participation in online or face-to-face reading groups. More than half (64 percent) of the respondents indicated that they were or had been members of a book club, and among these there was equal representation of online and face-to-face groups. Forty-five percent of the respondents lived in the United States and 47 percent lived in Canada. Eighty-five percent of all survey respondents identified as female.

The book club population of the respondents (154 people, 93 percent female) were asked their reasons for joining a book group and given thirteen options for responding (from which they could check as many as applied). Members of both face-to-face and online groups indicated that they joined their groups because they "wanted intellectual stimulation" and "to have fun." The next most frequent response was "to read books I wouldn't normally read." Over half the respondents said that they joined a book group because of a "need to talk about books." When asked the most satisfying aspect of their book group, the top responses were "social bonds," "access to new books," and "new ways of looking at the world."

The second part of Rehberg Sedo's study is a qualitative analysis of five face-to-face women's groups based on participant observation over a four-month period, group member responses to a questionnaire, focus group interviews, and fifteen interviews with key informants such as non–book group members, book club facilitators, booksellers, reporters, an author, a librarian, and a publisher's marketing representative. This variety of perspectives gives strength to the study and documents people often left out of such research, including those who choose not to participate. In this case, reasons given for not wanting to join a book group were fear that one's intellectual ability was insufficient, fear that it would diminish the pleasure of reading and make it more like taking a literature course, and a lack of interest in hearing others' thoughts on a work. Though these additional voices are mainly supplemental to those of the groups in her study, they introduce areas warranting elaboration through future research.

Rehberg Sedo found that the women in her study were heavy readers of various genres, not just those read by their clubs, and that they relied primarily on local networks of trusted friends and family members when choosing books to read. The groups in the study ranged in membership from six to twelve people, together totaling thirty-five Anglo-Canadian women. Attempting to explain what reading means to women who join book groups, the author draws on the notions of community and sisterhood. Rehberg Sedo asserts that book groups are unique among club or group types because they are purposeful groups that unite many types and topics of discussion under a single banner. Discussions are not restricted to one area but may include politics, religion, sex, and so on. She found that women join reading groups for two primary reasons: a desire to read more, "better," and more widely, and a desire to be with others in a "collegial environment that supports the desire to acquire and enhance their cultural competence."[19] In other words, these women seek intellectual stimulation as well as intimacy with other women. Book clubs, according to this study, serve as safe spaces where women can express their thoughts to others they trust.

"WHEN ADULTS TALK IN CIRCLES," BY JOAN BESSMAN TAYLOR

My dissertation, "When Adults Talk in Circles," reports on six years of participant observation in six open-to-the-public reading groups: a science fiction group, a mystery group, an African American group, a Great Books group, a literary fiction group, and a group devoted to contemporary fiction and nonfiction.[20] Participants in the study ranged in age from twenty-five to ninety and included both men and women. I refute Long's assertion that book group members do not acknowledge their interpretive processes. Through an examination of the role of the text in book discussion that draws on transcripts of discussion meetings, I identify two main categories of group interpretive processes: reading as dissection and reading as creation. When a book is deemed well written and complete, readers dissect the work as written to highlight how the work was accomplished. On the other hand, when a work has gaps or would benefit from elaboration or additional features, readers collectively create their ideal text through their suggestions for improvement. In this way, group members derive a satisfying experience from discussing a work that was not particularly liked, believable, or in keeping with their expectations.

A "good" book by literary standards may not make the best book for book group attention. Unpacking the notion of discussability, that is, the idea that some books are better suited for fostering discussion than others, I demonstrate that a work must have (or lack) certain features to be discussible, but that a book's discussability is not static. The same book might be discussible in one group and not another. "It is both the interaction between the work and the reader and the interaction between readers that account for discussability."[21] I recommend that readers' advisors, when asked by patrons for a "good" book, consider the question "good for what?" before responding. For book groups, aspects of nonappeal—those things that readers found problematic, did not enjoy, or thought needed revision or expansion—may be just as or more important than the traditional appeal factors advisors are accustomed to considering.

Conclusion

With the exception of my work and its wider discussion of group practices, most of the research on book groups has focused on a single organizing attribute such as romance reading, race, or gender and most often studied middle-class white women. This research coalesces in two main areas: studies of identity formation and the fashioning of the female self, and book groups as sites for negotiating cultural hierarchies of taste. Though the initial research has been done, there is plenty of room (and need) for additional research in the area. Work like that of mine and Griffin's that focuses on nonprivate groups will be of particular use and interest to librarians. Further analysis of the role of libraries and librarians in working with or hosting book groups would be especially informative.

LIBRARIAN'S VIEW   BY ANDREW SMITH

Oprah Winfrey focused attention on book groups and social reading clubs when she started the Oprah Book Club in 1996. It became a social phenomenon, bringing existing groups to the forefront while encouraging many of her viewers to form their own. But the history of communal reading extends far beyond Oprah; as Joan Bessman Taylor's literature review shows, book groups historically served both as venues for informal education and as catalysts for social movements. Today they might bring people from diverse backgrounds together or serve as an exclusive status symbol, depending on the intentions of their founders and members. Either way, book groups are part of what Robert Putnam calls "social capital"—small groups creating the bonds that build successful communities by allowing interaction with others.[22] As a profession that thinks of our institutions as community centers, librarians ought to be intimately involved with developing and sustaining book groups. Little evidence exists, though, to show that book groups think of libraries and librarians as a required resource for anything more than individual copies of books they don't want to buy. What do book groups want from libraries and librarians? And what can libraries and librarians do for book groups?

First, what do we actually know about book groups? Taylor's research review reveals a profound lack of library research or discussion about working with book groups. Instead, much of what we know comes from other disciplines. Because of that, few of the results are ones from which library practitioners can draw useful conclusions. Without much relevant and useful research to draw from, readers' advisors must turn to our own experience and what we witness in our interactions with users to develop and improve the practice of readers' advisory for book groups. As a reader services librarian at Williamsburg (Virginia) Regional Library (WRL), I work closely with book groups, and I've called upon that experience in writing this section. In attempting to answer the questions posed earlier,

---

Andrew Smith is readers' services librarian at Williamsburg (Virginia) Regional Library. He leads three book groups and regularly advises other groups in the Williamsburg area.

I offer some basics of readers' advisory for book groups and talk about the model WRL uses to provide materials to book groups.

Title Selection: The First Step

Pity the person whose turn it is to select the next book for their group's discussion—perhaps even to lead the group in that session. As hard as it is to find an enjoyable read for oneself, suddenly the individual is left confronting a universe of books and authors that must engage, if not please, several other people. And whether or not the nervous leader had been in complete agreement with other members over the titles the group has read in the past, most likely she or he has in mind the ideal of a good read followed by a lively discussion, closely shadowed by the fear that the book chosen will be a dud on both fronts. Even the most successful leader can suffer from this concern, especially when he or she is the sole selector of the titles. Oprah Winfrey temporarily suspended her book group after several selections earned her widespread disapproval. Where to turn for assistance?

According to Jenny Hartley's survey of British reading groups, book groups and their leaders turn to best-seller lists, media reports featuring the hot author of the moment, bookstores, friends from other book groups, perhaps even a long-held list of "books I ought to read." Unfortunately, as many book groups have found to their dismay, a good book group title is not merely one that has questions at the end, or even one that many other groups have liked. Nearly all those sources have commercial reasons for promoting titles to book groups and may even manipulate book groups into buying their books for discussion. Indeed, a publisher's spokesperson admits that they put their efforts into creating reading group guides only for titles that might be disparagingly, and unfairly, called "Oprah books."

Librarians, the one source that should not have any economic interest in the number of copies sold, are conspicuously absent from the list of Hartley's responses. That ought not to be the case. As librarians, we should be confident that we are among the resources book groups will consult before choosing a book. As readers ourselves, we should be engaged in helping book groups cultivate a deeper appreciation of books than that which a solo read provides. As a centerpiece of our communities, we should be encouraging the kind of interaction that becomes one of the building blocks of the "social capital" that many people feel to be missing from their lives. It seems, though, that we are failing those core purposes.

Many book groups don't come to us for ideas and suggestions because librarians are perceived as too busy or not interested enough to take the time. The obvious solution lies in applying our knowledge of both books and our local book groups to reach out and help them select the titles that offer the most opportunity for successful discussion. Because we have no financial interest in selling multiple copies of a certain title, we can and should focus on improving our knowledge about new and potentially "discussible" reads, finding the mid-list, small press, and underexplored authors whose books nonetheless represent opportunities for meaningful, satisfactory exploration by book groups without treading the same ground as every other group in the country. We already know how to find those ubiquitous book group title lists. We must take the role of searching out potential book group titles as seriously as we do our search for those individual titles we know will have local appeal in our libraries. For our own good, working with book groups ought to be a fundamental service libraries provide; where else are we going to find sociable people interested in reading, who are building community through small groups that are natural constituents and potential defenders of library services?

What Do Readers' Advisors Need to Know to Work with Book Groups?

From my post as readers' services librarian in the Adult Services Department at WRL, I have concluded that the three most important elements to book group patrons are resources, resources, and resources. When I talk about resources, I have in mind such diverse topics as materials that will allow leaders and group members to delve into the book under discussion; knowledge of a wide range of what Taylor calls "'discussible' titles";[23] and sufficient copies of those titles to meet the group's needs. Libraries are unquestionably expert in providing the first. Finding discussion questions for a specific title (or general questions, if necessary), pulling up author biographies, reviews, and perhaps criticism, providing maps, pictures, or other background material—these should be simple tasks for any librarian. When we look at the second and third items—patrons' expectations that we are knowledgeable about books for book groups and will have plenty of copies of the books they want—there often exists a serious disconnect between readers and libraries. I address both of these issues in the following pages, as well as points for conducting a readers' advisory interview with a book group.

Readers' Advisory Conversation Starters or
Questions to Ask the Book Group Leader

As a profession, we have developed generally accepted standards for working with individual readers, but there has been little discussion on adapting these strategies for working with groups of readers. It is time for us to accept that the two constituencies have distinct needs and begin to identify strategies unique to working with reading groups, since they are an important subset of library patrons who deserve services tailored to their unique needs. The first step in that process is to acknowledge that, although the interview for individuals is a good starting place, we must follow a different, more involved path to successful work with groups.

When confronted with a book group's request for a "good" book, Taylor recommends that we first ask ourselves the question "Good for what?" For a readers' advisor, it is an excellent question that reminds us to stop any other activities we're engaged in, take a moment to prepare, and focus on the conversation to come. By taking that mental moment, we are able to tune in to the response we get when we ask the patron to tell us about their most memorable discussions, the meetings that fulfilled the group's ideal purpose for existing. It will also help us remember that each group has unique needs and interests.

The next step is to initiate the actual readers' advisory transaction. Start by rephrasing Saricks to "Tell me about a good discussion you've had." Using this, we can learn far more about the group than a simple list of books they've read; we give ourselves the opportunity to listen for clues to the group's interests and its structure and to establish the next steps the interview might take. If the user names a title but doesn't detail why the discussion was good, the librarian must ask follow-up questions that reveal that information, even asking, "Why was this discussion better than other sessions you've had?" Knowing more about the special or memorable discussion sessions—not necessarily just books—aids the readers' advisor in selecting the follow-up questions that should eventually yield a list of suggestions for the group.

There are plenty of other questions the librarian might want to ask to help reveal the types of books previously enjoyed and the reasons for their success:

- Was the storyline, setting, or genre different from less-rewarding discussion books? If so, how was it different?

- Did the group find the characters or the plot to be the focus of their discussion? Was there a particular character that resonated with people?

- Was the setting—time or place—a factor in their conversation, and did individual members have a personal connection to either?

- Was there an issue or theme in the book that echoes a current event of interest? How did that connection influence the discussion?

- Did the group look at the style or mechanics the author used—for example, multiple points of view, unusual or descriptive language, foreshadowing, or other literary devices? Were they aware of those elements during their reading, or did a group member point them out during the discussion?

- Were there differing points of view in the discussion that convinced group members to alter their initial opinion of the book?

- Do other members of the group also think this session was remarkable?

Advisors also need some understanding of the group dynamics. Try asking some of these questions and listen carefully to the responses:

- Do the members view the group's primary mission as social or educational?

- Are they willing to experiment with styles or genres?

- Have they read only a particular type of book? Might they be in the mood for something different?

- Do they need works that provide story, characterization, or language that can be dissected for underlying structure or symbolism?

- Is the group leader expected to provide in-depth background material, questions, or other elements to manage the group closely?

- Are the members able to handle debate, controversy, or division without rancor?

These questions ought to provide the attentive readers' advisor with sufficient information to begin a preliminary list of titles or to articulate the appeal factors of specific suggestions the group may be considering. If the contact person's responses don't provide enough information, it is important for the librarian to do sufficient follow-up, including asking more. The advisor might also be able to communicate with other members of the group for more information. Finally, it is important for readers' advisors to communicate to the book group as a whole that they would like feedback on *any* titles they do suggest and that they would be happy to be involved in future suggestions.

The book group advisor must acknowledge that each individual group has a level of reading difficulty and quality that can define both the upper and lower boundaries of its interest. Although there is a general consensus among library staff who practice readers' advisory that the individual patron's reading enjoyment is paramount, professional discussions about book group reading can sometimes veer into the problematic territory of what makes a book "good enough" for discussion, and whether we have an obligation to steer book groups toward more challenging titles. Many of the prepackaged book lists, including those generated by libraries, publishers, prize committees, and book group consultants, lean toward the idea that there is a minimum level of quality—whether of writing skill, character development, or plot—that must be present for a book to be worth taking up for discussion. Although this discussion will continue, it is important for readers' advisors to let the book group take the lead in selecting its own reading and find its own range of comfort in the titles it chooses. Our primary role is to help groups find titles they'd like to read and to help them develop points of discussion; if they are dissatisfied with their choices, we must help them articulate which direction they would like to go next and start the process over.

As an example, one of WRL's Gab Bag books, *The Corset Diaries*, by Katie MacAlister, has been dismissed by several reading groups as "just a romance." Others have reported turning the subject matter into rewarding discussions of weight and body image, creating for themselves a useful examination of the culture and time it was produced in and the expectations or fears of the audience it was intended for. For those groups that didn't enjoy the book, we might steer them away from other genre books toward more typical book group fare or pay more attention to creating better discussion questions; for those that did enjoy the story and discussion, we might encourage them to try other genres or to look at their individual reading with the same kind of critical eye. Either way, the selection of the reading material and management of the discussion are the group's responsibility.

One vital difference between working with individual readers and book groups is the importance of "nonappeal" factors, which Taylor defines as aspects of a book that readers find affect their reading experience negatively but offer them more opportunity to tease out—or assault—the skill with which the author executed the story. Taylor's work on nonappeal factors offers valuable insight into the dynamic of reading groups that separates them from the readers we work with on a regular basis.[24] It is rare that a pleasure reader sticks with a book he or she does not enjoy reading; the external obligation to the group, however, often makes members read beyond their normal limits, pushing beyond the nonappeal factors simply to be prepared to criticize the book in the upcoming meeting. Book group members often informally report that, although they did not find pleasure in a particular book, they learned something new, enjoyed the challenge, and were glad to have read the book. This is an added dimension for groups—the act of talking about the book and sharing insights with other people—that does not exist for individual readers. Readers' advisors must factor in the key dimension of discussion and sharing the reading experience when talking with the book group leader and, most important, when presenting titles. The leader may often have to be told that not every member of the group will like the book. It may require "permission" on the part of the readers' advisor for leaders to acknowledge that and to learn to direct the conversation into exploring the nonappeal factors with dissenting members.

Providing Books to Groups

If and when a leader does come to the library looking for title suggestions, few libraries can guarantee a sufficient quantity of immediately available copies to meet the group's needs. Discussions on Fiction_L have revealed several options for provision of titles to book groups. In large systems, copies might be rounded up from branches scattered across a region. Some libraries, notably those in Georgia, are part of an interlibrary loan system that regularly sends copies of books for discussion from large and small libraries across the state to the requesting institution. The State Library of West Virginia maintains about 150 kits with copies and background materials for mailing to groups across the state. Still other libraries have collections of book group titles that individual members of registered groups check out for their discussions. This is the model used at WRL.

When WRL started its first book groups with a grant from our Friends, we began by purchasing paperback copies of the selected titles for the thirty people who initially signed up for the two groups. Following the discussion, book group members had the option of buying their copy for $3—the cost of a hardback book sold through our Friends book sale. It was a great bargain for the readers (and an accurate meter for the popularity of each title) but not a very good deal for the library. In addition to losing somewhere between $5 and $10 per book, we were left with the problem of storing the leftover copies and searching for a new purpose for them. On the suggestion of one of our staff members, we began putting the books into library tote bags, cataloging the whole bag as one record (with the cataloging designation [Kit]), and circulating them to reading groups in the community. In five years, we have grown from the initial nine titles to more than one hundred Gab Bags and have even had the dubious pleasure of weeding some of the lower-circulating titles to make room on crowded shelves.

Along the way, we have made some changes to accommodate the needs of patrons and to acknowledge the fiscal realities of the library. To maximize our funding, we cut our purchasing back to fifteen copies of each title and stopped selling individual copies. We extended our initial circulation period from six to eight weeks to give leaders more time to distribute copies and collect them for return. We began adding resource kits—notebooks with author biographies, reviews, and background material on some relevant aspect of the story—and put the Gab Bags on display for browsing rather than storing them behind the circulation or adult services desk. We have even extended our service beyond the Williamsburg area to all Virginia libraries, inviting them to request Gab Bag titles through the interlibrary loan system. We are also in the planning stages of implementing a Library 2.0 social networking program that will allow book groups to engage with other readers and the library by responding to the book, rating it for other readers, suggesting questions, discussion points, and resources, and learning more about other titles. By increasing the discussion audience from members of one book group to book groups all over the area, we hope to build that sense of a community of readers that is at the heart of book discussion.

At WRL I deal with all the book groups that come to the reference desk and freely pass out my card so that group members can contact me at any point. I find that simply encouraging them to get in touch with me is the best way to build the kind of ongoing relationship we want to develop. The one question we have not been able to resolve deals with advance reservations: since the Gab Bags circulate for eight weeks, we cannot set a title aside for a patron who wants to be guaranteed that a book will be available several months in advance. Putting it on reserve makes it unavailable to other groups working on a different schedule, and leaving it on the shelf means that another patron can reserve or check it out before the first patron's desired pickup. Coordinating that part requires one individual to schedule the reservation process well in advance, to keep an eye on the title, and to negotiate possible replacements with the book group. Although we have explored technological options through our OPAC, using an old-fashioned calendar and cultivating relationships with group leaders has sufficed—very few groups have missed getting the titles they wanted.

In spite of the possible difficulty with scheduling, patrons have responded enthusiastically to the Gab Bags collection. Area residents interested in starting new book groups have made use of the program to create a no-cost launch that eliminates the financial obligations that might deter potential members. Existing book groups have found that the diversity of titles offers a challenge to their reading, allowing them to experiment with authors or genres outside the book group titles they already knew. All the groups we have spoken to cited the convenience and savings of the Bags; the enriched content added by our resource kits has also been quite popular. In addition to the convenience of the multiple copies, patrons have told us that they like the variety of titles we offer. "Genre" titles from mystery, horror, and nonfiction (e.g., *Beekeeper's Apprentice*, *Cabinet of Curiosities*, and *Don't Let's Go to the Dogs Tonight*) check out as frequently as book group standards (*Memoirs of a Geisha*, *Corelli's Mandolin*, or *Angle of Repose*). Patron responses suggest that they like to be introduced to titles and authors they've never heard of or given guidance to develop a critical approach to books they didn't think could be discussed. The program's success can be seen in the numbers: between January 2002 and May 2007, the Gab Bags collectively have circulated more than nine hundred times.

Conclusion

There is no question that providing readers' advisory services and resources to book groups is an essential part of library practice that should be incorporated into every public library's mission statement and programming goals. It is essential that we as a profession begin to examine this phenomenon through the lens of our own discipline and that library school educators begin to examine the role of our institutions in the creation and sustenance of community reading. Simply put, we need more academics, students, and practicing librarians to analyze reading group dynamics and communicate their findings with each other. I would especially encourage those practicing librarians to look at what is working in their libraries and to share those best practices with each other via conferences and on electronic discussion lists such as Fiction_L and PUBLIB, or in published form in such readers' advisory–friendly journals as *RUSQ* or *Public Libraries*. When we accept the research that stems from a different set of needs than those of our profession, we do ourselves a disservice.

I have limited my discussion to the development of book group readers' advisory practices and a discussion of one model to provide resources to book groups; there are many other areas that our work with book groups should extend to: creation and leadership of library-sponsored groups, consultation with community book groups to help them improve their meetings, providing space for groups to meet, even serving as matchmakers between groups and individuals looking for community reading. To return to the question with which I began: what do book groups want? They want us to take their reading as seriously as anything else we do.

NOTES

1. David Laskin and Holly Hughes, *The Reading Group Book* (New York: Plume, 1995). The research on Oprah's Book Club falls outside the scope of this chapter. Nonetheless, some interesting studies include Cecilia Konchar Farr, *Reading Oprah: How Oprah's Book Club Changed the Way America Reads* (Albany: State University of New York Press, 2005); R. Mark Hall, "The 'Oprahfication' of Literacy: Reading 'Oprah's Book Club,'" *College English* 65, no. 6 (2003): 646–67; Janice Peck, "The Oprah Effect: Texts, Readers, and the Dialectic of Signification," *Communication Review* 5, no. 2 (2002): 143–78; and Kathleen Rooney, *Reading with Oprah: The Book Club That Changed America* (Fayetteville: University of Arkansas Press, 2005).

2. Jenny Hartley, *Reading Groups* (Oxford: Oxford University Press, 2001).

3. Ibid.; Pat Valentine, *Why Book Clubs?* (Perth: Pat Valentine, 1996).

4. Elizabeth Long, "Women, Reading and Cultural Authority: Some Implications of the Audience Perspective in Cultural Studies," *American Quarterly* 38 (1986): 591–611; "Textual Interpretation as Collective Action," in *The Ethnography of Reading*, ed. Jonathan Boyarin (Berkeley: University of California Press, 1993), 180–211; and *Book Clubs: Women and the Uses of Reading in Everyday Life* (Chicago: University of Chicago Press, 2003).

5. Long, *Book Clubs*, xvi, 22.

6. Ibid., 602, 603, 607. Kenneth Burke, "Literature as Equipment for Living," in *Perspectives by Incongruity*, ed. S. Hyman (Bloomington: University of Indiana Press, 1964).

7. Long "Women, Reading and Cultural Authority," 605.

8. Ibid., 605.

9. Frances Devlin-Glass, "More Than a Reader and Less Than a Critic: Literary Authority and Women's Book-Discussion Groups," *Women's Studies International Forum* 24, no. 5 (2001): 571–85; Marilyn Poole, "The Women's Chapter: Women's Reading Groups in Victoria," *Feminist Media Studies* 3, no. 3 (2003): 263–81; Lyndsie M. Howie, "Speaking Subjects: A Reading of Women's Book Groups," Ph.D. dissertation, LaTrobe University, 1998.

10. Devlin-Glass, "More Than a Reader," 572; Poole, "Women's Chapter," 256.

11. Devlin-Glass, "More Than a Reader," 571, 575.

12. Ibid., 572.

13. Michelle Diane Winter Sisson, "The Role of Reading in the Lives of African American Women Who Are Members of a Book Discussion Group," Ph.D. dissertation, University of Georgia, 1996.

14. Linda Griffin, "An Analysis of Meaning Creation through the Integration of Sociology and Literature: A Critical Ethnography of a Romance Reading Group," Ph.D. dissertation, University of Houston, 1999, vii.

15. Ellen Slezak, ed., *The Book Group Book: A Thoughtful Guide to Forming and Enjoying a Stimulating Book Discussion Group*, 3rd ed. (Chicago: Chicago Review Press, 1995).

16. Griffin "Analysis of Meaning Creation," 171.

17. Patricia L. Gregory, "Women's Experience of Reading in St. Louis Book Clubs," Ph.D. dissertation, Saint Louis University, 2000.

18. DeNel Rehberg Sedo, "Badges of Wisdom, Spaces for Being: A Study of Contemporary Women's Book Clubs," Ph.D. dissertation, Simon Fraser University, 2004.

19. Ibid., 143.

20. Joan Bessman Taylor, "When Adults Talk in Circles: Book Groups and Contemporary Reading Practices," Ph.D. dissertation, University of Illinois at Urbana-Champaign, 2007.

21. Joan Bessman Taylor, "Good for What? Non-appeal, Discussibility, and Book Groups," part 1, *Reference and User Services Quarterly* 47 (2007): 33–36; part 2, 48 (2007): 27–31.

22. Robert Putnam, *Bowling Alone* (New York: Simon and Schuster, 2000), 345.

23. Taylor, "When Adults Talk in Circles," 9.

24. Taylor, "Good for What?" (part 1), 33–34.

7

ROMANCE AND GENRE READERS

Why a chapter devoted to romance and genre readers? As seen in chapter 2, most people who enjoy leisure reading report reading some type of genre fiction. Yet genre readers, particularly romance readers, have never been as well served by the library as readers of "literature." One need only read Ross's introduction to *Reading Matters,* in which she details the history of the "fiction problem" and the related issue of series fiction, to realize that public libraries have always struggled with their mission.[1] Are they there to educate the masses or to provide what people actually enjoy reading? In the process, many libraries have consciously and subconsciously discriminated against genre fiction readers since the time of the dime novel. Readers' advisors, then, still need to think consciously about romance and genre fiction readers. Are their library collections and services really meeting their patrons' needs?

RESEARCH REVIEW   BY JESSICA E. MOYER

The 2005 Romance Writers of America (RWA) market survey revealed that romance novels made up more than half (54.9 percent) of all paperback sales in the United States, which accounted for $1.2 billion in annual sales. Romance accounted for more than a third of all fiction sales (39.3 percent), the largest single group. Mystery/thriller was a distant second, with less than 30 percent of the market share. In 2004, 2,285 romance titles were published.[2] How well are readers' advisory services prepared to work with romance readers? What, if anything, are libraries doing to attract and retain this large group of readers? Are any libraries spending 40 percent of their fiction budget on romance?

Reading the Romance, by Janice Radway

In 1984, Janice Radway wrote the seminal work on romance readers, *Reading the Romance: Women, Patriarchy and Popular Literature.*[3] Her ethnographic study of female romance readers was the first, and arguably the best, study of the single largest genre of popular fiction. More than twenty years later Radway's work continues to be the definitive study of romance readers.

Radway found that romance readers attained the majority of their books through mail order or at romance-friendly bookstores. She focused on Dot, owner of a midwestern romance bookstore. The reason Dot's customer bought from her over and over again? Because she was able to advise readers overwhelmed by the number of romance novels published each month. She provided friendly, reliable, and bias-free service to help her patrons find the books they wanted to read.

If Dot were a librarian, she would have been one of the best readers' advisors around, and she should serve as a model for any librarian working with genre readers. Dot's readers returned to her store again and again because they felt that she valued their questions and that the advice she gave was trustworthy. Librarians serving any readers should strive to do the same. Many readers feel overwhelmed by the selection in libraries and need assistance, and romance readers are no different. In fact, the proliferation of romances published each year, both inside and outside established lines, as well as the high consumption rates of many romance readers mean that romance readers may need even more help finding their next book. And they should be able to find that assistance (and plenty of books) at their local public library.

"Unrestricted Body Parts and Predictable Bliss," by Mary K. Chelton

Several years have passed since the initial publication of Radway's work. It is no longer taboo to talk about romance readers, but it is still not very cool. In 1991, Mary Chelton, then director of public libraries for Montgomery County, Maryland, wrote, "For a librarian, admitting to reading and *liking* formula romances is the professional equivalent of confessing a social disease."[4] From a background as a librarian and avid romance reader, Chelton wrote this article to help other librarians better understand why readers like these books and how to purchase and display them. Although not strictly a research article, this is an important contribution to the understanding of romance (and other genre readers) in terms of library services.

Chelton proposes that romance appeals to readers for four main reasons: predictability, sexual fantasy, humor, and escape. She observes that predictability is a critical aspect of most popular fiction; mystery fans expect the sleuth to solve the mystery at the end, just as romance fans expect the protagonists to get together and enjoy a happily-ever-after ending. Here, romance fans are just like fans of any other genre. Escape is important for all genre readers, but it seems especially crucial for romance readers, maybe because so much of romance is unreal. "I think people need relief from both responsibilities and self improvement at regular intervals," Chelton comments.[5]

Chelton goes on to explore the variations in romance, notably the differences between the various lines. She argues that it is critical for librarians to understand the differences between them and understand that each has dedicated readers. She provides an example of poor service, when all the lines are mixed together, with no regard for the different requirements of readers, and only "safe, sexless" titles are collected. Every book its reader, to quote Ranganathan; a romance series (sex and all) exists for each romance reader, and librarians need to know about and collect all varieties.

Chelton gives librarians some excellent tips for purchasing and weeding romance collections. She goes beyond the genrefication debate (see chapters 9 and 10 for full details) and advocates not only a separate romance collection but a unique organization—by series and publication number, not by author. Chelton argues that readers want to read a line in order and may also be interested in reading backward; one of the greatest things about libraries is that we don't go out of print and the backlist is always in stock. She also suggests that libraries subscribe to *Romantic Times* and use it as a tool to hand-select individual titles as an alternative to standing order plans for entire lines.

Modern Research

Chelton wrote her article in 1991. What has changed in fifteen years? Library service is improving. The 2005 Romance Writers of America survey found that 25 percent of readers obtained their most recent book at a library, up from 14 percent in 2002. Still, 36 percent were finding their books in bookstores, though this was a decrease from 44 percent in 2002.

And the romance market is still growing. More than a third of readers were under the age of thirty-five in 2004, and non-self-identified romance readers between eighteen and thirty-four were reported as the age group most likely to pick up a romance novel.[6] Libraries looking to reach younger readers would clearly do well to reach out to romance readers and advertise their romance collections.

"PUBLIC LIBRARY SERVICES TO THE ROMANCE READER," BY MARY BRYSON

Written more than twenty years after Radway did her first research on romance readers, Mary Bryson's master's paper is one of the most recent and most important research projects on romance readers.[7] Bryson conducted an online survey of romance readers, with an astounding 240 usable responses collected in a mere eight days. She focused on romance readers' reading habits and interests as well as their use and impression of library services. She found that, although some things have certainly changed since Radway conducted her research in the early 1980s, many things have also stayed the same. This is the first major study to update Radway's work and provides an important picture of modern romance readers and their use and impression of libraries, library services, and library collections.

Bryson's first survey question determined how dedicated respondents were to romance reading: "If you read romance fiction on a regular basis, do you consider yourself a romance reader?" Of the 244 respondents, 240 considered themselves romance readers, although several added qualifying remarks in the comments field. These remarks underline the bias many have against romance reading; readers admitted to being reluctant to class themselves as romance readers even when they regularly read romances.

The romance readers were also avid readers, which should make any librarian happy. More than 99 percent of the respondents read more than a book a month, and 48 percent read more than seven books a month. Such avid readers could very much benefit from readers' advisory services as they struggle to find enough good books to fill their reading habit. What types of romances were these avid readers enjoying? The popular subgenres were romantic suspense, historical, and contemporary, with most readers enjoying books from a variety of subgenres. The least popular subgenres among this group were inspirational and multicultural romances, but even these were read regularly by at least 10 percent of the respondents.

How do twenty-first-century romance readers select their next book? By far the two most popular methods in this group were browsing and reading book reviews, each with more than 50 percent of respondents regularly using these methods. One of the most interesting findings for librarians is Bryson's readers' heavy use of browsing. If romance readers come to your library, can they browse for books successfully? Sharon Baker found that browsing an integrated collection (all fiction together alphabetically by author), even one with genre labels, is extremely difficult for most readers and rarely successful; readers have trouble identifying the types of books they are looking for and regularly report frustration with the experience.[8]

Many of Bryson's readers reported reading online reviews and participating in romance reader networking sites as sources of inspiration for book selection. Bryson's survey was online as well, and she notes in her conclusion that "the heavy response to this small survey that was only available for eight days indicates that the online community of romance readers is ready to work with their libraries to improve services."[9] Since romance readers are clearly active online, one way librarians could better serve romance readers is to make sure the library's website is romance friendly and offers romance reading suggestions and ways for online romance readers to interact with librarians.

Bryson also found (mostly from the comments field) that many readers look for and continue to read authors whose books they enjoyed in the past. This finding is consistent with both Ross's and Baker's findings on how adult readers select books (see chapters 2, 10, and 11 of this book).

Use of recommendations was the third most popular selection strategy, employed by more than 40 percent of users. Fewer than 14 percent worked with library staff to select new books. This is an extremely disappointing number and one that might even be inflated, since this survey was distributed to several electronic discussion lists read by librarians. Why aren't more readers talking with librarians? The only bright spot is that this number is better than in Radway's work, which found almost zero library use among her informants. This is an even more disappointing result in the light of Bryson's next question: where did romance readers obtain their books? More than 50 percent reported regularly borrowing books from the library. This may be a great improvement over Radway's results, which indicated that romance readers almost never borrowed library books; clearly librarians are doing a much better job stocking romance novels than they were in the early 1980s. Even so, Bryson's respondents, though using the library, were still not asking librarians for assistance. We need to find out why.

How else are readers obtaining books? Many of Bryson's respondents were purchasing from stores (more than 61 percent), and nearly a third purchased books online. Clearly, although libraries are serving a significant portion of romance readers, they are not yet reaching the majority. Many romance readers are also members of book clubs, both romance-focused clubs and clubs that read other genres or more general fiction. In Bryson's survey, most club members also used the club meetings as a source of inspiration for new titles, reflecting the importance of networking with other genre readers. This result also indicates that many of Bryson's readers also read in other popular fiction genres such as science fiction, fantasy, and mystery.

Interestingly, Bryson's readers indicated that they would be comfortable discussing romance reading with library staff, with nearly 75 percent indicating that they would be at least somewhat comfortable. If that really is the case, why are they not asking librarians for recommendations and reading assistance?

When asked about their local library, nearly all respondents indicated that their library had some romance books, but only 58 percent of those libraries had the romance collection separate from general fiction. In terms of the types of romances collected, a majority of the libraries collected some category and series titles, which indicates that most libraries are considering the needs of regular romance readers.

How much do romance readers actually rely on the library for their romance reading needs? Not as much as librarians would like. Nearly a third of Bryson's respondents did not rely on the library's collection in any way, and an additional 45 percent relied on the library only somewhat. Comments indicated that readers primarily used library collections for browsing for something new or unknown, which indicates that libraries that do not support browsing of their romance collection may be driving away possible patrons.

Why else might reliance on library collections be so low? In her final question Bryson asked readers to rate their libraries' collections with the following descriptive terms: outdated, unbalanced, hidden, up-to-date, well balanced, easily located, sparse, too few titles, well stocked, and lots of titles. More than a third of the respondents rated their library's collections as up-to-date and easy to locate. But more than a quarter found their local collections to be outdated, sparse, unbalanced, and containing too few titles. More than 15 percent of respondents felt their library hid the romance collection. The mixed nature of the results likely indicates that some librarians have excellent romance collections that are easy to find and use, while others have poor collections that do not appeal to modern romance readers. Clearly libraries are moving in the right direction, but many still have a ways to go before they are satisfactorily serving the world's largest group of genre fiction readers. As Bryson observes, "With a reading habit of seven plus books a month, the majority of these readers would benefit from the library's collections and readers' advisory services."[10] Modern romance readers are ready to work with libraries, as indicated by the many responses to Bryson's survey and the willingness of most readers to talk with librarians. All libraries need to do now is reach out to romance readers and indicate a willingness to improve their collections and services to better serve this large group.

"ROMANCE COLLECTIONS IN NORTH CAROLINA PUBLIC LIBRARIES," BY AMY FUNDERBURK

Also in 2004, Amy Funderburk conducted a study on the relationship between reviews and presence in collections for romance and other genre novels.[11] Using only award-winning titles, she investigated the number of copies in North Carolina libraries and the presence of reviews in standard library sources (*Library Journal, Booklist, Publishers Weekly, Kirkus,* and *New York Times Review of Books*). Funderburk found that overall only 32 percent of romance award winners had been reviewed, but when she limited the search to the years after 1995 (when *Library Journal* started a romance review column) she found that nearly 65 percent of romance award-winning titles were reviewed, which was nearly the same review rate as award winners in horror and westerns. Still, this does not even come close to the review rate of science fiction and mystery award winners, which were consistently at or above 90 percent. This is great news for science fiction, fantasy, and mystery readers—award winners are regularly being reviewed.

Since 1995, romance novels are being reviewed more often by the review sources most often used by librarians, and significant gains have been made. But Funderburk also found that romance titles were likely to be held in North Carolina public libraries only if they were reviewed in a standard source, so we clearly have a long way to go. Librarians concerned about creating an updated, diverse, and well-balanced romance collection (of the type Bryson's readers desired in their public library) need to look for reviews in places other than the usual sources (see the Librarian's View in this chapter). Also, since some genres are clearly collected more evenly than others (viz., award-winning titles in science fiction, fantasy, and mystery), libraries need to consider whether expressing such a clear preference for one genre type over another is really best serving their patrons.

"LEADING A GENRE STUDY," BY SUE O'BRIEN, AND "ROMANCING YOUR READERS," BY JOHN CHARLES AND CATHIE LINZ

What can libraries and librarians do to improve this situation? Two practice-oriented articles address this question. In "Leading a Genre Study," Sue O'Brien discusses one way for librarians to improve their knowledge of a genre: lead or be a part of a genre study.[12] O'Brien led a mystery genre study for the Adult Reading Round Table and uses her experience and many examples to illustrate this continuing education technique. Genre studies are best done in groups but can also be partaken in by individual advisors eager to improve their knowledge of a genre. Use O'Brien's article along with Saricks's *Readers' Advisory Guide to Genre Fiction* to start an individual genre study or to learn how to lead a group study.[13]

In "Romancing Your Readers: How Public Libraries Can Become More Romance-Reader Friendly," librarian, romance reviewer, and RWA Librarian of the Year John Charles, along with former librarian, RWA library liaison, and romance author Cathie Linz, offer some helpful tips on making your library more welcoming to romance readers, in addition to explaining the appeal of reading romance novels.[14] This makes a nice update to Chelton's earlier article, reflecting the changes in library services and collections since 1990. Charles and Linz offer "Five Simple Steps to a More Romance-Reader Friendly Library," which are both useful and thoughtful enough to be repeated here in their entirety:

1. Become more familiar with the romance genre and its subgenres. Read reference books on the genre, read romances themselves, and talk to romance readers.

2. Purchase romance fiction for your library's collection. While this might sound somewhat simplistic, if you don't have a good romance collection, you won't get many romance readers in your library.

3. As you select romance fiction for your library, try to purchase a range of titles from all of the romance subgenres. Series or category romance fiction should also be a part of your library's collection.

4. Catalog your romance fiction. Simply because the majority of romance titles currently published are paperback originals, they tend to be lost in libraries that don't catalog paperback fiction. If you don't know what you have, how can your readers?

5. Market your romance collection to readers. Whether through booklists and bibliographies, displays, programs or even book

discussion groups, let your patrons know you [and your library] value romance fiction and its readers.[15]

In additional to these excellent suggestions, Charles and Linz explain the most common and "persistent misperceptions about romance fiction still harbored by some misguided library staff." They explain that sex is not the sole ingredient in romance fiction and that current romance novels have a wide range of sensuality, from totally chaste to extremely steamy. Nor, they explain, are all romances alike. Just like other genre fiction (murder mysteries, police procedurals, etc.), romances rely on a few conventions and plot ingredients (every romance features some kind of relationship), but the actual stories vary widely. "Each [book] is a unique reading experience."[16] Charles and Linz briefly explore the current trends and subgenres in romance publishing, noting that in 2005 there was a growing interest in paranormal romance, an increasing influence on romance by the chick lit and women's fiction genres, a rising popularity of tough heroines, and more interest in romance series. They also include a selected list of recommended titles by subgenre. This article is highly recommended reading for all readers' advisors and touches on many of the issues explored in this chapter's Librarian's View.

LIBRARIAN'S VIEW   BY KATIE DUNNEBACK

The Romance Reading Community

According to statistics last updated in the winter of 2005 on behalf of the Romance Writers of America, Corona Research found that approximately 64.6 million Americans had read at least one romance novel in the previous year. Twenty-five percent of those readers checked out books from their local library.[17] Romance readers span all ages, socioeconomic brackets, education levels, and genders. This is a community that is passionate about reading. It is vital for librarians to tap into the romance reading community. They are already readers. They are current, future, and potential voters. They are advocates for libraries and librarians. They can be library supporters.

Katie Dunneback is currently a consultant with Southeastern Library Services in Bettendorf, Iowa. She is a longtime member of the Romance Writers of America and has published short romance novellas under a pseudonym.

Romance readers are also well used to the censure of being known as readers of romance. Think about what is said about readers of the various popular fiction genres. Who usually is the most looked down upon? Which group is usually the most stereotyped in a negative way? Who is the most often accused of reading "trash"? Romance readers have dealt with years of prejudice from every source, including library staff. How hard is it to return to a place where a staff member has loudly and publicly denigrated the patron's reading choices? Or even a library that less loudly, but still clearly, makes it known that romance reading isn't "real" reading? This still happens in libraries all over the world, sometimes less obviously than in the past, but the signs will still be clear to a sensitive reader.

In this section I discuss collection development for romance and other popular fiction genres, ways to make your library "romance friendly," and readers' advisory for romance readers and conclude with a list of resources for further information. Although this chapter has a romance focus, nearly all of the comments and suggestions included here apply to readers of other genres, such as science fiction, fantasy, mystery, and even inspirational fiction.

Review Sources and Collection Development

In library school, students are taught to use authoritative review sources when making collection development decisions. When buying any type of genre fiction, it is often hard to find sufficient quantities of authoritative reviews. *Booklist, Library Journal,* and *Publishers Weekly* all review genre fiction but in limited quantities. *Booklist* and *Library Journal* are especially helpful when sourcing reviews of original mass-market paperback titles. What to do, though, when more than one review source is needed or when what is available in these sources isn't enough to expend the budget? Librarians building genre collections must look outside the library world.

Every genre has specialized magazines that often contain reviews. For romance, the best known of these is *Romantic Times Book Reviews*. They have been publishing since 1981 but have changed names twice since 2002—from *Romantic Times Magazine* to *Romantic Times Bookclub* in 2002 and again to *Romantic Times Book Reviews* in 2006. Another long-standing print review source of the romance market is *Affaire de Coeur* magazine. Both of these magazines have loyal followings.

Within the past five years, the number of romance-centric review websites has exploded. Those that began during the explosion are more likely to be electronic format friendly, since their popularity followed the growth in the electronic book market. These are also the sites most likely to have reviews of small press books; *Romantic Times* and *Affaire de Coeur* have review policies that often require small press authors to pay for advertisements.

Of the web-based review sites, the two older and best known are All About Romance (AAR) and The Romance Reader. AAR has a strong following, but it also has a reputation for purposefully inciting conflict within the industry. Its *Desert Island Keeper* (*DIK*) feature is a reliable resource for readers' advisory. The Romance Reader is less known now than it was five years ago, but this is most likely because its focus is strictly on print books. It does have the benefit of longevity (since 1996), adding to its image as an authoritative resource. And, since the focus of popular reading collections in libraries is print, it is a top resource to consult.

The two websites that have emerged as leaders in the newest generation of review websites are Romance Junkies and Fallen Angel Reviews. Both have been in business since 2003 and review a wide range of romance genres. They both got their starts in response to filling the need for reviews of electronic books. Both quickly expanded and now cover both print and electronic books of all genres. Both sites accept paid advertisements, but they do not require that an ad be purchased for a book to be reviewed.

What does all this mean for the librarian? The sources for reviews have multiplied, but they may not be considered authoritative sources like *Booklist* or *Library Journal*. One can hope that education and awareness of other librarians and administrators will help to change this problem. Romance readers are not the only group of readers whose collection development needs cannot be met using traditional library sources. Additionally, websites like these cannot be ignored, for readers are often alerted to new titles of interest from these sites. Whereas electronically published authors' survival depends on their presence on the Internet, print romance authors have long had an online presence. Authors often spend a significant, if small, portion of their promotion budget on web-based advertisements. Skimming through these sites (or other similar sites) for what is being advertised in addition to reading reviews should become regular habits of any librarian responsible for genre fiction.

This brings us to the issue of budget allocation in terms of formats. "Paperback or hardcover?" is one of the most difficult questions faced by librarians doing collection development in genre fiction. Within romance, as in other popular genres, the majority of titles are released only as mass-market paperbacks, so librarians must be prepared to purchase paperbacks and libraries must be prepared to process and shelve paperbacks just like hardcovers. If romance is popular with the service community (extremely likely in every public library), librarians cannot rely on donations of this type of book to supply the collection. It often takes years for an author to get published in hardback, and by that point he or she has built up a loyal following. Even the most successful authors publish in paperback. One example is Nora Roberts. Although her single-title romances and J. D. Robb titles are now initially published in hardback, her romance trilogies are still first published as mass-market paperbacks. Fans of hers will want to read the newest book, no matter the format, as soon as it comes out. Donations rarely come in close enough to a publication date for this fulfillment strategy to be effective, another reason it is a poor collection development strategy.

Mass-market paperbacks are also popular with readers because of their portability. There is a trade-off, however, since hardbacks tend to be physically easier to read. The compromise for these two issues seems to be the emergence of the trade paperback. Its larger size accommodates larger font and spacing of text, and it is smaller and more flexible than the hardback. The biggest drawback is the limited subgenre selection. More and more publishers are bringing authors out in trade paperback rather than making the jump to hardback from mass market, but three subgenres still dominate the trade paperback women's fiction market: chick lit, spicy/erotic romance, and erotica.

Once format policies have been finalized, the next step is balancing subgenres. Once again, take a look at which books are being checked out and talk to the regular romance readers. Attempt a proportional budget and be willing to readjust as necessary. Librarians usually lack the time or opportunity to do in-depth analyses of the circulation of the collection, although easily generated reports created by modern integrated library systems (ILS) are making it much easier for librarians to gather important information about their collections (see chapter 11).

You can do informal surveys to observe the popular subgenres every day. Review reports from the ILS or weed using "last circulation date" and "total circulation" as indicators. Or carve an hour out of your workday to browse through the popular fiction collection, randomly picking out titles and checking those same indicators. Battered books are ones that are (or used to) circulate well. Paperbacks with uncracked spines are easy indicators of unread titles. Review the "recently returned" shelf or shelving carts to see what patrons have checked out or just looked at recently. Make sure to check the hold shelves or daily pull lists to see which books are never even making it back to the shelves.

Sometimes a subgenre may be of interest but a particular author may not be. Experiment with different authors when choosing titles from subgenres. When grocery shopping, notice which titles are displayed for purchase. Patrons will be in asking for them. Finding a balance in providing patrons what they are searching for is an art and one that can be mastered. It just requires a willingness to be observant and open to change.

Trends

As with any marketplace, romance publishing is subject to trends of what's hot and what's not. Managing the collection to not only respond to, but anticipate, trends patrons may be interested in can be frustrating. Once again, the answer is being tuned in to the service community and what's happening in the romance genre at large. The added factor in anticipating trends, however, is also being tuned in to popular culture in general. Right now, the two hottest trends in the U.S. romance publishing market are Christian/inspirational and erotic romance. These are two seemingly disparate subgenres, but in American culture in general, spirituality and sexuality are heavily discussed mainstream topics.

In July 2006, *Publishers Weekly* ran an article titled "It's Not Just You—It Really Is Hot in Here." In it, the author discusses the evolution of erotic romance and the force it has become in today's romance marketplace. Almost every major New York–based publisher now has an erotic romance imprint or publishing directive.[18] Inspirational romance, though just as strong a force as erotic romance, has not quite rated the development of individual imprints at the major publishing houses. Tracy Farrell, then senior editor of Harlequin's Steeple Hill imprint, noted in 2002 the uphill battle Steeple Hill faced getting its books into Christian Booksellers Association bookstores because of Harlequin's non-Christian focus. She also remarked that many Christian publishing houses already had their own romance imprints.[19]

Trendy subgenres come and go. One potential indicator of how long a trend will last is how quickly it rises to the top of the "must have" genres. Chick lit, a publishing phenomenon that began with *Bridget Jones's Diary* and *Sex and the City* in the late 1990s, is now losing the ground it quickly gained. In a *Publishers Weekly* interview about the name change of the Avon Trade Paperbacks imprint to Avon A and focus from primarily chick lit to one appealing to a broader demographic, Avon publisher Liate Stehlik stated that "what women are reading is changing."[20]

Maybe the largest and most enduring subgenre of romance is historicals. Historical romances broke out from the pack in 1979 with Kathleen Woodiwiss's *The Flame and the Flower*. Historicals have been a favorite subgenre ever since. Within the publishing industry, the demise of the subgenre is also an equally popular discussion. Abby Zidle, then editor at Harlequin's HQN imprint, noted that it is harder for new authors to break into historicals, "but we've been saying this for 15 years."[21]

One way for librarians to track which genres are popular is by checking the listing of special interest chapters on the Romance Writers of America website. Currently there are chapters dedicated to supporting writers in the subject areas of regencies, Celtic, chick lit, erotic, futuristic, fantasy, paranormal, gothic, inspirational, general historical, mystery, suspense, and medical.[22]

Marketing the Collection

The shelving of fiction is a perpetual point of debate among librarians. Everyone has their own opinions on what methods work best. This debate is fully reviewed in chapter 10 of this book. Purchasing the proper titles is the first half of the battle of providing what the service community wants to read. Making those titles easily accessible is the second half. Crowded shelves from which it is hard to remove books restrict access. Weeding older, low-use, and worn titles helps to alleviate this problem. Interfiling formats in which mass-market paperbacks are constantly getting pushed behind larger formats restrict access. Constant attention and shelf straightening or the separation of formats reduce this risk. Improper cataloging restricts access. The points outlined in chapter 10 ease patron and staff frustrations and increase accessibility of genre fiction collections.

Regardless of how books are shelved, it is vitally important that library staff provide effective finding aids for patrons. Finding aids that are readily available, preferably within or near the collection, serve the dual purpose of alerting patrons to the location of items and also effectively marketing the library's collection. Creating aids specific to genre readers and collections is an excellent way to show patrons that your library is welcoming of genre readers.

One of the most effective formats for finding aids is bookmarks, which patrons can quickly scan for information and then take with them to use. Bookmarks do not have to be expensively designed and printed on four-color cardstock; they can be attractively designed with any desktop publishing program, printed on colored paper or plain cardstock on the library copier, then cut up and placed out for patrons to use. Inexpensive in-house laminating of lightweight colored paper is another good option. Use the resources at your disposal when creating a marketing tool, and as long as it is done well your patrons will pick it up. One of the best feature about bookmarks is that they can be placed inside books. Place a handful of them in titles of the authors listed to promote read-alikes. Guerrilla marketing tactics are just as valid in the library as in other venues.

When creating subject-based finding tools, design the look to reflect the tone of the subject. Dark, gritty, romantic suspense bibliographies may have an image of a knife dripping blood, heavy black—but still readable—type, and printed on a light red (not pink!) paper. Sunny yellow paper, curlicue title font, and flowers are not what readers of Allison Brennan are looking for in bookmarks but would be perfect for a list of books that includes Alesia Holliday's titles.

Informal displays are another potential marketing tool. Staff-picks shelves are of interest to patrons because they are interested in what the staff are reading. They also show patrons that staff members read in their preferred genre. A related display would be a patron-picks shelf. The easiest way to do this is to designate an area for the display and put up a sign inviting people to place their picks on the shelf. This strategy may take a while to implement, but it is a community builder and one in which many romance readers will be happy to participate.

A favorite trick of booksellers is placing books face out on the shelves in order to draw attention to particular titles in the sea of spines. In libraries, it can be hard to practice this in the middle of a shelving scheme, but it is possible. Designated display areas allow for the highlighting of particular themes. Small displays (as few as three or four featured titles can do) on small tables or even book carts in the stacks can work. Or use the increasingly available end-of-shelving-unit display kits to highlight a particular subgenre at the point of access. The key to a successful display is to include with the books a finding aid that features more titles related to the theme. This allows patrons to bypass the books if they don't find them intriguing, to look further if the theme does catch their interest, or to save the aid to use later. More important, a premade list can help staff easily refill the display. A display (regardless of size) only works well if it is regularly restocked.

Although it is definitely preferable to have at least one staff member—be it a librarian, administrator, or clerk—who is passionate about each of the genres in the library's collections, this is not always possible. It is important, though, that all staff members be willing to assist patrons in finding the books they are looking to read. An open, friendly, and welcoming staff is the best marketing tool for any collection and essential for a successful readers' advisory service.

Readers' Advisory and Romance Readers

As with any genre, a librarian who is not familiar with romance may feel uncomfortable doing readers' advisory. Readers' advisors need to be prepared for all readers regardless of genre, and this section provides some tips for working with romance readers. It can be particularly helpful to know some of the most common questions to help prepare. The number one question romance readers are likely to ask is about series order. These can be remarkably complicated questions, for some series are written by different authors (2005's highly successful 2176 series from Lovespell), or all the titles sound alike. It sometimes seems that Jodi Thomas only writes books with Texas in the title, so how can anyone figure out which are in the desired series? Author websites are the most authoritative sources for such information and are generally easy to find. Other reliable resources include Kent District Library's *What's Next?* database, Vancouver Public Library's *Sequels* reference book series, currently on its fourth edition, and subscription database *NoveList*.[23]

Another question that might make a librarian uncomfortable discussing romance is sensuality. The amount of sensuality varies widely in romance, and reader preferences vary just as widely. For romance readers' advisory, level of sensuality is as important as readers' mood and must be addressed for a successful transaction. It is best to be up front about this topic, for romance readers know that the genre offers a wide range of sensuality, and it is even more important for casual readers of romance who may not (or may not be able to) bring up this critical issue with a readers' advisor. The best question for the direct approach is to ask, "How hot/spicy/sensual do you prefer?" If an indirect approach is necessary, a discussion of favorite romance authors can help, but this requires the readers' advisor to be knowledgeable about romance. For example, if the patron prefers authors like Linda Howard, Sherrilyn Kenyon, Lora Leigh, and Nora Roberts, they probably have a high tolerance, if not preference, for more sensual and erotic stories. At the opposite end of the spectrum are patrons who prefer Debbie Macomber, Jeanette Oke, and Karen Kingsbury.

One drawback of this author-based approach is that authors may change sensuality levels as they write for different publishers, imprints, or even series. For example, Lynn Kurland's early novels include explicit, though not graphic, sex scenes, but she has since stated that she now intentionally keeps her stories to a PG rating.[24] Kurland is an example of an author who appeals to readers of both extremes of the sensuality spectrum. Most readers choose her books purely based on the type of subgenre she specializes in: time travel romance.

Romance readers can be hard to draw into a readers' advisory exchange because they may be reluctant to talk about their preference for the genre in public. Most readers' advisory service desks are both busy and public. This is where creating a romance-friendly environment is important. In an ideal world, *all* genre readers will feel equally welcome in the library. When it is obvious that a library specializes in one or two genres over others, it is vitally imperative that the staff do everything within their power to reach out to the nonspecialization readers.

This also ties into marketing the collection. Creating, and prominently displaying, bookmarks and other read-alike tools for all genres is one avenue. Using large, centrally located display areas to feature specific genres is another. The Romance Writers of America passes out "Romance Reader Friendly" buttons at conferences. Have staff wear these or similar buttons to help patrons feel more at ease approaching them for help. If a staff member is knowledgeable about romance, promote that person as one to talk to the next time the patron comes in. Knowing there is a fellow enthusiast on the library staff can encourage patrons to be more forthcoming. During staff training days, remind all staff who the point persons are for all genres. This is not to discourage staff members from helping patrons but to give them the confidence to refer the patron to a more knowledgeable staff member if they feel stymied. Additionally, few readers' advisory transactions are onetime events. Patrons need to feel that they can return many times for reading assistance, and directing them to a specific staff person can help make a return visit easier. This may also be the time to promote your library's other readers' advisory resources, such as the library's website or online readers' advisory service (see chapter 12).

The two biggest publishers of readers' advisory texts, Libraries Unlimited and the American Library Association, both have titles available for romance fiction. Unfortunately, they are from 1999 and 2000, respectively. Updated versions of these titles are direly needed to reflect recent changes in the genre and promote the many new authors. For those with teenage romance readers, Libraries Unlimited produced a book targeted for this market in 2004, *Rocked by Romance*.[25] Until updated versions of the general titles have been made available, Libraries Unlimited's *Genreflecting* (6th ed., 2006) book and companion website are a good alternative.

Conclusion

The romance genre can be overwhelming because of both its size and its diversity. It is important for librarians to remember, as with most popular fiction decisions, that it is the desires of the service community that must be respected. There are many resources available for librarians and library staff interested in learning more about the romance genre, and a short list is included below. A well-informed staff, no matter the genre, is one that will best serve the community.

Further Resources

GENERAL RESOURCES

The Romance Wiki, www.romancewiki.com
Romance Writers of America, www.rwanational.org
RRA-L, Romance Readers Anonymous Listserv, www.toad.net/~dolma/

REVIEW WEBSITES

Affaire de Coeur, www.affairedecoeur.com
All About Romance, www.likesbooks.com
Coffee Time Romance, www.coffeetimeromance.com
Fallen Angel Reviews, www.fallenangelreviews.com
Joyfully Reviewed, www.joyfullyreviewed.com
Just Erotic Romance Reviews, www.justeroticromancereviews.com
Paperback Reader, www.paperbackreader.net
Road to Romance, www.roadtoromance.ca
Romance Junkies, www.romancejunkies.com
The Romance Reader, www.theromancereader.com
The Romance Studio, www.theromancestudio.com
Romantic Times, www.romantictimes.com
TwoLips Reviews, www.twolipsreviews.com

READER/WRITER BLOGS AND WEBSITES

The Misadventures of Super Librarian, http://super_librarian.blog spot.com

Romancing the Blog, www.romancingtheblog.com

Smart Bitches Who Love Trashy Books, www.smartbitchestrashybooks .com

ACADEMIC WEBSITES

Bronwyn Clarke, http://bronwynclarke.com/blog/

Teach Me Tonight, http://teachmetonight.blogspot.com

NOTES

1. Catherine Sheldrick Ross, "The Company of Readers: The 'Fiction Problem,'" in *Reading Matters: What the Research Reveals about Reading, Libraries, and Community,* by Catherine Sheldrick Ross, Lynne E. F. McKechnie, and Paulette M. Rothbauer (Westport, Conn.: Libraries Unlimited, 2006), 10–17.

2. Romance Writers of America, 2005 Market Research Study on Romance Readers, http://www.rwanational.org/cs/the_romance_genre/romance_literature_statistics/ readership_statistics.

3. Janice A. Radway, *Reading the Romance: Women, Patriarchy and Popular Literature* (Chapel Hill: University of North Carolina Press, 1984; 2nd ed., 1991).

4. Mary K. Chelton, "Unrestricted Body Parts and Predictable Bliss: The Audience Appeal of Formula Romances," *Library Journal* 116, no. 12 (1991): 44.

5. Ibid., 48.

6. Romance Writers of America, 2005 Market Research, 3–5.

7. Mary Bryson, "Public Library Services to the Romance Reader: An Online Survey of Romance Readers," Master's paper, University of North Carolina, School of Information and Library Science, 2004. Available online at http://hdl.handle.net/ 1901/91.

8. Sharon L. Baker, "Will Fiction Classification Schemes Increase Use?" *RQ* 27, no. 3 (1988): 366–76.

9. Bryson, "Public Library Services," 34.

10. Ibid.

11. Amy Funderburk, "Romance Collections in North Carolina Public Libraries: Are All Genres Treated Equally?" Master's paper, University of North Carolina, School of Information and Library Science, 2004; statistics from 21–23. Available online at http://hdl.handle.net/1091/44.

12. Sue O'Brien, "Leading a Genre Study," *Public Libraries* 38, no. 6 (1999): 384–86.

13. Joyce G. Saricks, *The Readers' Advisory Guide to Genre Fiction* (Chicago: American Library Association, 2001).

14. John Charles and Cathie Linz, "Romancing Your Readers: How Public Libraries Can Become More Romance-Reader Friendly," *Public Libraries* 44, no. 1 (2005): 43–48.

15. Ibid., 44.

16. Ibid., 44, 45.

17. Romance Writers of America, 2005 Market Research.

18. Bethanne Kelly Patrick, "It's Not Just You—It Really Is Hot in Here," *Publishers Weekly* 253, no. 29 (2006): 23–26.

19. Suzanne Mantell, "Reinventing the Wheel?" *Publishers Weekly* 249, no. 26 (2002): 38.

20. Lynn Andriani, "Avon Gives Itself an A," *Publishers Weekly* 254, no. 10 (2007): 11.

21. Suzanne Mantell, "That First Romance," *Publishers Weekly* 252, no. 24 (2005): 22.

22. Romance Writers of America, Special Interest Chapters, http://www.rwanational.org/cs/about_rwa/chapters_listing/special_interest_chapters.

23. Kent District Library, *What's Next?* http://www.kdl.org/libcat/WhatsNextNEW.asp; Vancouver Public Library Online, *Sequels*, 4th ed., http://www.vpl.ca/branches/LibrarySquare/prl/Sequels/sequels.html.

24. Lynn Kurland's author website, *Frequently Asked Questions*, http://www.lynnkurland.com/faq.html.

25. Carolyn Carpan, *Rocked by Romance: A Guide to Teen Romance Fiction* (Westport, Conn.: Libraries Unlimited, 2004).

8

READERS' ADVISORY INTERVIEW

The readers' advisory interview, or conversation, as Joyce Saricks eloquently argued in *Booklist*, is both an essential and an understudied area of readers' advisory.[1] Readers' advisory services have generally been considered a subset of reference services, and thus the readers' advisory interview just a special reference interview, but very little has been written about the unique nature of the readers' advisory interview.

RESEARCH REVIEW   BY JESSICA E. MOYER

Readers' Advisory in Library and Information Science Textbooks

I begin this research review by looking at two of the most popular reference textbooks, *Reference and Information Services* and *Conducting the Reference Interview: A How-to-Do-It Manual for Librarians*, both of which address the readers' advisory interview. These texts are used regularly in both library and information science courses and in-service training programs and are likely the first place most students or librarians encounter information about the readers' advisory interview. I follow this with a review of *Readers' Advisory Service in the Public Library*, which is frequently assigned in courses focused on readers' advisory.

REFERENCE AND INFORMATION SERVICES, BY RICHARD E. BOPP AND LINDA C. SMITH

Bopp and Smith's *Reference and Information Services* briefly addresses readers' advisory services.[2] The introductory section provides a definition and overview of readers' advisory services and acknowledges the recent growth. An additional two pages on readers' advisory services can be found in the reference interview chapter. This very brief overview of the readers' advisory interview emphasizes the importance of listening and understanding the user and acknowledges that most of these transactions take place in public libraries and often involve return visits. Although this is an acceptable introduction to readers' advisory, the fact that only three pages of more than six hundred are devoted to readers' advisory demonstrates a lack of both interest and respect for readers' advisory as an important part of reference services. Bopp and Smith will have a new edition in 2008, one hopes with additional space and respect devoted to readers' advisory.

CONDUCTING THE REFERENCE INTERVIEW, BY CATHERINE S. ROSS, KIRSTI NILSEN, AND PATRICIA DEWDNEY

Conducting the Reference Interview is refreshingly different.[3] It devotes an entire section to the readers' advisory interview and interweaves readers' advisory throughout the rest of the book. Ross is an expert on readers' advisory, and this is evident in the breadth, depth, and quality of information about the readers' advisory interview. This is an excellent source for librarians or students new to readers' advisory, providing an overview of readers' advisory services, tips for conducting a readers' advisory interview, and a case study with comments for analyzing a readers' advisory transaction. The case study in particular is a welcome addition that could be used by itself in a classroom or work training situation, as could the next section, a series of exercises based on comments from actual readers (interviewees from Ross's reading studies). Particularly for those without the time to read all of Saricks's, *Readers' Advisory Service in the Public Library*, this is an excellent alternative.

READERS' ADVISORY SERVICE IN THE PUBLIC LIBRARY, BY JOYCE SARICKS

Students who are lucky enough to take a class with a readers' advisory focus are often assigned Saricks's *Readers' Advisory Service in the Public Library*.[4] In addition, this book is regularly used for professional development and in-service activities, making it the single title most known by library staff. Fortunately, it is also one of the best resources on readers' advisory in general and has excellent information about the readers' advisory interview. The emphasis is entirely practical, based on Saricks's and Nancy Brown's work as readers' advisors in public libraries. Additionally, the first edition (with Brown) was published in 1987, before the majority of the research reviewed in this chapter or even in this book was published. Because of its practical nature, I do not discuss it further here other than to recommend it as an excellent resource for students and practitioners.

Readers' Advisory Interview and Services

"THE NATURE OF THE READERS' ADVISORY TRANSACTION IN ADULT READING," BY KENNETH SHEARER

In 1996, Shearer published the first study of readers' advisory interviews.[5] In this first chapter of *Guiding the Reader to the Next Book,* he recounts the results of several class projects inspired by Joan Durrance's work on patron satisfaction with reference transactions.[6] Shearer modified Durrance's project strategy and had students ask a readers' advisory question at a public library. Students were instructed to say they had read and enjoyed *To Kill a Mockingbird,* by Harper Lee, and ask for something similar to read. They recorded the responses and wrote a narrative of their experience, and the assignment played a key part in classroom discussion. Shearer repeated this assignment with a few variations with several classes from 1992 to 1994 and reports the results.

Shearer's work reported in this chapter was the first of its kind for readers' advisory research. Although he used a research model long employed by reference researchers, his is the first project to use it explicitly for readers' advisory. He acknowledges that this is not the most rigorous research design, nor is it in any way quantitative. But this is often the case with the early research works, and the perhaps flawed results are still of great significance; they are not, however, particularly positive. Students were initially directed to ask for a librarian, which resulted in so many awkward situations that this instruction was dropped from later assignments. Many readers' advisory transactions were conducted not by librarians but by circulation staff who were personally heavy readers and handled most of the books as they went in and out of the library. (The lack of professionalism in readers' advisory transactions is also discussed by May in her 2000 article in *Library Journal* and in a chapter in *The Readers' Advisor's Companion,* both discussed below.) Shearer's most important result is that staff (or librarians) who asked the patron/student why they liked the book were the ones most positively reviewed by the students, who also overwhelmingly responded that they would return to these persons for more help in the future. Students who were not asked why they enjoyed the book rated the overall transaction lower and were much less likely to indicate a willingness to return to the same person.

"LIBRARIANS' ABILITIES TO RECOGNIZE READING TASTES," BY DUNCAN SMITH

Guiding the Reader to the Next Book also includes one of Duncan Smith's first articles on his studies of videotaped readers' advisory transactions,

"Librarians' Abilities to Recognize Reading Tastes."[7] Even though Smith uses an entirely different research design, he does a remarkably similar study to that conducted by Shearer. Using a case study methodology, Smith videotaped a reader talking about her reading likes and dislikes and a recent book she had read. He then shared the recording with two readers' advisors, who responded to the reader and made suggestions for additional reading. Smith then returned to the reader with the suggestions and videotaped her responses. Much of the chapter is a discussion of the advisors' responses and the reader's reactions to their suggestions. Smith relates this transaction to other research in reference transactions, providing a useful theoretical basis for studying readers' advisory.

Unlike Shearer's project, Smith's shows readers' advisors in a much more positive light. Critics might call this not only an ideal readers' advisory transaction but a readers' advisors' dream scenario. How many librarians have time to sit down with a reader and do a personal reading history and readers' advisory interview—and then time to go ahead and create personalized book lists based on their interviews? The reality: not that many. Many libraries' service desks are too busy for librarians to spend extended time with a single patron, and most patrons are too busy to spend a long time talking with a librarian or waiting for a personalized book list to be assembled. Instead, most patrons want something they can get off the shelf and take home, preferably getting out the door of the library within fifteen minutes of walking in. This doesn't give the librarian much chance to conduct the idealized situation Smith presents. Still, this chapter is worth reading because it models an ideal readers' advisory transaction. Particularly for beginning librarians, students, or those otherwise new to readers' advisory, this chapter provides a detailed model for a one-on-one readers' advisory interview.

STUDIES OF READERS' ADVISORY SERVICES BY MARY K. CHELTON AND ANNE MAY

In recent years, Mary K. Chelton and Anne May have spearheaded several studies of readers' advisory services in New York libraries.[8] May believes that it is important for libraries to pursue better service to fiction readers as the library takes on an increasingly recreational role. In her study "Readers' Advisory Service," responses to requests for readers' advisory assistance were varied, from delighted to irritated; most staff seemed uncomfortable with the requests. May also found that no staff members conducted a full-fledged readers' advisory interview. Few asked questions about the appeal of the books or "probed into which elements were critical to our selection or appreciation of fiction."[9] Though most did offer some type of help, time expended on these queries was varied, and few offered follow-up. May's patrons were satisfied with the transaction if the staff person was friendly or helpful but dissatisfied if staff were condescending or showed irritation. May also found that staff were reluctant to use readers' advisors tools. When they did use reference tools, the first choice was the OPAC. Few used other readers' advisory tools and none used websites. One interesting (and distressing) finding of her research (and Shearer's) is that staff with an MLS did not do better than paraprofessionals. This result could have serious implications for library science education and should be of concern to all librarians.[10]

In many of the situations described by May's students, staff responded in a way that would be entirely unacceptable in a reference interview yet seemed an acceptable response in a readers' advisory transaction. This is a disturbing trend in which leisure readers are not treated the same way as patrons with a reference question—disturbing especially when fiction accounts for more than half of the circulation in most public libraries.

"READERS' ADVISORY: MATCHING MOOD AND MATERIAL," BY CATHERINE ROSS AND MARY K. CHELTON

Although "Readers' Advisory: Matching Mood and Material" has no references or citations to research literature, it added an accepted and important aspect to the readers' advisory interview.[11] Based on Ross's work with heavy readers and Chelton's on readers' advisory interviews, this article was the first to suggest that mood is relevant to readers' book selection and something readers' advisors must ask readers about for a successful transaction. They suggest asking a question like "What kind of book are you in the mood for today?" This would not replace Saricks's opening question—"Tell me about a good book you've read recently"—but would go beyond with the realization that readers are not always looking to repeat one reading experience, that their moods vary over time. Ross and Chelton argue convincingly that readers' best reading experiences and the best readers' advisory transactions result when the readers' current mood is taken into consideration by the advisor.

"READER DEVELOPMENT," BY BRIONY TRAIN

A recent general discussion of readers' advisory services can be found in the U.K. publication *Reading and Reader Development,* in the chapter "Reader Development," by Briony Train.[12] Drawing heavily on Saricks's and Brown's work, Train provides a brief overview of the readers' advisory interview, focusing on the difference between a conversation for readers' advisory and an interview for reference, as part of a lengthy chapter on readers' advisory. She also briefly addresses the problems of recommending versus suggesting titles to patrons. Addressing the issue of quality, Train observes the difficulty of assessing a readers' advisory transaction. Each reader will have a unique experience with a book, and their opinions of the suggested titles will also vary widely; so, unlike reference suggestions, there is no "right answer" in a readers' advisory interaction. Train reminds us that it is not an advisor's job to make a judgment of quality on behalf of the reader. This is a good overview source, but since it was written before Saricks's new edition in 2005 and provides little new information, its most important contribution is as a British view of readers' advisory services.

Improving Readers' Advisory Interview Skills and Professional Development

TALKING WITH READERS, BY DUNCAN SMITH

How do librarians learn to improve their readers' advisory interview skills? One method is set out in a workbook titled *Talking with Readers*, developed by the Minnesota Office of Library Development and Services and *NoveList* under the direction of Duncan Smith. Using the self-assessment and development guide model that is in use in Minnesota, this guide focuses on supporting the growth and development of readers' advisors and readers' advisory services in libraries of all sizes. The workbook identifies the competencies needed to deliver readers' advisory service. These competencies were identified by Minnesota librarians engaged in readers' advisory work. The workbook also contains self-assessment activities, next steps for improving your readers' advisory abilities, and resources to expand your knowledge of this important service area.[13]

The full workbook and supplementary materials are available to Minnesota library staff or *NoveList* subscribers as a PDF file. Smith wrote a companion article for *Reference and User Services Quarterly*, "Talking with Readers: A Competency Based Approach to Readers' Advisory Services," which places the workbook and the entire initiative into the current state of readers' advisory, explains its purpose, and comments on the various sections.[14]

Smith's article identifies the four areas of competence for readers' advisors, including "the readers' advisory transaction," which is the focus here. He frames the readers' advisory interview as a conversation rather than the interview taught to reference librarians. Readers' advisory librarians are not seeking "the right answer" but are seeking possibilities for the reader, many of which may be right. Smith refers to readers' advisory librarians as consultants rather than experts (reference librarians). He also proposes that readers' advisory is more qualitative and that this needs to be evident in the readers' advisory transaction.

Smith explains that he developed the workbook to assist in the move from conceptual competencies to actual readers' advisory practice in libraries: "Talking with Readers is a first step in providing library staffs with a structured approach for moving readers' advisory from a 'non-methodical, information, and serendipitous response' to a service grounded in our profession's knowledge skills, abilities, and standards of effective practice."[15] He elaborates on each of the identified competencies in sections called "Whys and Whats," designed to be used by individual librarians or groups as part of a continuing education plan.

Talking with Readers links knowledge with practice in other ways as well. After each section, multiple-choice questions are presented to help advisors confirm that they understand the information they have read. Other sections check knowledge of popular authors and advisory resources through lists that prompt staff to evaluate their own knowledge. Smith's workbook is clearly a well-researched and thoughtfully produced program for learning about readers' advisory in general and the interview in particular. It would be most useful for self-directed and motivated students of readers' advisory or as part of a larger, formal training program.

LIBRARIAN'S VIEW   BY DAVID WRIGHT

When it comes to what's been written about the ins and outs of advising readers face to face, the idea of a scholarly and practical divide is largely a false dichotomy, since most of what is available on the subject is deeply pragmatic, created by and for practitioners in the field. The books and articles of respected readers' advisory authority Joyce Saricks are based on her own library's work with readers as well as her discussions with other

---

David Wright is a readers' advisory librarian at the Seattle Public Library and has written for the NoveList *database,* Booklist, Library Journal, Reference and User Services Quarterly, *and elsewhere. He is a member of the Readers' Advisors of Puget Sound and the RUSA CODES Readers' Advisory Committee.*

working librarians through the Adult Reading Round Table of Illinois. Her research was largely hands-on, and her conclusions were drawn from ongoing trial and error with actual library patrons. Many subsequent articles, including responses and addenda to Saricks's work, have followed the same path.

By the way, if you are hoping this article will teach you the actual process of conducting a readers' advisory interview, let me disabuse you right now. If you need more information on the how-to-do-it aspects of the readers' advisory interview, I suggest the best place to start is by reading the first half of Joyce Saricks's excellent and thoughtful *Readers' Advisory Service in the Public Library.*

In addition to direct instruction on readers' advisory interview techniques, there has been much research, both academic and market based, of readers' behavior and tastes that is of interest and use in our field.[16] There have also been studies of the current state of readers' advisory interactions in our libraries, together with arguments for the importance of such service to our profession's future. All of these articles can help us improve our readers' advisory interactions, as is discussed below, but only if we *read* them, and this brings us to our threshold issue. Most librarians don't read articles or books like this one. Here lies a paradox, inasmuch as you, dear reader, are clearly an exception to this tendency. It may be presumed that—unlike some of your colleagues—you are someone who takes regular, edifying dips into the professional literature, and that you already understand your vital role as "information gatekeeper" and readers' advisory booster to the unlettered masses. For playing this thankless role, I salute you: keep it up! In all seriousness, you are a credit to your organization and a big help to its staff, whether they know it or not.

Why don't librarians read more professional literature? Out of many reasons not to, a few may suffice: it's boring, we're busy, and life is short. Why *should* we read it? For them that do and them that don't, the crux is the same. It is not a question of whether such works represent the fruits of empirical research or the considered, hard-won suggestions of helpful, experienced colleagues. The question is, just what effect, if any, will words on the page (or screen) have on what we actually *do* all day? Is professional reading worthwhile; does it have much bearing on our working lives? For many of us, it doesn't much seem to. I believe that it can, but whether it does is largely up to us. Books such as this one can assist the busy librarian by reviewing and summarizing the literature, steering us toward useful writing. What they can't do is help us get better at readers' advisory in any way at all, unless, of course, we really want to.

Writing about the readers' advisory interview falls into two general categories: prescriptive, or how we should do it, and descriptive, or how we actually do it. Let's begin with the latter.

Zen and the Art of the Reader's Advisory Interview

Most of the hard-core research about readers' advisory transactions consists of academic studies in which shadowy cabals of incognito students fan out and infiltrate nearby public libraries, approaching unwary staff with disingenuous requests for "a good book" or "something to read." They then painstakingly record the treatment they receive at our hands, which is sometimes thoughtful and responsive but as often as not falls into the range of cavalier, callous, indifferent, inept, intimidated, intimidating, or insulting. These valuable studies (or as certain Nassau County and North Carolina library workers like to refer to them, "nightmarish ordeals") reveal that libraries on the whole are even more clueless about readers' advisory transactions than we are about doing reference interviews—no small feat given that similar studies of reference effectiveness tend to hover around a 50 percent success rate.[17] These sobering data can and should be welcomed as cures for complacency and stirring summons to action, though on a blue Monday they're just as likely to be a defeatist's death knell. What possible difference could our own efforts at readers' advisory make?

Aside from giving us a healthy dose of humility, this descriptive research gives us specific information about just how we most typically fail in our patrons' eyes. Interestingly enough, despite the fundamental differences between reference and readers' advisory interviews, they seem to share the same prevalent error: we don't listen; we don't hear. Our eagerness (or panic, or indifference) prompts us to talk when we should be listening and to push books on the reader as though we were selling rather than sharing them. How liberating it is for the anxious advisor to realize that the basic requirement of a good interview is simply to converse with others about books. But for that to happen, we need to clear some welcoming space in our attention. This is not always easy amid the bustle of a busy library, but it is crucial for doing meaningful advisory. These conversations are ongoing and we may not have a perfect suggestion at every turn, but when we treat our patron with respect, attention, and enthusiasm, we make it clear that we value and serve readers and thus lay the foundation for good things to come.

If you'd like to learn about still more ways that the readers' advisory transaction can crash and burn, in 2006, Neil Hollands wrote a great piece in which he enumerated seven "faulty assumptions" of the traditional model of readers' advisory.[18] Although the article may somewhat overstate the case against face-to-face advisory in pursuit of promoting a new online model, Hollands makes some excellent points that should help in improving online and live interactions, both vital venues in making readers' advisory services available to a wide range of readers.

The central message of these studies—that we are failing at readers' advisory—may well be lost on those who need it most. I refer to those who are either already crippled by the sense that they don't have any talent for talking with readers or have long since been hobbled by the conviction that they do. In mastering the art of advisory, the thorniest crisis of confidence may not be having too little of the stuff, but too much. A wise middle course for the advisor is to remember that we are seldom as good or as bad as we think we are. Zen masters talk a lot about "beginner's mind" (or *Shoshin*), which basically means to be fully engaged in what you're doing without being distracted by your own prior knowledge, assumptions, or opinions—the idea being that whatever hard goal you seek (and I know many of you are convinced that doing good readers' advisory must be about as difficult as attaining Nirvana), no matter how green or seasoned you may be, you should strive to approach each transaction in a spirit of open-minded discovery, with a willingness to fail and to learn.

It may come as some comfort to the many librarians who feel themselves unworthy or inept at advisory to realize that the ultimate goal is not to become an expert or literary guru but merely to become a more experienced beginner. It is truly one of the blessings of readers' advisory that there will always be more to learn and more to try. It may be that we have been working in libraries and getting paid for it for some time now and feel a bit silly or fraudulent at the notion that we might still have things to learn about how to do our jobs. It's a natural thing to feel, but we certainly wouldn't want our personal physician or legal advisor trapped in the same delusion. If you find yourself among those advisors who have grown more comfortable engaging with readers, to the extent that other staff start to brand you as the resident "expert," take my advice and *don't believe them.* In a field that brings us into contact with new personalities and stories each day, the assumption of expertise can be a crippling, deadening condition, distancing us from coworkers and patrons alike. Learn as you go, but wear your experience lightly. "It is the readiness of the mind that is wisdom."[19]

On the other hand, nothing can sabotage a readers' advisory transaction faster than an advisor's obvious lack of confidence. When confronted with a librarian who stares and stammers as though he had just been handed a spent nuclear fuel rod rather than a request for a good book, it is little wonder that most readers will spare us—and themselves—any future awkwardness by staying well away. As Anne May points out in her study, readers who share their literary enthusiasms and tastes with us are entrusting us with some surprisingly personal aspects of themselves, and it is entirely fitting that we cultivate the sangfroid and relaxed interest of a good bedside manner.[20] Becoming easy with our role as perpetual beginners can help us cultivate this ease with patrons in addition to helping us avoid those ruts that seem to litter the library landscape.

Against Fundamentalism, Against Science

In addition to descriptive studies, there is a large and growing body of work that offers prescriptive how-tos on conducting the readers' advisory interview. The best-known example of this is Joyce Saricks's seminal *Readers' Advisory Service in the Public Library*, now in its third edition. The topic has also been given extensive treatment by Duncan Smith and the *NoveList* crew in their workbooks *Talking with Readers* and the less epic *RA-101 Lite*. Readers' advisory interviews also crop up in an ongoing succession of articles and chapters and woven into the text of various other resources such as Saricks's *Readers' Advisory Guide to Genre Fiction*. I want to warn against one potential pitfall of hitting the books and reading up on the readers' advisory interview that lies in wait for even the most assiduous of students; indeed, they are the most vulnerable. I'm talking about the pernicious tendency to view these well-intentioned aids as dogma and/or science.

Readers' advisory is an art, not a science. To call it an art is not to equate it with whimsical, subjective improvisation; artists practice rigorously and struggle mightily to master various techniques and skills in pursuit of their craft. Rather, it is to caution us against adopting a hidebound approach toward people and books. I'm often struck when I talk with library students by just how rigorously and literally many of them seem to take readers' advisory texts, as though genres were classified by means of differential calculus and appeal characteristics were unalterable Holy Writ. In their zeal to serve, they baffle the unsuspecting patron with arcane jargon such as "benchmark author" or "appeal factor" or terrify them with the prospect of something that seems more like invasive psychotherapy than a casual conversation about books.

Anyone who insists that a readers' advisory interview must be conducted *just so* or in such and such a fashion should be viewed with amiable skepticism. For instance, I cannot tell you how many successful readers' advisory conversations I've had where few if any descriptive terms were used. When a patron is in a rush or not especially communicative, it is not at all uncommon to rely on the shorthand of their most and least favorite authors, drawing quick mental Venn diagrams around folks they have liked and disliked. Most of our readers' advisory teachers, if they've worked in the real world, understand this. We don't do advisory in a vacuum, and the best interview strategies certainly vary depending on whether we are talking with a harried mother with screaming kids in tow, a laconic longshoreman, an adventuresome young iconoclast, or a loquacious retiree who could use a book but only if she can first tell us about the latest escapades of her dachshund.

Books, articles, and workshops can be inspiring, but the real answer doesn't lie in our ability to retreat, but to advance. To boldly baby-step where no readers' advisor has gone before: this is where the readers' advisory rubber meets the road.

The Library as Laboratory

So much of our success or stagnation as librarians and advisors comes down to our own individual initiative. Surely it will have struck many of us upon landing our first real library job what a staggering range of service standards we found in operation. I am not talking about the official service standards, a copy of which no doubt sleeps on some shelf in some binder assembled by some administrative committee some time ago. I mean the *actual* standards—the manner in which patrons are greeted and treated by staff. This seems to veer wildly from outgoing friendliness to restrained hauteur, from obsequious servitude to sheer indifference to ill-disguised contempt, all depending on the initiative and mind-set of the individual librarian. As we learned the ropes, we will have seen inspiring models for imitation and discouraging examples to avoid—and found ways to profit from both, we hope. The autonomy afforded us by our profession can be a blessing and a curse; we typically regard it as a blessing for ourselves and a curse for those few misfits and burnout cases whom we feel should really be "brought into line."

The readers' advisor's "classroom"—that part of our job that is the most private, autonomous, and off limits to others—is the readers' advisory interview. Our actual interactions with patrons tend to be subject to a tacit and largely unconscious hands-off policy with regard to help or criticism from any quarter, be it other staff, the professional literature, or even the promptings of our own conscience. In contrast, we seem to have little problem sharing ideas and adopting input in more peripheral and public areas of readers' advisory. We regularly beg, borrow, and steal from each other when it comes to themes for displays, discussion questions, book lists, or program ideas, areas where it would never occur to us to go it alone. I belong to a local readers' advisory roundtable that has met quarterly for the past several years, and in all that time we have looked at almost every aspect of readers' advisory *except* the readers' advisory interview. When it comes to the crux—how we interact with our patrons—that is often perceived as being nobody's business but our own. We keep our hands off each other and off ourselves. *Why is this?* Are these conversations too intimate to reveal, too subjective to share, too complicated to get into, or too delicate to withstand scrutiny? Or are we merely afraid of being revealed as frauds, found out to be less than exemplary, not quite the experts we feel we ought to be? Here again, a premium for expertise can block the way forward, whereas adopting the outlook of a perpetual beginner can free us up to learn and develop.

One alternative, instead of developing our skills at talking with readers, is simply not to do readers' advisory interviews at all. They are breathtakingly easy to avoid. The easiest way to eliminate almost all of those messy readers' advisory interviews is simply to remain as you are and go about your business. Most of your patrons wouldn't dream of asking for help looking for a good book, and your boss probably doesn't expect it either. I am always a little amused by presentations on how to do readers' advisory that begin by citing that proverbial dreaded question: "Can you recommend a good book?" In my experience, if you've waited for readers to ask for help, you have already missed the majority of the readers' advisory interactions that could be taking place in your library.

You know that folks seldom ask for a good book; they ask for the best seller that isn't on the shelf, or where the mysteries are, or they don't ask anything at all but simply browse a display or the stacks, minding their own business and assuming you'll mind yours. Yet these scenarios are in fact the most typical openings to a readers' advisory transaction. The successful advisor must hawk her wares at every turn, approaching browsers and striking up friendly conversations. Some patrons, of course, prefer to be left alone, and others may enter into a long-lasting advisory relationship with us. Almost all will appreciate the attention. If we don't initiate the interview, we're sending a tacit message that in our library readers are on their own. Remember this: the readers' advisory interview is most often initiated by the interviewer, not the interviewee. And remember this as well: the only way to get better at readers' advisory interviews is by *doing* them.

A useful way of looking at these brash sorties beyond the safe haven of the reference desk is to view the library as a laboratory, a place to improvise, play, experiment, to *try* things. This approach can apply to all sorts of services we provide, but the readers' advisory interview is the most volatile and exciting of our experiments. It may be that your library has some formalized training in readers' advisory, but most of the time for most of us these experiments rely upon our own initiative. Fortunately, we tend to have quite a bit of autonomy when it comes to our actual interactions with patrons. As for *what* to try, here's where all these essays and books about the readers' advisory interview can come in handy, not as a set of rules or marching orders but as a cookbook loaded with potential recipes.

The word *essay* means "to try," and the godfather of the essay was Michel de Montaigne, whose motto was "Que sais-je?" or "What do I know?" (The guy had never heard of Zen, but he certainly knew a thing or two about beginner's mind.) There is no shortage of writers out there professing to teach us how to do readers' advisory interviews, many of whom are listed in this chapter. None of them can do us any good if we don't actively reconstitute their dry words into deeds and try them out. Rather than just reading about what others have done, go and do the same yourself. Between colleagues and patrons and strangers on the bus, you will have no shortage of guinea pigs to try things out on. You may find some great strategies on your own, and you will also find some brilliant ideas from others that don't work so well for you. Perhaps you will even be inspired to join the conversation with an essay of your own, because your own experiences talking with readers are the best kind of research around.

Sure, it's scary to push yourself beyond your comfort zone. But seriously, what's the worst that can happen? You can crash and burn and reveal yourself as a fraud with little knowledge of literature or readers? Okay, that *is* pretty bad, but consider this: those descriptive studies show that patrons really appreciate it when we try, regardless of what we're able to come up with for them. The real shame is not to have tried at all. It hardly matters to ignored patrons whether our failure to reach out to them was owing to our being an ossified desk ogre who loathes all things human or a well-meaning public servant who is a little intimidated by the learning curve. The end result is the same: they weren't served. So try. And here's the best part: once you try and fail, you will have just mapped out a new area for experimentation and growth. It's like a game: Let's play library! Let me do one thing different and see what happens. You don't necessarily have to go lock yourself in a room and hit the books. Just dip in, sample, taste. Adopt promising techniques and adapt them to your own style and personality. Use the tools rather than letting the tools use you. Articles can be great for this, but even a sizable book is really just a collection of articles, if you smash it into pieces.

Of course, there is nothing remotely original in what I'm suggesting. Over a decade ago, Kenneth Shearer talked about the same thing. He referred to it as taking a "practice audit" stance:

> In order to do the best job possible, professionals assess the relevance of what they read in the literature and hear in continuing education sessions; they selectively try aspects that seem most promising on the job. They then critically observe what works and what doesn't. . . . They regulate their behavior to reconfigure what mix works best in their practice.[21]

Or, they try stuff out, keep what works, and toss the rest. This is all very clearly laid out and seems almost common sense, but Shearer's chapter has one failing compared to mine: you probably haven't read it. To be fair, you're only partially to blame here, for his title—"Reflections on the Findings and Implications for Practice"—is about as inviting as oral surgery.

We can also take a library-as-laboratory approach to the descriptive research by doing a little informal descriptive research of our own. It may well be that the most meaningful, life-altering benefit of such research lies not in the articles it produces but in the experience of the students who do it, and the only way to partake in that benefit is to go forth and do likewise. We librarians are already notorious for taking busman's holidays, but asking questions is anathema to most of us. We grouse and groan about how folks never ask us for help but can barely conceive of doing so ourselves, and this should tell us something. At the high-profile library where I work, I see scores of visiting librarians each week. They slink around filling their pouches with book lists like marsupials at a trade show, either never interacting with us or posing sidelong questions about our administration, code of conduct, or web access software. Yet I suspect those who take the most away from their visits are the ones I never spot as fellow librarians, those few who are using the opportunity to take a walk in their patrons' shoes. We should all do some secret shopping from time to time. What better way to gain a real sensitivity to our patrons' experiences and situations than to take a turn at being them?

Try this sometime soon: go to a library you've never been to in your area, in a sincere quest for something good to read. Does anyone approach with an offer of help as you browse the stacks or invite you with their demeanor? If not, step up, ask them for help, and see what happens. Try the same thing in a bookstore or two, maybe a big chain store and a local independent, if there are any left in your area. At their best, librarian advisors and mercantile "hand-sellers" play the same game, for both are seeking to bring the customer back again and again. When you find exemplary booksellers or librarians, get to know them, talk shop with them, and learn their secrets. Sample the research coming from publishers and booksellers, which often has more to say to readers' advisors (and in plainer language) than academic writing.

Conclusion

There really is no conclusion to this ongoing conversation, but this particular chapter has gone on long enough, don't you agree? Here's the deal: there are plenty of folks out there writing analysis and practical instruction on the readers' advisory interview. Although you don't know them, these folks are your colleagues, and at least one of their motivations is to help us all get better. Some have more experience than you, some less. Some write so much that it makes you wonder where they find the time and what they do all day while you're helping people and putting out fires, and even who *they* are to tell you anything. Some may offer you the considerable gift of a different or broader perspective than you are likely to have from your place in the trenches. Some of their ideas will come in handy for you, some not. It makes little sense for me to suggest which are more practical and which less, for I know from experience that a wide variety of approaches is needed to reach both advisors and advisees. We're not honing a scalpel's edge here, we're loading a shotgun. The only way I know of finding out what works for you is to engage these writers and play around with their ideas in your work, adding their writings to the various places you go to refuel, get inspired, and find new directions. I've been working in public libraries for a decade now and have engaged in several hundred of what could be called readers' advisory transactions, ranging from swift chats to fairly intimate hour-long heart-to-hearts. Nevertheless, I'm still a true beginner at this, with much to learn and many strategies left to try, not a few of which are lying around in books and articles I haven't yet read. Ultimately, all these interview techniques are tools that help us all inspire and invite readers to share, to hear what they're telling you, and to help facilitate their reading lives. They are ways for us to connect with other people, and that is what makes our workdays fun and meaningful in the first place.

NOTES

1. Joyce Saricks, "Rethinking the Readers' Advisory Interview," *Booklist,* April 1, 2007, 24.

2. Richard E. Bopp and Linda C. Smith, *Reference and Information Services: An Introduction,* 3rd ed. (Englewood, Colo.: Libraries Unlimited, 2001).

3. Catherine Sheldrick Ross, Kirsti Nilsen, and Patricia Dewdney, "The Readers Advisory Interview," in *Conducting the Reference Interview: A How-to-Do-It Manual for Librarians* (New York: Neal-Schuman, 2002), 162–75, 180–84.

4. Joyce Saricks, *Readers' Advisory Service in the Public Library,* 3rd ed. (Chicago: American Library Association, 2005).

5. Kenneth D. Shearer, "The Nature of the Readers' Advisory Transaction in Adult Reading," in *Guiding the Reader to the Next Book,* ed. Kenneth D. Shearer (New York: Neal-Schuman, 1996), 1–20.

6. Joan Durrance, "Reference Success: Does the 55 Percent Rule Tell the Whole Story?" *Library Journal* 114, no. 7 (1989): 34.

7. Duncan Smith, "Librarians' Abilities to Recognize Reading Tastes," in Shearer, *Guiding the Reader,* 89–125.

8. Mary K. Chelton, "What We Know and Don't Know about Reading, Readers and Readers' Advisory Services," *Public Libraries* 38, no. 1 (1999): 42–47; Duncan Smith, "Reinventing Readers' Advisory," in *The Readers' Advisor's Companion,* ed. Kenneth D. Shearer and Robert Burgin (Englewood, Colo.: Libraries Unlimited, 2001), 59–75; Anne K. May, "Readers' Advisory Service: Explorations of the Transaction," in Shearer and Burgin, *Readers' Advisor's Companion,* 123–48. See also Anne K. May, Elizabeth Olesh, and Anne Miltenburg, "A Look at Readers' Advisory Services," *Library Journal* 125, no. 15 (2000): 40–43.

9. May, "Readers' Advisory Service," 144–45.

10. Library science education in this area is explored in Shearer and Burgin, *Readers' Advisor's Companion,* chaps. 1–2, and Jessica E. Moyer and Terry L. Weech, "The Education of Public Librarians to Serve Leisure Readers in the United States, Canada and Europe," *New Library World* 106, nos. 1/2 (2005): 67–79.

11. Catherine Sheldrick Ross and Mary K. Chelton, "Readers' Advisory: Matching Mood and Material," *Library Journal* 126, no. 2 (2001): 52–55.

12. Briony Train, "Reader Development," in *Reading and Reader Development: The Pleasure of Reading,* by Judith Elkin, Briony Train, and Debbie Denham (London: Facet, 2003), 30–58, quote from 39.

13. Duncan Smith et al., *Talking with Readers: A Workbook for Readers' Advisors,* a cooperative project of *NoveList,* the Minnesota Office of Library Development and Services (Department of Children, Families, and Learning), and Minnesota library staff; available on *NoveList.*

14. Duncan Smith, "Talking with Readers: A Competency Based Approach to Readers' Advisory Services," *Reference and User Services Quarterly* 40, no. 2 (2000): 135–42.

15. Ibid., 141.

16. For example, see Ross and Chelton, "Readers' Advisory."

17. Durrance, "Reference Success."

18. Neil Hollands, "Improving the Model for Interactive Readers' Advisory Service," *Reference and User Services Quarterly* 45, no. 3 (2006): 205–12.

19. Shunryu Suzuki, *Zen Mind, Beginner's Mind* (Boston: Shambhala Press, 2006), 113.

20. May, "Readers' Advisory Service."

21. Kenneth D. Shearer, "Reflections on the Findings and Implications for Practice," in *Guiding the Reader*, 180–81.

9

TOOLS FOR READERS' ADVISORS

Why do readers' advisors need tools? Joyce Saricks answers this important question in appendix 2 of her *Readers' Advisory Guide to Genre Fiction:*

> I believe they are important because they provide us with added memory. No matter how good we are at remembering titles and authors, there are times every day when our minds go blank. . . . If we can go to a reference source, book or electronic, and look up information for a reader, we have reinforced that this reader has asked a "real" question. . . . Reference sources confirm that this is a serious query and that there are places to look for an answer. This can make a real difference with readers and staff.[1]

Saricks make a strong case for readers' advisors to use tools in readers' advisory transactions; using tools makes it clear to both patrons and other library staff (and administrators) that readers' advisory is just as "real" and valid an adult public service as reference. So what tools do readers' advisors use? And which ones work best?

RESEARCH REVIEW   BY JESSICA E. MOYER

This section is not an overview of all the tools available to readers' advisors.[2] It is a review of research about which tools readers' advisors use and which ones they have the most success with. Many tools are also created for use by patrons, so we also look at research about the ways patrons do (or do not) use readers' advisory tools to assist in their fiction selection. This chapter's Librarian's View gives much more detail about individual tools. One important exception is the online catalog, a subject reserved for chapter 10.

This review of research on tools is broken into four broad sections: print tools, free websites, reviews, and electronic resources. Because many of the tools are available in different forms and many of the publications discuss more than one type, there is significant overlap between some of the sections.

Print-Based Tools

Print-based readers' advisory tools have been around since the beginning of the readers' advisory renaissance in the 1980s. Betty Rosenberg's first edition of *Genreflecting* was published in 1982, and the title's sixth edition came out in 2006.[3] A glance at recent Libraries Unlimited or ALA Editions catalogs reveals many new books for all types of readers' advisory assistance, from *Fluent in Fantasy* to *Make Mine a Mystery*.[4] Anyone doubting the importance of print tools to the practice of readers' advisory service need look no further than a 2004 article in *Reference and User Services Quarterly*, "Recommended Readers' Advisory Tools":

> The core collection consists of materials that the committee considers essential to providing readers' advisory service. These are the basic tools that librarians will need in order to begin the process of working with readers, and libraries should make these titles among the first acquisitions for a readers' advisory collection.[5]

Of the eight titles in the core collection "general list," all are available in print, and only two (*Fiction Catalog* and *What Do I Read Next?*) were also available electronically at the time of publication.

"HELPING READERS FIND BOOKS," BY CHRISTINE L. QUILLEN

The only research-based publication that includes print-based readers' advisory tools is Christine Lynn Quillen's master's thesis for the University of North Carolina in 2001.[6] Quillen methodically and objectively compares Amazon.com, *NoveList*, *Now Read This*, and *What Do I Read Next?* using the electronic version of the latter, and this type of comparison cannot be found elsewhere in the research literature. Only by objectively comparing various readers' advisory tools can librarians really know which ones work best and which ones to turn to first when working with a patron. This model for evaluation is a significant contribution to readers' advisory research and one that should continue to be used by advisors everywhere.

Quillen's findings are that all four are good sources for assisting with readers' advisory questions, but each has drawbacks. She gives the highest marks to *Now Read This,* noting that its limited scope actually makes it easier to use and navigate, particularly for patrons. She also notes the extremely important aspect of appeal factors, which are present throughout this work. Quillen recommends making a copy of this and *Genreflecting,* which she notes is similar in content, available to patrons near the fiction collection. It is interesting that, after such an exhaustive evaluation, it is a print-based product that tops the list. Quillen's work highlights the value both readers and librarians place on print, a value with important implications for the readers' advisory profession.

Free Websites

In "Helping Readers Find Books," Quillen notes that Amazon.com provides a wealth of information, from customer and professional reviews to genre headings, subject lists, and links to all other books by the same author. When she was doing her research, Amazon.com was also the only source for book cover images, which are now a common feature in online catalogs and frequently included in *NoveList* and other electronic tools. The commercial nature of Amazon.com brings some limitations not found in most library-oriented products, but Quillen observes that it does provide (for free) a great deal of information valued by readers. She suggests that creators and vendors of readers' advisory products start adding more of these patron-desired qualities to their products. (See more on Amazon .com in the chapter 10 Librarian's View.)

Outside of Quillen's research, there is nothing that studies the use of Amazon.com by librarians. But any discussion with a group of librarians will quickly reveal that they all use it on occasion, and many use it regularly. Clearly this is an area in which there is a great need for additional research. For one, do librarians use Amazon.com before they use tools their library has purchased? If so, why?

In addition to commercial sites like Amazon.com are dozens of other extremely useful websites, many of which were created by librarians, but there is no published research on their use. The United Kingdom has provided readers' advisory across the world with a valuable and useful free website, Whichbook.net, which is part of the national readers' advisory program, Branching Out, and associated organization Opening the Book. Whichbook.net was designed to be used mainly by patrons who do not regularly visit the library, namely, young professionals under forty and visually impaired, disabled, or homebound patrons. The idea is that they can use Whichbook.net to discover leisure reading books that they can then reserve at their local library. Most of what has been written about Whichbook.net is not research based but practical, describing how it was created, the target audience, and how it can be implemented in U.K. libraries. This fairly new product (released in 2002) was based on a great deal of research done at Loughborough University, and we can only hope that research on this intriguing tool is in the works. Anecdotal evidence suggests that Whichbook.net is not often used by U.S. librarians, possibly because they just don't know about it.[7]

"READER DEVELOPMENT AND ICT," BY ANGELA BIRD AND LUCY A. TEDD

A recent U.K. article, "Reader Development and ICT: An Overview of Projects in Welsh Public Libraries," provides an overview of the ways libraries can and are using technology and the Internet to provide additional readers' advisory services.[8] Readers' advisory has long been promoted at the national level in the United Kingdom, ever since the involvement of Opening the Book in readers' advisory services in the late 1980s. More recently, readers' advisory and technology have become closely connected with the advent of the People Network, a national initiative like the Bill and Melinda Gates Foundation, to provide free public access computers and Internet in all public libraries.

Bird and Tedd's article focuses on the effect this program has had on Welsh public libraries and the difficulties and opportunities created for readers' advisory services. They report on a questionnaire filled out by the reader services librarian (readers' advisory point person) at each of the twenty-two Welsh library authorities. Because of the high level of response (twenty of twenty-one currently active positions), these results give an actual view of what is happening in terms of readers' advisory services across Wales, making these results and this article useful for both researchers and practitioners. Overall, Bird and Tedd find that Welsh libraries are increasingly taking advantage of the high levels of Internet access by library patrons to promote and provide readers' advisory services, providing excellent models for the future of readers' advisory services. All the libraries surveyed have been (or soon will be) trained in using Whichbook.net, and the link is prominently displayed on all library web pages. Libraries are also promoting remote use of databases such as *NoveList* and working hard to reach potential patrons under age forty.

In addition to promoting readers' advisory for adults, Welsh librarians are using the Web to reach out to children through websites and portals designed to lead children to good books. This article is full of examples of excellent programs and even includes several screen shots of the mentioned websites. I recommend it for any library wishing to increase the use of technology for readers' advisory services, create a readers' advisory web presence, or do more to promote readers' advisory services and reach out to younger patrons where they are.

"ICT AND READER DEVELOPMENT," BY DEBBIE DENHAM

"ICT and Reader Development," in Elkin, Train, and Denham's *Reading and Reader Development*, also provides an overview of recent projects in U.K. public libraries that involve reading promotion and technology, including the Essex library project "Ask Chris" and the national website Stories from the Web, which is also mentioned in the earlier article on Welsh libraries.[9] Even this research-oriented book is able to do little more than describe these tools because of the complete lack of research beyond their initial development.

"THE HISTORY OF FICTION_L," BY ROBERTA JOHNSON AND NATALYA FISHMAN

The other free web-based tool regularly used by U.S. librarians is Fiction_L,

> an electronic mailing list devoted to readers' advisory topics such as book discussions, booktalks, collection development issues, booklists and bibliographies, and a wide variety of other topics of interest to librarians, book discussion leaders, and others with an interest in readers' advisory. Fiction_L was developed for and by librarians dealing with fiction collections and requests.[10]

Even though Fiction_L may be the single most used tool for North American advisors, the only article written about it is Johnson and Fishman's history and description published in 2002.[11] Fiction_L is ripe for study.

Reviews

Many librarians already read reviews as part of their selection duties, and most libraries subscribe to at least one review journal, such as *Booklist* or

Library Journal. Reviews have also started to appear in electronic tools such as *NoveList* as well as on Amazon.com. Reading reviews is a good way for librarians to stay up to date with current books and popular authors, but how much do reviews help readers' advisors? Two master's papers from the University of North Carolina attempt to answer this important question.

"AN ANALYSIS OF CHRISTIAN FICTION REVIEWS . . . ," BY SHANNON SALTER

In 1997, Shannon Salter studied Christian fiction reviews and their inclusion in prominent readers' advisory tools.[12] Salter created a list of all Christian fiction titles reviewed in *Library Journal* and *Booklist* from 1994 to 1996, then searched *Fiction Catalog, NoveList,* and *What Do I Read Next?* to determine availability of reviewed titles. What this study reveals is both the usefulness of reading reviews to learn about a specific genre and the usefulness of three readers' advisory tools in accessing books in a specific genre. Salter notes that, if librarians are buying books based on reviews in traditional review sources, then the tools they are using for readers' advisory services need to provide access to those titles. This paper was written in 1997, and there have been many changes to these readers' advisory tools and the review journals over the past ten years, but their general scope, contents, and audience have stayed the same.

Salter found that *Library Journal* and *Booklist* were providing similar contents; they were equally evaluative and reviewed a similar number of books. She noted that *Library Journal* "includes more concise statements of positive or negative reviews and clearly recommends or does not recommend most titles." In conclusion, she advised that reviews state clearly both that a title is Christian fiction and into which other genres it might fall, such as romance, historical, mystery, or any popular genre.

Salter concluded that *NoveList* was the best of the three sources for Christian fiction. It listed the largest number of her selected titles and had the highest number of religious subject headings, which makes it easy for readers' advisors to immediately identify Christian fiction as well as lead to other similar titles. *What Do I Read Next?* was a distant second: "It describes itself as a guide to current genre fiction which should not exclude Christian fiction titles. As this research shows, 57% of the [reviewed titles] . . . were classed into one of the genres included in *What Do I Read Next?*" Perhaps this weakness has been remedied in the ten years since Salter studied this resource. *Fiction Catalog* is actually the tool least likely to have changed since 1997, because it has been published in the same format for the same audience for nearly one hundred years. Salter found it to be the least useful of all three tools. Only one title of all the Christian books reviewed in *Library Journal* and *Booklist* could also be found in *Fiction Catalog*. Clearly this source is not at all useful for readers' advisors working with Christian fiction readers.

"A CONTENT ANALYSIS OF BOOK REVIEWS FROM A READERS' ADVISORY PERSPECTIVE," BY ALEXANDRA E. DUDA

In 2005, Alexandra Duda studied book reviews from the readers' advisory perspective.[13] She provides a different perspective on book reviews and updates some of Salter's work. Duda gathered four hundred reviews from *Booklist, Library Journal, Kirkus Reviews,* and *Publishers Weekly* and analyzed their contents for statements of literary comparison. She found that *Library Journal* and *Booklist* reviews had the highest percentages of nonneutral comparisons, statements that make a judgmental comparison to other authors, books by the same author, or books by other authors—in essence, statements about read-alikes. Duda concludes that *Library Journal* and *Booklist* reviews are the most useful for readers' advisors.

Duda notes that such nonneutral book reviews are quite effective as electronic resources. A keyword review search for "Nora Roberts," for example, should bring up reviews of books that would be similar reads for Nora Roberts fans as well as books by Roberts. Nonneutral comparison statements can make reviews into a true readers' advisory tool, for they can be searched and studied over time and no longer just used for collection development or current awareness.

Even research less than two years old can be out of date. Since Duda wrote her thesis, *Booklist Online* has been released, and one of its stated goals is to use reviews as a readers' advisory tool. The conclusions of Duda's paper are helpful for librarians who read reviews, librarians writing reviews, and editors making content policies.

Electronic Tools

Following the same trends as reference, electronic tools for readers' advisory have become an increasingly important part of readers' advisory work. Developed by former librarian Duncan Smith, *NoveList* was the first electronic product created exclusively for readers' advisors and has been available for many years. As such it has a loyal following, is available in many libraries, and is the product that has been the most studied and refined over the years. Still, there is little published research about this or any similar products, in part, no doubt, because any company-produced research can be considered proprietary and remain unpublished. The few published works about *NoveList* focus primarily on its use as a staff development tool, as do all the wonderful articles in the "For Librarians" sections of *NoveList*. The only exception is Quillen's paper (see above).

In evaluating the two electronic subscription-based products, *NoveList* and *What Do I Read Next?* Quillen notes that both can be overwhelming on initial contact and may be especially off-putting to do-it-yourself patrons. She suggests that these are both best used by librarians trained and versed in their subject-based orientation and, more important, notes that the needs of readers looking for leisure reading books often go beyond subject headings. Still, that same subject-based orientation can be a lifesaver for a librarian working with a patron who wants mysteries featuring cats based in the modern United States.

In 2006, two major new electronic readers' advisory tools were introduced. *Reader's Advisor Online* was created by Greenwood Press and Libraries Unlimited, with much of the content coming from *Genreflecting* and the Genreflecting series print titles. *Booklist,* long a resource for reviews, also went online in 2006 with *Booklist Online.* Both products are so new that no research has been published about them. Mary Wilkes Towner takes an in-depth look at them in the following Librarian's View.

LIBRARIAN'S VIEW   BY MARY WILKES TOWNER

The most critical elements in providing effective readers' advisory services are tools. These are the books, databases, and websites that help us find the right book for the right patron at the right time. Without tools readers' advisory could never become a truly professional service because it would rely solely on staff members' own reading preferences and interests. Just as effective reference librarians require a variety of reference tools, effective readers' advisors also need a variety of reliable readers' advisory tools. In my part of this chapter, I discuss the different types of these resources, highlight some examples, talk about patron use, and

---

Mary Wilkes Towner is an adult services librarian at the Urbana (Illinois) Free Library. She teaches on-campus and online sessions of a course on adult popular literature at the University of Illinois Graduate School of Library and Information Science.

think about what might be available in the future. The focus is on the most effective ways popular tools can be used by patrons or librarians. Because of space considerations I limit my coverage to selected works and online resources that target leisure reading and teach us how to find books our patrons want. I apologize if I have omitted some of your favorites.

Tool-wise, this is a wonderful time to be a readers' advisor. More and more resources are being developed that allow us to do our job better. These range from books to help us learn our trade, to print and online works that help us find those elusive books our patrons want to read, to resources patrons enjoy using themselves. Some are in print and some are online. Some are free and some cost money. But they're all useful, in varying ways. One of your most important jobs as a readers' advisor is to discover the different tools that are out there, develop a basic collection for you and your library, and learn to use the different tools effectively, both as a librarian and as a patron.

Discovering, Identifying, and Choosing the Right Tools for You

Where do you go to find out what's available now? The chapter "Readers' Advisory Reference Tools" in Joyce Saricks's *Readers' Advisory Guide to Genre Fiction* is an excellent resource, as is the 2004 article "Recommended Readers' Advisory Tools," compiled by the Collection Development and Evaluation Section's (CODES) Readers' Advisory Committee.[14] Though both are several years old, they do a good job of listing the major print tools and providing some basic information about online resources. For more recent information, I recommend "Establishing and Promoting Readers' Advisory in Small and Medium-Sized Libraries," also created by the CODES Readers' Advisory Committee in 2006 and available online.[15] I appreciate this particular article because the recommended print items are chosen for usefulness and arranged by cost. There is an ample list of websites for book alerts, genre fiction, and general readers' advisory information. The handout also includes names of publishers that frequently produce readers' advisory materials and a list of the existing fee-based online resources. This is exactly the type of basic, current information that we need.

Right now, there are many new readers' advisory tools plus several in development or planning stages. Just trying to keep on top of it all can be challenging. New editions of print tools are published regularly, and online tools change rapidly. I personally utilize several strategies to become aware of new tools and changes to old ones. I read or skim

Publishers Weekly, Booklist, Library Journal, the *New York Times Book Review, BookPages,* and fan genre magazines, making sure to read any reviews, articles, or ads about new readers' advisory tools. I look at fliers and the publishers' catalogs my library receives. I browse publishers' displays at conferences. I meet with the publishers' salespeople who come to visit the library. I follow discussions in Fiction_L. And, since library blogs often highlight important and very current news snippets, I subscribe via RSS to several different ones, using "readers' advisory" as a search term in my aggregators.

If you do hear about a new readers' advisory tool, make the effort to find out everything you can about it. Here are some points to consider when evaluating a potential tool:

- What do I need to do my readers' advisory job?
- What do we need in our library to support readers' advisory for both staff and patrons?
- Does this particular tool fit well with the needs we've analyzed?
- Will our patrons actually use this tool?
- What can we afford?
- Is there a free version that will fill this same need?
- Which format is best for my library, print or electronic?

Once you have identified a potential purchase, how do you decide? Peer recommendations are valuable. Reviews (almost always written by other librarians) can also be good resources. Some of these reviews are in library professional journals. Other, more spontaneous reviews can be found online. For professional reviews, check out Carol Tenopir's regular "Online Databases" column in *Library Journal.* In the September 1, 2006, issue she discusses *Reader's Advisor Online* and contrasts it with Amazon.com.[16]

If you go online for peer reviews, your first stop should be Fiction_L (http://www.webrary.org/rs/flmenu.html). Fiction_L is the premier electronic mailing list for all things readers' advisory. Librarians and fiction lovers from around the world inhabit this high-traffic list. They discuss a broad range of readers' advisory topics—including the pros and cons of new readers' advisory products. The Morton Grove (Illinois) Public Library maintains the accompanying Fiction_L website, where posts and book lists are archived and searchable.

Readers' advisory–centered workshops and study groups are available in many areas. If you are based near one, join it. The Adult Reading Round Table (ARRT) is an excellent example of a regional readers' advisory organization (www.arrtreads.org). ARRT members stay connected through regular meetings and a newsletter, and the group annually conducts genre studies. Most important, ARRT and similar groups provide an efficient way to network locally. Have a question about a readers' advisory resource? Call a colleague and ask for information.

Print Tools

If you are learning about readers' advisory as a service and how to provide it, a most valuable introductory source is Joyce Saricks's *Readers' Advisory Service in the Public Library*.[17] This basic text covers all the nuts and bolts, from what readers' advisory is, to appeal factors, to conducting a readers' advisory interview.

For beginning genre study there are two must-haves. The first is Saricks's *Readers' Advisory Guide to Genre Fiction*.[18] This textbook covers genres in depth, discussing appeal factors, characteristics, working with readers, and major authors and titles. It gives strategies for improving one's genre grasp, including similar reads in other types of fiction and the five-book challenge. Even though it is several years old, it still is an excellent resource for understanding the major genres. The second book is Diana Tixier Herald's *Genreflecting: A Guide to Popular Reading Interests*.[19] This volume continues the Genreflecting tradition, breaking down genres into subgenres and giving major authors and titles. In addition, the sixth edition has been enhanced by the contribution of brief topical essays by guest authors. Either one of these sources will provide an excellent introduction to the major genres of leisure reading.

ALA Editions and Libraries Unlimited provide two of the major readers' advisory series. The ALA Readers' Advisory Series includes such titles as *Mystery Readers' Advisory*, *The Romance Readers' Advisory*, and *The Horror Readers' Advisory*.[20] These focus on the genres and subgenres, give annotations and examples, and discuss working with readers. Libraries Unlimited publishes the Genreflecting Advisory Series, with genre guides created in the style of *Genreflecting*. The scope of this series is broad, covering general fiction, traditional genres, Christian fiction, Jewish fiction, and Canadian fiction. Nancy Pearl wrote two significant works for this series—*Now Read This* and *Now Read This II*, which cover mainstream fiction.[21] Two recent print titles I find particularly useful are Sarah Statz Cords's *The Real Story: A Guide to Nonfiction Reading Interests* and John Mort's *Read the High Country: Guide to Western Books and Films*.[22] The annotations in Cords's book are intriguing and provide one of the few appeal-oriented access points to nonfiction leisure reading materials. And as a Baby Boomer inundated by all things western in the 1950s, I appreciate Mort's inclusion of film. Media ties in heavily with cross-appeal for genre reads. I see cross-media advisory as a coming trend in readers' advisory and an area in which, with the exception of Mort's book, there is a nearly complete lack of tools.

What Do I Read Next? A Reader's Guide to Current Genre Fiction is one of the other major print resources and is published by Thomson Gale. These annual volumes survey titles of interest published during the previous year. The books are indexed by author, subjects, era, and characters and are given annotations. Read-alikes and other books by the same author are also provided. Since this has proved such a popular title, Thomson Gale has spun off *What Do I Read Next?* into individual genre volumes, such as *What Do I Read Next? Multicultural Literature.*[23]

Another category of book you want to have on hand could best be described as lists of best books or personalized reading lists. Nancy Pearl's *Book Lust: Recommended Reading for Every Mood, Moment, and Reason* comes to mind.[24] Though not traditional readers' advisory tools, these are fun to read and greatly enjoyed by patrons and book club devotees.

The great thing about these print tools is that they're perfect for patrons to use too. Some readers want suggestions from a librarian; others like to browse. And all of these books are eminently browsable. Hand them to patrons looking for good books to read. If you're busy and can't spend extended time with a potential reader, suggest looking through the pages as a strategy to intrigue the patron. Equally important is to shelve these in a public area near the fiction, where they can be discovered by serendipity or by readers reluctant to approach the desk. And don't forget to publicize them in displays that also market your readers' advisory services.

What about the OPAC?

Any librarian providing readers' advisory services already has a powerful readers' advisory tool at hand—the online catalog. With the recent addition of features like enhanced subject headings, reviews, links to summaries, and cover images, the OPAC has become even more useful for this purpose. One of the best features of the OPAC is that search results are scoped to your library or system. Do take care, though. Mary K. Chelton, in her article "Readers' Advisory 101," writes, "The librarian uses the OPAC as a crutch to keep the hands busy and the eyes away from the user when the brain stops. This is just plain bad service."[25] As usual, she's right; librarians do have the tendency to turn immediately to the OPAC to answer questions, forgoing active listening, because of our "computer dependence." A far better strategy is to listen to the patron, discover what he wants, and then go with him to a public computer where the two of you can work together. You can help satisfy his quest and spread the joy and satisfaction of using the OPAC (or other readers' advisory tools) at the same time.

Fee-Based Online Sources

Since readers' advisory has increased in popularity as a library service, several publishers have developed online sources. Some of them are based on similar print works and some of them are totally new concepts. And most are increasingly user friendly. It is important for us as readers' advisors to urge database publishers to continue this trend. Public librarians are noticing that patrons are accessing our collections more and more in the online environment. If we are going to market our huge fiction and leisure reading collections effectively, we need to do outreach to all, including remote access to readers' advisory tools. But this works well only if the database is easy to use—and easy to find.

NoveList and *What Do I Read Next?* have been the two major online readers' advisory sources for several years. They are both incredibly rich in content, but I agree with Quillen that their primary value is for librarians. Both of these databases have learning curves that will deter usage by casual patrons. Since both have been discussed by Quillen and are familiar to most advisors, I limit my comments on them to focus on some of the newer or less popular tools.

NOVELIST AND NOVELIST K–8

NoveList and its recent spin-off, *NoveList K–8,* are now provided by EBSCO Publishing. *NoveList* was one of the first online readers' advisory tools and has grown in size, content, and popularity throughout the years. Although librarians and patrons can search for books by author, title, series, and plot, the major richness of *NoveList* is in the extras. Patrons will find annotated book lists, read-alikes, and book discussion guides. *NoveList* can link search results to each library's OPAC. Teachers and librarians will find enriching readers' advisory resources and training materials. Many of the major names in readers' advisory are contributors to the *NoveList* content. I find *NoveList* to be overall authoritative, with deep content.

In April 2007 (during the writing of this chapter), EBSCO and *NoveList* announced a new product for 2008—*NoveList Plus. NoveList Plus* will be an enhanced version of the original database that for the first time will include nonfiction. According to the press release, *NoveList Plus* will be an all-inclusive upgrade and will have a new interface and additional features requested by users. This is something to watch.

WHAT DO I READ NEXT?

This database is the popular online version of the Thomson Gale print series of the same name. According to the Thomson Gale March 2007 "Product Update Bulletin,"

> Recent additions have improved *What Do I Read Next?* with more than 125,000 titles included in the database, combining best-seller lists, librarian's favorites and national/international award-winning titles. Adding to the content, there are now nearly 68,000 plot summaries, awards information from hundreds of national and international awards and coverage of nearly 35,000 non-fiction titles.

This database emphasizes book finding and offers search elements similar to those indexed in the print version. The interface is straightforward, and users quickly learn the navigation.

FICTION CATALOG

The 2004 RUSA article "Recommended Readers' Advisory Tools" cites *Fiction Catalog* as an important resource for librarians. Many of us are familiar with the print edition of *Fiction Catalog,* but the publisher, H. W. Wilson, also produces an online version. The Wilson website gives this description:

> The selective list presented in *Fiction Catalog* features [more than 8,000 entries for] classic and contemporary works of fiction recommended for a general adult audience, written in or translated into English. The best authors and their most widely read works in literary and popular fiction . . . including mysteries, science fiction, fantasy, Westerns, and romance.

This database is available via WilsonWeb, which is a utilitarian and rather plain interface. WilsonWeb offers all the content of the print editions and current updates, accessible by basic bibliographic elements plus special searches, such as Dewey Decimal number, keyword, and document type. Users can retrieve excerpts from reviews and MARC records, and the results can be linked back to the library's OPAC to check ownership and status. Librarians on Fiction_L discussed this tool in January 2006 and had mixed opinions as to its best use. The book version seemed to be the librarians' choice for use in the stacks, where it is most commonly used for weeding.[26] Conclusion: this is a tool sculpted primarily for use by librarians; the presentation style in both the print and online versions may not attract patrons.

READER'S ADVISOR ONLINE AND READERS' ADVISOR NEWS

Libraries Unlimited, a strong source of print readers' advisory materials, has become an online presence with two of its latest products. In 2005, it established *Readers' Advisor News*, a free quarterly e-newsletter available via e-mail or on the company's website (http://rainfo.lu.com/news .aspx). The newsletter is intended to serve several purposes, but two of the most significant are to help keep readers' advisors and readers' advisory educators up to date on new research and professional issues, and to promote readers' advisory in libraries and in library and information science education. The articles contained are quite brief and to the point, excellent for continuing education.

The *Reader's Advisor Online* (*RAO*, http://rainfo.lu.com) debuted in 2006. Based on the Genreflecting series of readers' advisory books, this database is geared toward the readers' advisory practitioner. It has great professional resources and depth on content, but like *NoveList* and *What Do I Read Next?* there is a learning curve that would slow down a casual browser. I recommend reading two recent reviews of *RAO*, the previously mentioned article in *Library Journal* and the *Booklist* review "RA Corner: Reader's Advisor Online."[27] In addition, I want to highlight some of what I consider to be the valuable features of this database. First of all, *RAO* currently includes in its readers' advisory Materials section the full text of eighteen Libraries Unlimited readers' advisory titles, most of which come from the Genreflecting series. These titles alone make *RAO* a bargain. The online edition can be a money—and space—saver for libraries wanting to increase their readers' advisory services. I like the fact that the folks who have selected the database contents and read-alikes and editors' recommendations are the Genreflecting book series authors and other experts in the field. Additionally, members of the advisory board are among the best-known and most active readers' advisors today.

The advanced searches, requiring a bit of practice, can be honed to take advantage of incredibly detailed genres. And when you do an advanced search, you get back a subject-clustered and weighted list of read-alikes. Some of the search refinements I appreciate are being able to limit by diversity (e.g., "Canadian") and limit to elements (e.g., "suitable for a book group"). If you use the browse function, you can peruse categories such as "award" or "author read-alikes." Another useful feature is being able to save titles and then print customized book lists.

Libraries Unlimited has chosen some excellent marketing strategies for *RAO*. One of the most important for me is that Libraries Unlimited has given free access to readers' advisory classes. This gives educators and future librarians/potential database purchasers a great opportunity. In April 2007, Libraries Unlimited added a blog—the *Reader's Advisor Online Blog*. This will be part of *RAO*, but access will be free to everyone. The plan is to include product announcements, best-seller news, readers' advisory articles, selected book and publishing news, and "fun stuff" geared both to book lovers and to advisors.

FICTION CONNECTION

Fun to use? Lots of patron appeal? If that's what you're looking for, try *Fiction Connection* (www.fictionconnection.com), an extra free module provided to all Bowker's BooksInPrint.com library and bookseller customers. The award-winning interface is intuitive to both staff and patrons, offering several options and pathways to discover books.

The first screen a user sees at log-in contains a large, colorful "tag cloud." Many web users are familiar with tagging, which summarizes blog, database, or bibliographic content by assigning individual weighted words. For librarians, it is similar to basic subject headings. Words are grouped together to form the tag cloud. The larger the word or the more striking the color, the more associations are attached. To browse *Fiction Connection*, choose an attractive word and click on it. You'll be taken to a list of all items with that tag, sorted by relevance.

This visual method of selection can be quite appealing, and the juxtaposition of words can spark interest in other topics. *Fiction Connection* presents six selective clouds—topic, genre, setting, character, location, and time frame. Each cloud can be expanded to show alphabetically all the subtopics contained. For more traditional users, *Fiction Connection* provides an alternative: a friendly keyword search box is positioned above the tag cloud.

The search results screen is equally fascinating and provides three different ways to access books matching the search. All the matches, sorted by relevance, occupy the middle of the screen. They can be resorted by date, author, or title. Each result gives a thumbnail book cover, author, title, and brief annotation. Click on the title or cover and you get a full *Books in Print* summary plus reviews, subject headings and elements, and edition information. Return to results to click on the "Find similar" button and get read-alikes. The right side of the search screen provides the results clustered into groups and subgroups that allow the user to refine the search. Besides typical limits such as genre, *Fiction Connection* can narrow the results to character traits, reading level, awards, media mentions, and best sellers. The left side of the screen provides a visual search, similar to tag clouds. The chosen search term is in the middle, linked by lines to other terms associated with it, creating a starlike effect. The other terms might be an associated word, or a translation, or a spelling variant. Click on one of those elements for further investigation. This visual approach is intuitive for many people and allows them to conduct in-depth searches without worrying (or understanding) about traditional search strategy. Everything is well labeled. And it's fun.

What about the content? It's strictly a book search and review source without any supplementary readers' advisory resources. *Fiction Connection* allows patrons to more easily search fiction (and biographical works) contained in the immense BooksInPrint.com database.

Fiction Connection succeeds well as a readers' advisory tool because the content is good and the interface is attractive, easy to use, and designed with options to fit every type of searcher. Both patrons and librarians will enjoy using it. It has been successful enough that Bowker introduced an associated product in summer 2007—*Non-Fiction Connection.* This new database requires a separate subscription but will use the same interface as *Fiction Connection.* The focus is narrative nonfiction ("character-driven and reads like fiction with good storylines"). One difference from *Fiction Connection* is that users are asked to begin their search by entering the title of a book they've already enjoyed.

BOOKLIST ONLINE

Booklist Online (www.booklistonline.com) is a fairly recent addition to the online readers' advisory tool scene. At first I was skeptical about its value for readers' advisory. Wouldn't the focus on reviews make it more a service for librarians? But then I started thinking about Amazon.com and the fact that I use the summaries and reviews it provides all the time for ready reference. So I looked at the source again through patron-focused eyes.

Users need a subscription and have to log in to get full value from this site. The emphasis on reviews is heavy. However, the quick search function is easy to navigate and allows searches by keyword as well as author, title, and ISBN. This keyword capability is useful for readers' advisory questions and allows librarians and patrons to identify books for which they might just have partial information. A fairly comprehensive advanced search feature is also available, as are browse functions, links to *Booklist* columns, and articles about prize winners. Added features for each review or article allow you to print or e-mail, find similar books, find other writings by the same author, or link directly to Amazon.com to check on an item's availability. *Booklist Online* is a useful adjunct to the print journal for librarians.

Booklist Online offers some options that are particularly appealing to leisure readers—Top 10 lists, read-alikes, and a web feature called *Story behind the Story*. There's a book blog—*Likely Stories*—that highlights a staff member's takes on books and book news. The most interactive feature is the *Booklist Book Club*. This is a collection of online forums, or bulletin boards, on which members can post comments about books, authors, and all things literary. *Booklist Online* is partnered in this endeavor with the Downers Grove (Illinois) Public Library, which has an active book discussion and readers' advisory service. Books being discussed at the library will be added to the forum, and Downers Grove staff moderate the discussion. These forums (along with the blog) are open to everyone, but you do need to register to post. This interactivity takes *Booklist Online* a step beyond most of the fee-based online readers' advisory sources.

NEXTREADS AND BOOKLETTERS

NextReads (www.nextreads.com), an offshoot of *NoveList,* offers annotated reading lists delivered right to a patron's e-mail address. Library patrons can sign up for any of more than twenty monthly or bimonthly topical newsletters. Libraries can also link directly to these reading lists from their websites. All the major fiction genres are represented, but one of the strengths of this product is that it also promotes nonfiction and audiobooks. Patrons interested in armchair travel, popular culture, or business and personal finance will be pleased to find that their reading tastes are remembered here. And younger patrons are not forgotten: *NextReads* provides lists of kid's books, picture books, and young adult books. Check out the *NextReads* website for a fuller discussion of all the newsletters available. These lists are created by librarians, who use review information, holdings, and other materials when selecting titles. Besides best sellers, the lists contain information on new books, provide read-alikes, and can be based around a theme, promoting some of the older works in your collections. Best of all, you can link each title back to your library's catalog, so patrons can instantly find the status of an item.

Work for staff can be minimal, making this an appealing product for busy or understaffed libraries. Patrons manage their own e-mail subscriptions. *NextReads* sends out information ahead of each newsletter's release, so unowned titles can be ordered and newsletter links to the OPAC created. All the e-mail and web pages can be visually branded and customized with the library's own logo and template. The *NextReads* website also contains a robust section on marketing the product to patrons. And, in spring 2007, version 2.0 was released. The new version allows newsletter creation and more options in editing the lists.

BookLetters (www.bookletters.com), a product much like *NextReads*, has been around since 2003 and is brought to us by the same folks that create the *BookPages* magazine. The concept is to provide valuable, seamless content for library websites. The cover art and content come from a variety of sources, but primarily Bowker. *BookLetters* contains a five-year archive of *BookPages.*

BookLetters provides newsletters to be read online or e-mailed. These *BookLetters* products can be branded and customized to replicate the look of the website. Individual titles can be linked back to the library OPACs. Coverage ranges from genre, to nonfiction, to best sellers, to Spanish-language materials. The library controls which lists are made available, and the librarians can edit all aspects.

BookLetters also provides author interviews, award lists, an events calendar module, and *Book Letters Daily,* an e-mail book club. Some of this content—the interviews and award lists—are also available without charge on the *BookLetters* website. You can even sign up for free for one of twenty-six e-mail lists.

Both *NextReads* and *BookLetters* newsletters are colorful, with book covers and annotations. Librarians have mentioned both services favorably on Fiction_L. The concept of outreach to patrons, offering customized book information on the Web or by e-mail, lets you creatively promote your library's leisure reading collection. Patrons will think of your library even when they are not inside the physical building. Both are recommended, so choose on the basis of contents, time, and cost.

The Future: Upcoming Tools

Right now OCLC is researching two FRBR-based projects that have great readers' advisory and patron access potential. *Fiction Finder* (http://fictionfinder.oclc.org), in beta testing, gives access to almost three million fiction items of differing formats and languages in the OCLC WorldCat database. You can search *Fiction Finder* by author, title, ISBN, and other elements. There's also a browse function that retrieves titles by genre, fictional character, subject, or setting. You can use a traditional search or a subject tag cloud. Results give summaries, number of different editions, and bibliographic information. A corollary project is *WorldCat Identities* (http://orlabs.oclc.org/Identities/), also in beta testing. Users start at a tag cloud of the top 100 identities (i.e., authors) in WorldCat, plus a search box. Once you identify an author, *Identities* gives huge amounts of information gleaned from OCLC bibliographic records, including an overview of holdings, time line, most widely held items, titles, languages, and even cover art. For both these databases, once you limit to the specific edition of interest, you can link directly into a search in WorldCat's online free version *Find in a Library* (www.worldcat.org). Based on the ZIP code, town, or state you enter, you are presented with a list of the nearest libraries holding the edition. Using these two tools plus WorldCat, soon our patrons will be able to carry out advanced searches and locate titles all from outside of the library.

Free Internet Sources

Ricki Nordmeyer, a readers' advisory specialist at the Skokie (Illinois) Public Library, suggests several useful readers' advisory sites in "Readers' Advisory Web Sites."[28] Her focus, however, is more on the presentation and concept of a library website than on the content of the selected resources themselves. And this is where we need to begin. If we're going to recommend Internet sites, we need a method of compiling them so we don't keep searching for useful resources over and over again. We can start by keeping a list for ourselves to use, but why not share them with our patrons by creating a readers' advisory website on our library homepage? Just as it's a good idea to shelve our print tools at the point of use, why not provide a similar service for our online patrons?

What resources should we select? There are tons out there. Each library has to choose what fits it best. I like resources that are both useful to me doing readers' advisory and enjoyable to patrons. Ease and transparency of use are important. Let's not forget that more and more websites exist that provide social networking, which is all the rage right now—especially to the younger generations of our library patrons. Below I list five great sites for librarians and five great sites for patrons, with brief explanations of why I chose each one. "Establishing and Promoting Readers' Advisory in Small and Medium-Sized Libraries," the RUSA CODES handout I mentioned earlier, also has an excellent selection of websites.

WEBSITES FOR LIBRARIANS

Amazon.com. What can I say about the online megastore? I use it every day. It's fast, it's free, and it's stuffed full of information that librarians need to get hold of quickly. Patrons love it. Amazon.com is a great companion to the wholesaler databases most of our libraries subscribe to. It provides bibliographic information, book covers, and summaries and some professional reviews, stock availability, account tracking, and discount pricing for in- and out-of-print titles. It's a great tool for title verification. Amazon .com has its own unique features. "Search inside" a book to see sample pages and read an excerpt. Most of the CDs for sale have sound clips. And Amazon.com gives readers a recommender system. You get recommendations based on both your purchases and the purchases of others who bought the same book. Not all the suggestions are on target, but many are interesting. Additionally, customers can write reviews, rate books, assign tags, and share book lists. These "man on the street" reviews can be very helpful in collection development—or just in deciding whether you want to read a book. All in all, a very useful site for readers and librarians.

What's Next? (http://www.kdl.org/libcat/WhatsNextNEW.asp). One of the most frequent questions I get from readers is, What's the next book in this series? Although my library owns the excellent Merle Jacob and Hope Apple reference guide *To Be Continued: An Annotated Guide to Sequels,* that work is now seven years old and doesn't contain current titles.[29] An incredibly useful tool is available on the Internet (and in print version, if you want a hard copy). *What's Next?* is an updated series search database developed and maintained by the Kent (Michigan) District Library. You have the option to search by author, title, or series name and limit by genre or age category. Results are presented by series name and listed in reading order. Become familiar with this gem. It's a great time-saver.

Fresh Press: Books and Authors in National Media (http://freshfiction .com/medias.php). Part of the larger website Fresh Fiction, this page provides a daily listing of books and authors appearing on more than sixty-five nationally broadcast television and radio programs. You can visit the site or sign up for a daily e-mail newsletter. Summaries and publishing information are available for each title. This site is particularly useful for librarians trying to track down that elusive book for the patron who can't quite remember the author or title she just heard about on television. A site offering similar media interview information is ABA's *Bookselling This Week Media Guide* (http://news.bookweb.org/mediaguide/).

Stop, You're Killing Me: A Website to Die for . . . If You Love Mysteries (*SYKM*, www.stopyourekillingme.com) is an excellent example of a genre website. It advertises itself as "a resource for lovers of mystery, crime, thriller, spy and suspense books. We list over 2100 authors, with chronological lists of their books (nearly 25,000 titles), both series and non-series." Navigation is good, and it's easy to browse quickly. There is a search feature, but the link is not prominent. The content is wonderful. You can browse by author, character name, or award winners. Indexes allow you to explore mysteries by location, job of the sleuth, historical period, and diversity of the series character. You can find author and category read-alikes. Links to current mystery magazines are provided. *SYKM* offers both information on upcoming hardcover and paperback releases and a semimonthly newsletter, highlighting additions to the site. A great place to discover all things mystery.

All About Romance—Sensuality Ratings Guide. All of us who've suggested romances to patrons know how hard it is to raise the issue of the amount of sexual content desired. The well-explained Sensuality Ratings Guide is part of the larger site, All About Romance: The Back Fence of Lovers of Romance Novels (http://www.likesbooks.com/kissburn.html). This useful website contains more than 6,000 romance reviews, all coded and searchable by the level of sensuality contained, along with a grade, designation of type, and publishing information. This is a great place for librarians to double-check the "heat" of an unfamiliar author. Patrons will also enjoy the larger site All About Romance because it has lots of other features, such as author interviews and message boards.

UNIQUE SITES YOUR PATRONS WILL LOVE

Whichbook.net. All of us who provide readers' advisory are familiar with different appeals that attract patrons to certain books. Mood is always the most difficult to match, because mood is subjective and changes frequently. Today's satisfying read might just not be appealing tomorrow.

Whichbook.net advertises itself as "a completely new way of choosing what to read." And it does that by addressing mood.

How does Whichbook.net work? The opening screen presents twelve sliders, with contrasting moods or elements. You can explore four at a time. Where you position the slider between the two extremes indicates your interest. Choices include funny/serious, sex/no sex, expected/unpredictable, and short/long. You can limit results by large print and audiobook. After you position all the sliders, click "go" and get suggestions that match. Whichbook.net will return matches, with reader comments, extracts, and parallel reads for that title. And if you live in the United Kingdom you can request the book. Don't like the results you got? Try again. Or, you can try the other choosing option, which lets you specify character, plot, and setting.

The product is well designed. The basic application requires Flash, but the site offers text-only and large-text access too. Books in the Whichbook .net database "are all fiction and poetry in paperback written in or translated into English and published since 1995" and are selected by a team of 150 with library or literature backgrounds. The project has a strong public library focus.[30] Whichbook.net helps readers and their advisors find great books based on those elusive elements that make reading experiences unique. It's a site to watch.

LibraryThing (www.librarything.com) lets you create a personalized library online, accessible via the Web from anywhere in the world. Just as in a real library catalog, your books are linked to bibliographic information, including subject headings, provided by Amazon.com, the Library of Congress, or one of many other libraries. You can add your own tags to make your records unique. The service is free if you enter fewer than two hundred books and only $25 for a lifetime membership and unlimited collection. Best of all, you are helping form a larger cooperative library. You can share your book lists, swap reviews, join groups, and get fiction and nonfiction recommendations from folks whose reading tastes or tags are similar to yours. LibraryThing has a unique "Unsuggester Service." Put in a title and you get back a list of the books least likely to be in your library. If your patrons like LibraryThing, they might also enjoy Shelfari (www .shelfari.com), another interactive social media site.

What Should I Read Next? (WSIRN, www.whatshouldireadnext.com) is a British collaborative recommendation system similar in concept to LibraryThing. Registered readers have contributed more than 20,000 favorite books to this database. The more books entered, the more certain titles are associated with each other. Enter a search on a title you liked. The database will return titles that mass opinion has declared you probably will enjoy, even though they are not exactly read-alikes. You don't need to register to use WSIRN, but you do if you want to add titles. Does this system work? Your patrons will have fun finding out.

Story Code (www.storycode.com) is another cooperative recommender product, based on the premise "that the many are smarter than the few." Contributors spend about five minutes coding each book, answering roughly forty questions covering general information, the amount of effort to read, plot and narrative style, personal views, and recommendations. Moving a slider to the left or right, measuring the strengths of each element, creates the coding. It's just like taking a personality test. What you get back is a list of recommendations ranked by percentage matched to the elements you coded in your book. Coders also assign readability and age ratings. You don't need to register to code books or get recommendations. Registration allows you to save your reading log; more features for registered users are planned for the future. Patrons with an analytical bent will enjoy exploring this site.

Reader's Robot—Reviews That Reveal the Appeal (http://www.tnrdlib .bc.ca/rr.html). Created in 1996, *Reader's Robot* is one of the first readers' advisory online tools. Twelve years later it's still with us and now contains recommendations on more than 7,300 books. Browse and search by keyword, genre, and subgenre. A newer enhancement allows search by appeal factors, including some that address mood. *Reader's Robot* is a collaborative source. Anyone can submit books to the databases and search the results. To contribute, pick the genre for your entry, answer a set of questions about the subgenre and types of appeals the book contains, and add setting and time period, some subjects, and a brief plot.

Conclusion

The concept of this book I most appreciate is the emphasis on research. We are librarians providing readers' advisory, but there have been few studies that document what we're doing or explore the data to see if we could do our job better. More research needs to be done on reader preference and how readers pick what they enjoy reading. Access to well-thought-out readers' advisory tools—both print and electronic—is critical to our success in providing readers' advisory service. We need to identify the best. We need to take advantage of Internet and Web 2.0 interconnectivity to develop enjoyable online tools that could benefit our patrons. Online tools in particular have the potential to be beneficial, both for cost considerations and for use by multiple levels of users. We librarians need to be aware of tools under development that will enhance our services.

Since technology and our library interests are changing so quickly, it is hard to predict what our readers' advisory tools will become in the future. RSS feeds, podcasts, and V CASTs are underutilized at this point. The media in all its permutations—games, movies, audiobooks, graphic novels—is rapidly becoming an additional focus for readers' advisory and certainly has an essential connection with books and reading. Neither patrons nor readers' advisors should be format bound—and neither should our tools.

NOTES

1. Joyce Saricks, "Appendix 2: Readers' Advisory Reference Tools," in *The Readers' Advisory Guide to Genre Fiction* (Chicago: American Library Association, 2000), 395–96.

2. A concise, objective, and thorough overview of nine general readers' advisory tools can be found in appendix 2 of the *Readers' Advisory Guide to Genre Fiction* (ibid.). Even though it is several years old, nearly all these tools can still be found in public libraries, and several are still being updated and used regularly by readers' advisors.

3. Betty Rosenberg, *Genreflecting: A Guide to Reading Interests in Genre Fiction,* 1st ed. (Littleton, Colo.: Libraries Unlimited, 1982); Diana Tixier Herald, *Genreflecting: A Guide to Popular Reading Interests,* 6th ed. (Westport, Conn.: Libraries Unlimited, 2006).

4. Diana Tixier Herald, *Fluent in Fantasy: A Guide to Reading Interests* (Englewood, Colo.: Libraries Unlimited, 1999); Gary Warren Niebuhr, *Make Mine a Mystery: A Reader's Guide to Mystery and Detective Fiction* (Westport, Conn.: Libraries Unlimited, 2003).

5. Collection Development and Evaluation Section (CODES) Readers' Advisory Committee, "From the Committees of RUSA: Recommended Readers' Advisory Tools," *Reference and User Services Quarterly* 43, no. 4 (2004), quote from 295.

6. Christine L. Quillen, "Helping Readers Find Books: An Evaluation of Four Readers' Advisory Resources," Master's paper, University of North Carolina, 2001.

7. Rachel Van Riel and Tom Forrest, "Helping Choice Along," *Australasian Public Libraries and Information Services* 15, no. 4 (2002): 180–81; Rachel Van Riel, "A Book to Match Your Mood, Forager Information System Allows Readers to Select Books Based on Psychological Attributes," *Library Association Record* 101, no. 5 (1999): 292–93.

8. Angela Bird and Lucy A. Tedd, "Reader Development and ICT: An Overview of Projects in Welsh Public Libraries," *Journal of Librarianship and Information Science* 36, no. 4 (2004): 159–74.

9. Debbie Denham, "ICT and Reader Development," in *Reading and Reader Development: The Pleasure of Reading,* by Judith Elkin, Briony Train, and Debbie Denham (London: Facet, 2003), 171–97.

10. Morton Grove Public Library, Webrary, Readers' Corner, Fiction_L welcome page, http://www.webrary.org/rs/flmenu.html.

11. Roberta Johnson and Natalya Fishman, "The History of Fiction_L," *Reference and User Services Quarterly* 42, no. 1 (2002): 30–33.

12. Shannon Salter, "An Analysis of Christian Fiction Reviews in *Library Journal* and *Booklist* and the Inclusion of These Reviewed Titles in *Fiction Catalog, NoveList,* and *What Do I Read Next?*" Master's paper, University of North Carolina, School of Information and Library Science, 1997, quotes from 23–24.

13. Alexandra E. Duda, "A Content Analysis of Book Reviews from a Readers' Advisory Perspective," Master's paper, University of North Carolina, School of Information and Library Science, 2005. Available online at http://ils.unc.edu/MSpapers/3044.pdf.

14. CODES, "Recommended Readers' Advisory Tools," and Saricks, "Appendix 2: Readers' Advisory Reference Tools."

15. American Library Association Reference and User Services Association Collection Development and Evaluation Section Readers' Advisory Committee, "Establishing and Promoting Readers' Advisory in Small and Medium-Sized Libraries," 2006 Annual Program, http://www.ala.org/ala/rusa/rusaourassoc/rusasections/codes/codessection/codescomm/codesreadadv/Handout1.doc.

16. Carol Tenopir, "Readers Who Like This Book," *Library Journal* 131, no. 14 (2006): 29.

17. Joyce Saricks, *Readers' Advisory Service in the Public Library,* 3rd ed. (Chicago: American Library Association, 2005).

18. Saricks, *Readers' Advisory Guide to Genre Fiction.*

19. Herald, *Genreflecting.*

20. John Charles, Joanna Morrison, and Candace Clark, *Mystery Readers' Advisory: The Librarian's Clues to Murder and Mayhem* (Chicago: American Library Association, 2000); Ann Bouricius, *The Romance Readers' Advisory: A Librarian's Guide to Love in the Stacks* (Chicago: American Library Association, 2000); and Becky Spratford and Tammy Clausen, *The Horror Readers' Advisory: The Librarian's Guide to Vampires, Killer Tomatoes, and Haunted Houses* (Chicago: American Library Association, 2000).

21. Nancy Pearl, *Now Read This: A Guide to Mainstream Fiction, 1978–1998* (Englewood, Colo.: Libraries Unlimited, 1999); and *Now Read This II: A Guide to Mainstream Fiction, 1990–2001* (Englewood, Colo.: Libraries Unlimited, 2002).

22. Sarah Statz Cords, *The Real Story: A Guide to Nonfiction Reading Interests* (Westport, Conn.: Libraries Unlimited, 2006); and John Mort, *Read the High Country: Guide to Western Books and Films* (Westport, Conn.: Libraries Unlimited, 2006).

23. Edith Maureen Fisher et al., *What Do I Read Next? Multicultural Literature* (Detroit: Thomson Gale, 1997).

24. Nancy Pearl, *Book Lust: Recommended Reading for Every Mood, Moment, and Reason* (Seattle: Sasquatch Books, 2003).

25. Mary K. Chelton, "Readers' Advisory 101: A Crash Course in RA: Common Mistakes Librarians Make and How to Avoid Them," *Library Journal* 128, no. 18 (2003): 38–39.

26. Morton Grove Public Library, Webrary, Reader's Corner, Fiction_L archives, *Fiction Catalog,* http://www.webrary.org/MaillistF/msgcur/2006/1/Re.FictionCatalog.html.

27. Tenopir, "Readers Who Like This Book"; Kathleen Stipek, "RA Corner: Reader's Advisor Online," *Booklist,* January 1 and 15, 2007, 152.

28. Ricki Nordmeyer, "Readers' Advisory Web Sites," *Reference and User Services Quarterly* 41, no. 2 (2001): 139–43.

29. Merle Jacob and Hope Apple, *To Be Continued: An Annotated Guide to Sequels* (Phoenix, Ariz.: Oryx Press, 1995).

30. For more information on this U.K. project and the book list, see http://www.openingthebook.com.

10

CATALOGING, CLASSIFICATION,
AND BROWSING

Cataloging and classification is a broad area that encompasses many important topics related to readers' advisory. The topics discussed in this chapter include subject headings for fiction, the creation and use of OPACs to access fiction, and, probably the most controversial, shelf classification and arrangement of fiction, often referred to as genrefication.

RESEARCH REVIEW   BY JESSICA E. MOYER

Unlike many other areas in readers' advisory, issues related to cataloging and classification have produced an abundance of research. Unfortunately, much of it was completed more than ten years ago and almost none has been done in the twenty-first century—just when cataloging, like many other areas of library services, has undergone many significant changes. OPACs now resemble Amazon.com instead of being difficult-to-use text-based systems. Subject headings are no longer limited by the amount of space on a card or in a file. And readers are accessing library catalogs from outside the library at least as often as they use the OPAC within the physical library. So, although there is a great deal of important research to discuss in this area, this is also an area of significant need for more research.

In this section, I discuss classification of fiction, subject headings for fiction, and cataloging fiction together because the research in these areas uses "classification" to mean assigning genres to fiction for shelving or assigning subject headings to works of fiction as part of the cataloging process. I include a discussion on browsing because the manner in which books are classed and shelved is integral to the ways readers browse shelves.

Cataloging

GUIDELINES ON SUBJECT ACCESS TO INDIVIDUAL WORKS OF FICTION, DRAMA, ETC. AND THE OCLC/LC FICTION PROJECT

With the introduction of computer-based cataloging systems in the 1960s and the subsequent proliferation and ease of use, many of the rules of cataloging based on the restrictions of having to type cards for each new item are no longer necessary. Now that cataloging systems have evolved to the point where there are no real restrictions on size and space, catalogers are finally free to add as many subject headings as they deem necessary to describe a work fully. No longer should every romance novel in the library have the single subject heading of "love stories—men and women." Recognizing this, in 1990 ALA published the *Guidelines on Subject Access to Individual Works of Fiction, Drama, Etc.,*[1] and in 1991 the Library of Congress partnered with OCLC to start the OCLC/LC Fiction Project. Since the Fiction Project's inception, participants have enriched more than 14,000 bibliographic records, and more than 916 new and changed subject headings have been approved and added to the Library of Congress subject headings. This is an ongoing project, and according to the Fiction Project website

> there is currently an ALA ALCTS CCS SAC [American Library Association, Association for Library Collections and Technical Services, Cataloging and Classification Section, Subject Analysis Committee] subcommittee editing a revision of the original guidelines. Some of the genre terms need refinement and further definition. The subcommittee invites interest, comments and suggestions regarding the guidelines and the genre headings. . . . A cross-reference structure will greatly enhance the usefulness of the genre headings, especially with the addition of on-line scope notes in the public access catalogs.[2]

Outside this current project, there has been very little done in this area since 1997.[3]

Fiction Classification Research

"DOMAIN OF ADULT FICTION LIBRARIANSHIP," BY L. YU AND A. O'BRIEN, AND "ADULT FICTION READING," BY JESSICA E. MOYER

Two published literature reviews, "Domain of Adult Fiction Librarianship," by Yu and O'Brien, and my "Adult Fiction Reading" include sections on cataloging, classification, and browsing as they relate to fiction reading.[4] Yu and O'Brien provide comprehensive reviews of works published before 1995, notably the groundbreaking work of Annelise Pjetersen in Denmark and the fiction classification system developed by Claire Beghtol.

"USE OF FICTION CATEGORIES," BY GAIL HARRELL

In 1996, one of the most important books in the area of readers' advisory research was published, *Guiding the Reader to the Next Book*, edited by Kenneth D. Shearer of North Carolina Central University. Chapters 6, 7, and 8 of that book are dedicated to the subjects of fiction cataloging, classification, and browsing.

In chapter 6, "Use of Fiction Categories," Gail Harrell argues that arranging fiction by categories is one of the easiest ways to guide patrons, especially in tight budget times when there is not enough staff time to conduct a readers' advisory interview with every patron.[5] Most of the chapter is devoted to a discussion of the genres and types used by various libraries around the country, making this a valuable resource for librarians. Harrell believes that genrefication, following her suggestions, is an important step for libraries to take until a single classification scheme is adopted for use in all libraries. The results of her survey provide librarians interested in undertaking a project of this kind the commonly used genres and categories.

Harrell's focus is on the lack of a single scheme for fiction classification, which she thinks is critical because readers can more easily find the kind of books they are looking for without having to talk to a librarian. Harrell supports some type of genrefication of fiction. She thinks using LC or Dewey to organize fiction is not only useless but a barrier to the reader, an opinion shared by many and moderately well supported by the research. She also believes that a simple alphabetical scheme is not an adequate solution.

Harrell has done extensive research on the various classification schemes for fiction used in U.S. libraries. The bulk of her chapter describes her research process, primarily surveys, and the results. She discusses the various genres and classification schemes uncovered by her research and suggests those that might be the most useful for public libraries looking to better organize their collections. Although this research was done well and is a strong contribution in describing various schemes for classification, it does little to explain why a library would choose one scheme over another or to offer compelling reasons for libraries to better classify and arrange their fiction. Still, it is an excellent starting point for any library considering reclassifying and arranging their fiction, since Harrell's categories are based on research from libraries across the country, making them more applicable to a variety of libraries.

"GENREFICATION," BY JEFFREY CANNELL AND EILEEN MCCLUSKEY

The next chapter in Shearer's book is an excellent follow-up to Harrell. "Genrefication: Fiction Classification and Increased Circulation" is a case study of a library that broke out all its fiction (and some nonfiction as well) by category, with many categories being the same as those researched by Harrell.[6] After the project was completed, fiction circulation increased by 36 percent. Cannell and McCluskey believe genrefication is an important step for libraries to take. Once OPACs, electronic readers' advisory tools, and fiction classification schemes have developed to the point that readers are able to "browse" genres electronically, genrefication may not be necessary. But until these electronic tools are available in all libraries, genrefication serves an important function to fiction readers. This important work provides quantitative evidence of what happens when a library reorganizes its leisure reading collection. As noted earlier, quantitative evidence is often lacking in library research, and readers' advisory research is no exception. Because this is a case study, the results cannot be easily applied to other libraries; fortunately, there are other studies that address the impacts of genrefication.

"GENRE FICTION CLASSIFICATION," BY AMY J. RICHARDS

In 1999, in a study similar to Cannell and McCluskey's, Richards found that Durham County (North Carolina) Public Library patrons responded favorably to a genre-based rearrangement of fiction over the previous alphabetical arrangement by author's last name.[7] She reports that patron satisfaction increased; users found the library much easier to navigate; "information overload" decreased; and users felt it was easier to find books, even though initial results did not show the circulation increases reported by Cannell and McCluskey.

In 2005, Kerri Huff did a follow-up study at Durham County and included a patron survey and review of circulation statistics.[8] Huff found that patrons continued to report satisfaction with the new system and circulation continued to increase steadily. This follow-up report is unique to the library literature and thus of greater importance. It shows that initial rises in circulation and reports of patron satisfaction were not just the result of a reorganization but instead have persisted over several years, confirming Richards's findings over the long term.[9] These studies, along with several done in Europe,[10] support the idea that genrefying the collection makes it easier for patrons to find books and that patrons like to have leisure reading materials arranged in genres. Librarians are not always as cognizant of patrons as they should be when buying and arranging books, and this research reminds us that readers appreciate it when it is easier for them to find the materials they came to the library for in the first place.

"FEEDING WITH THE SPOON," BY JARMO SAARTI

Of all the work done in Europe in this area, one study in particular deserves further mention, "Feeding with the Spoon, or the Effects of Shelf Classification of Fiction on the Loaning of Fiction," by Jarmo Saarti, which took place in Finland.[11] Saarti discusses a multiyear experiment on the loaning of fiction conducted in two branches of the Kajaani public library and the nearby library of Kuhmo. Starting in 1991, the fiction in Kuhmo and one of the branches was broken into eleven categories, or shelf classifications, while the other branch kept its original organization. Over the course of the next two years, all the fiction in all three libraries was thoroughly indexed and cataloged, for the first time. For all books, subject headings were given for genre, themes, main characters, settings, and time. Sometimes additional headings were added about other important facts of the book, such as readability. The results of this quasi experiment had two parts: how patrons accessed materials and how library staff used the fuller cataloging and indexing for fiction.

After three years, patrons and staff at all three libraries were surveyed and interviewed. Overall, staff were satisfied with the changes. The changes to the cataloging and indexing of fiction in the online catalog made it easier and faster for them to answer patron questions and find materials. Patrons were generally happy with the new system, once they got used to it, since it made it easier to find genre fiction on their own. Patrons did report needing to use the online catalog more often, to determine in which area a particular book was located or where the rest of an author's works could be found. Generally, however, patrons were satisfied with using the OPAC for that purpose because of the changes made during the cataloging part of the project. Saarti's paper is significant as an actual experiment with a control library and two experimental libraries. Thus, unlike all previous studies, his results could be compared against a control and over the course of several years. Thus his results are more broadly applicable than case studies like those of Richards or Cannell and McCluskey.

Most interesting, Saarti found that most fiction that was borrowed could be categorized as recreational, or nonliterary, works. As many as 80 percent of the books borrowed were of this type, and that was what most patrons were looking for. They found it easier to find recreational fiction when it was broken into genres. Librarians worried that patrons were not being encouraged to read more serious fiction because it was now so easy to find recreational fiction. Patrons were happier because it was now so easy to find what they were actually looking to read. It is clear that most patrons wanted and continue to want to read recreational fiction and that librarians everywhere need to remember that many patrons are not interested in literary fiction. As this study clearly demonstrates, shelf arrangements, cataloging, and indexing all need to keep recreational readers in mind, since they constitute most public library patronage, whether in Finland, the United Kingdom, or the United States.

Browsing

Why is genrefication so important and successful? As all the aforementioned authors note, smaller, more focused collections are easier for patrons to browse. What makes them easier to browse? Why is browsing important to patrons? These major questions underlying the issue of genrefication have been well researched, though unfortunately not since 1996.

"A DECADE'S WORTH OF RESEARCH ON BROWSING FICTION COLLECTIONS," BY SHARON L. BAKER

Sharon L. Baker has done most of and the most important research on fiction classification as it relates to how patrons browse, particularly for leisure reading materials in public libraries. The most thorough review of her work can be found in "A Decade's Worth of Research on Browsing Fiction Collections."[12] Baker observes that most readers (as high as 86 percent) who come to the library come to find books by browsing. Today, this is fairly well accepted fact in the world of readers' advisory, but twenty years ago it was a revolutionary idea. And the reason it is accepted as fact is Baker's research. Without her work, the idea that patrons like to browse would be just that, an idea, backed up only by anecdotal evidence. Another major contribution to this area is Baker's finding that patrons learn to use whatever shelf arrangements libraries provide, even though those arrangements are not necessarily the most conducive to effective and successful browsing.

Baker also asks whether it is important to support browsers and answers with a resounding yes. Most library patrons want to browse for leisure reading materials and are unwilling or unable to ask library staff for help, and not all libraries are willing or able to provide readers' advisory services at all times for all readers. When libraries do not support browsers, patrons may leave with unsatisfactory selections or even with empty hands and go elsewhere, like a bookstore, to find the kind of books they want to read. If browser and leisure readers make up as much as 80 percent of adult public library patrons, as the research above suggests, then libraries must cater to their desires.

What does this all have to do with cataloging and classification? Baker reports that the single most important thing a library can do to help browsers is make the fiction collection more accessible, and she suggests several practical strategies that are also well supported by her research:

Weed out older, unused, and unattractive titles. If the titles are still circulating, replace them with newer, more attractive volumes. Baker finds that the actual size of the fiction collection in many libraries can be greatly reduced without getting rid of the titles patrons are actually looking for. Sometimes there can be a big difference between what librarians think patrons want to read and what they actually read, something we need to keep in mind.

Use modern automation systems than can generate detailed reports on noncirculating items as a place to start weeding.

Make sure collection development practices are actually meeting the needs of patrons (see more on collection development in chapter 11).

Move the titles around. Research clearly shows that books on top and bottom shelves circulate less than books on shelves at eye level, and the closer books are to the door the better they circulate. Shift the whole collection, or even a part of it, to get top-shelf books to eye level and different areas of the collection closer to the front door and circulation areas.

Design and prepare displays carefully to be truly successful. Displays are critical. Patrons like displays, and materials on displays circulate. Theme-based displays are often successful, especially when they cross genres.

Create, update, and fine-tune book lists, again making sure that they are actually meeting patron needs and that the library can support the requests that may come from such lists.

Take advantage of the return bookshelf. Baker reports some interesting research from Britain that found that 46 percent of all circulation came from one small area, the recently returned books. Nothing is more compelling a recommendation than that someone else checked out a book. Plus, these areas are usually quite small and near the circulation area, both factors that increase browsing success.

When organizing your collection, recognize that more than half the patrons seeking fiction are usually looking for a particular genre.

The last suggestion bears most on the topics of this chapter. Baker reports that most patrons (as many as 70 percent) want books to be separated by genre. She notes that the research shows that using genre stickers in interfiled collections brings similar initial circulation increases, but patrons greatly prefer (and are much happier with) physically separated collections. For librarians who want to promote cross-genre reading, book lists and displays are more successful than interfiled collections, particularly in medium-sized and larger fiction collections, and meet the needs of the more than 70 percent of patrons who wants books organized by genres. Baker concludes this chapter with tips for creating fiction subdivisions, many of which are similar to those suggested by Harrell.

Baker convincingly shows that the single most important thing a library can do to make its browsers and fiction readers happier is to genrefy the collection. Because of Baker's work and the work done in Europe, any library that has not already genrefied its collection should seriously consider doing so right away. The question of whether to break out a fiction collection into genres has been well researched, and any library considering such a move should do no more than consult the literature referenced in this chapter.

Recent Developments

"ICT AND READER DEVELOPMENT," BY DEBBIE DENHAM

As valuable as Baker's research was, it ended in 1996. Since that time, much of the new research in cataloging and classification has been done overseas, mostly in Europe, just as it was in the early 1980s when Annelise Pjetersen was doing her innovative work on Bookhouse in Denmark. A great deal of interesting readers' advisory research has been done in Great Britain in the past decade, and much of it has involved the authors of the excellent *Reading and Reader Development*, by Elkin, Train, and Denham, associated with the University of Central England, Birmingham.[13] In "ICT and Reader Development," Denham explores areas of convergence between information and communications technology (ICT) and reader development (readers' advisory), and in the subsection "Access to Fiction" she tackles the areas of cataloging and classification. She reviews research that shows readers' difficulties in navigating strictly alphabetical arrangements, highlighting the work of Lyn Sear and Barbara Jennings. Unlike Baker, Denham does not think that genrefication is the solution; she points out the difficulties that can arise when assigning a genre, especially since there is no national or international standard.

Denham takes on the tricky issues of cataloging fiction and using the OPAC to do more than locate a known title or author, basing her comments on the work of Pauline Rafferty and Jane Faux to provide an excellent overview of the research in this area. Denham points out that, although British libraries and catalogers now use the same ALA guidelines as U.S. librarians and the OCLC/LC Fiction Project, there is still a great deal of room for subjectivity. Subjectivity is a big concern when it comes to fiction because readers who find that works they enjoy are not classified well or in the way they think they should be can be offended or dismayed enough to stop using the library.[14] Denham goes on to discuss fiction classification schemes, which she notes that everyone agrees are important, but not how they are to be developed; do they come from the literature or from the user?

According to Denham, if libraries are assigning fiction to genres as an organizational scheme, the next big issue is in which category to assign books. Each book can be assigned only one category, thus highlighting only one aspect of the novel's content, which once again may irritate readers. For example, Nora Roberts is seen by most of her readers as a romance novelist, and they expect her books to be found in romance. Yet her Eve Dallas series is much more crime fiction than romance, and her series written under the name of J. D. Robb are much more science fiction oriented. Where do they go? Will crime readers object to seeing her books in crime? Will her romance readers find the Eve Dallas series in the crime section? What about the reader who wants to read *all* her books, no matter the genre; how many places will they have to look? Will they even know to look in more than one place?

These are challenges readers' advisors and catalogers must consider, especially now that cross-genre books are all the rage. Jasper Fforde's books about Thursday Next are a wonderfully frustrating example. Thursday is a detective and she is busy solving a mystery, but the kidnap victim is Jane Eyre and Thursday has to go into *Jane Eyre* to solve Jane's kidnapping. So is it a mystery novel or a fantasy? Or is it science fiction—Thursday's father is a rogue operative of the ChronoGuard, a time-traveling police force, and Thursday has a pet dodo she built at home, using one of the first home cloning kits for extinct animals. Plus there is a love interest, Landon, whom Thursday hasn't spoken to in ten years. *The Eyre Affair* is popular and can be found in most public libraries in the United States and Britain, but where will the reader find it? An informal survey of the Fiction_L mailing list found that it is classed most commonly as mystery, general fiction, and science fiction.

Rafferty and Faux then move on to technology-based systems that can be used to overcome some of these difficulties. The original system was Bookhouse, which was developed and implemented by Pjetersen in Denmark. Bookhouse is based on how librarians and users talk about fiction—subject, frame, author's intent, and accessibility—and is remarkable for both the amount of research put into its development and its completely innovative design, predating modern web-based OPACs by more than a decade. Beghtol also developed an important system, which is based on literary warrant but unlike Bookhouse is often considered too complicated for a library to implement easily or for leisure readers to use. In fact, outside the initial project there is no record of any library ever having attempted to implement Beghtol's system.

More recently, the Branching Out project was responsible for launching Book Forager, now known as Whichbook.net, a web-based fiction retrieval system similar to the North American product *NoveList* in that it uses a multidimensional subject approach that is not restricted to genre. Also like *NoveList*, book information is inputted by librarians and literature specialists all over England. Denham's "Access to Fiction" section concludes with a case study of Whichbook.net, which is still in development but uses some interesting ways to access fiction. Nowhere in the search criteria can readers pick a genre like mystery; instead, plot types are described (e.g., as quests, or against the odds). Unlike *NoveList*, this resource is free, and it may be worth the time of any readers' advisor to explore it, since it could end up being the perfect choice for tricky patrons. It may also be useful for patrons who care a lot about mood and character and not much about genre. See the chapter 9 Librarian's View for a detailed discussion of Whichbook.net.

"CONSTRUCTING REFERENCES FROM THE BOOK TO THE READER IN FICTION SEARCHING," BY L. YU AND A. O'BRIEN

In 1997, Yu and O'Brien went beyond studying different shelving arrangements in libraries and even genre-based cataloging with one of the few real experiments in readers' advisory.[15] Although an excellent study and article, it is not very accessible to most readers' advisors, both because of the journal it was published in and the scientific language of the article. Yu and O'Brien studied an electronic system that attempts to better help readers select books and overcome the problems and limitations of browsing. Based on information cues used by fiction readers, such as author, title, cover, subject index, abstract, and reviews, Yu and O'Brien tested three versions of a hypertext fiction-searching and -browsing system, using three hundred participants in three groups. They found that readers were willing to use their search and browsing system and that

> composite information cues which consist of bibliographical information, descriptive information and analytical information seem to be able to establish a more comprehensive system of references from the books to the readers' reading context than bibliographic or descriptive information alone and are therefore more helpful in predicting the relevance of the book.

They also found that when readers were provided with more cues, they depended less on their own knowledge. They observed that readers were able to select several books and then checked them out, indicating that the selected books met their needs and reduced the amount of browsing. One of the most interesting results was that the reader group provided with the most cues tended to choose less popular and familiar authors and overall expanded their selection of books in both type and author. These researchers theorize that the additional clues allow readers to take greater risks in selecting unknown titles or authors because of the greater information about the title than they could obtain from the search system.

Yu and O'Brien's research is interesting for many reasons. They based it on the type of information readers use in selecting books, not the type of information librarians think readers use; again, for such studies to be really useful, they must be based on what readers say and do and how they actually go about finding books, whether it is browsing or using an electronic system. Yu and O'Brien also recognized the limitations of genre classifications and browsing, which have in the past been ignored by their proponents, and developed a system that attempts to remedy these problems in such a way that readers actually use it and find it useful for obtaining leisure reading materials. They also found that readers both want and need additional information beyond that traditionally provided in an OPAC record, in order to be most successful in finding leisure reading books with a limited amount of browsing. This research tells readers' advisors and catalogers exactly the type of information we need to be pestering OPAC developers to include in their systems and what type of additional information is important for catalogers to add to their records. And since this article was published in 1997 it appears to be having an effect. Many OPACs now offer libraries the option of automatically having book covers and review information added to each record, both of which are important to readers. And, as is noted in the beginning of this chapter, the active, ongoing OCLC/LC Fiction Project continues to enhance fiction records with more descriptive subject headings, something, according to Yu and O'Brien, readers use and appreciate.

LIBRARIAN'S VIEW   BY NANETTE WARGO DONOHUE

Genrefication

The research tells us that genrefication is good for our users and that browsers prefer it as an organizational method—but how far should we go? One of the main issues when libraries choose to shelve fiction by genre is deciding what defines each genre. If we are delineating genre, there must be some guidelines or boundaries, but the likelihood of all librarians (and readers) coming to the same conclusions about what typifies their favorite genre is low. Therefore, the decision must be made locally. This means that a library choosing to label or classify its fiction in a collection separate from general fiction is going to have to make some decisions— some of them simple and some quite difficult.

Most readers' advisory librarians are aware of the basic parameters of the major genres in fiction and could rattle them off with little or no difficulty. But with the growth in niche materials in the major genres, the ranges of traditional genres are increasingly broad and diverse. What was typical of a genre ten years ago may be less typical today. Consider, for example, erotic romance. These novels defy many of the "typical" conventions of romance fiction and are more sexually explicit than most romance novels. Still, they are considered part of the genre (partially because traditional romance publishing houses have embraced the format) and are a rapidly

---

Nanette Donohue is technical services manager at Champaign (Illinois) Public Library and a 2002 graduate of the University of Illinois Graduate School of Library and Information Science.

growing and increasingly popular niche within romance fiction. On the other end of the spectrum is inspirational romance, which frequently (but not always) has a Christian focus. The readers of erotic romance may rarely delve into a Christian romance, and the readers of a Christian romance would likely be disinterested in an erotic romance. Though the target audiences of these books may rarely, if ever, cross over, both types of books are included under the romance classification. Whether the continued specialization in genre fiction is a problem for browsers remains to be seen, but it should be investigated further.

This raises an important question: how far do we take genrefication? Can we go too far? Many libraries have started to create "inspirational fiction" collections to meet the browsing needs of their users. The problem with a label like "inspirational fiction" is that it's vague. It means something slightly different to everyone. One person's "inspirational" may be another person's "offensive." In "A Decade's Worth of Research on Browsing Fiction Collections," Baker cautions librarians to use headings that are easily understood by patrons.[16] If the phrase "inspirational fiction" can mean different things to different readers, is it clear enough to be used in our libraries? I don't think that librarians intend to be vague when assigning materials to an "inspirational fiction" collection, but should we be clearer? If the "inspirational" is strictly Christian in nature, should we simply call the collection "Christian fiction"? Like any other genre collection, there is a good deal of variety in theme, tone, and plot within inspirational fiction. Readers who are looking for books similar to the Left Behind series may not be satisfied with Lori Wick or Beverly Lewis, authors commonly found in inspirational or Christian fiction collections.

I suspect that the purpose of genrefication in most libraries is to steer our users toward books that are similar to other books they have enjoyed. But as genres continue to expand, it becomes increasingly difficult to use genrefication as a simple form of readers' advisory. Consider the variety in the basic genres; romance, Christian fiction, mystery, speculative fiction, and western fiction are all broad genres that continue to expand in scope. There is no one-size-fits-all solution available, and I predict that genrefication is becoming less and less useful as a readers' advisory tool. So where do we turn?

Because of the increasing democratization of publishing brought on by print-on-demand publishers as well as writers' ability to post material on the Internet inexpensively and easily, librarians can expect to see continued growth in the quantity and variety of niche materials. We can also expect our users to request some of these materials.

One important aspect of genrefication is ensuring that the appropriate people are aware of what we consider a part of a specific genre. The majority of the time, the person who is cataloging or processing the materials and the person who is serving in a readers' advisory capacity are not the same. If catalogers are to make decisions about where to classify items within the collections, they should be aware of the readers' advisory staff's vision of what typifies the genres. For example, should a crime-related thriller go in the mystery section, or is the mystery section reserved for detective novels and police procedurals? What should be done if an item crosses genres, such as the aforementioned J. D. Robb novels or *The Eyre Affair*? Readers' advisory librarians and catalogers need to work together to develop guidelines to answer these questions consistently.

Readers' advisory librarians—and any public service staff, for that matter—should also be prepared to educate users about how genrefication decisions are made in the library. Perhaps another nearby library has different parameters for fiction classification, and the user cannot find the item because it is considered part of a different genre (or not part of a genre at all). Our decision-making processes may not always be clear to our users, so staff should be ready to provide guidance and give explanations when needed. There are several options for providing explanations, including signage, printed guidelines, or even book lists.

Providing Subject Access to Fiction

If genrefication based on shelf placement will become increasingly difficult, what are some other options? Increasing searchability is one of the first options that comes to mind. But before we consider how to increase searchability, we must consider how users are connecting with materials. In *Guiding the Reader to the Next Book,* Baker cites a 1986 study that states that 86 percent of readers do not use the card catalog when selecting books.[17] This study was conducted in the days of card catalogs, and we are now in the era of the online catalog. Many of our users are at least somewhat familiar with searching for information online, but they may not be familiar with searching for information the way we provide it. Library online catalogs are not intuitive for most patrons. There is certainly a difference between searching Google or Amazon.com and searching most libraries' online catalogs. A key question we must ask ourselves is, do users connect with materials through browsing, or are they using our online catalogs with greater frequency? There haven't been any recent, published studies that seek to answer this important question.

Even if our patrons are using the catalog to locate fiction, catalogers are sadly limited when it comes to providing subject access to fiction. Although the situation has improved in recent years, it is still difficult to capture the "aboutness" of a work of fiction using the Library of Congress subject headings, which are the predominant controlled vocabulary used in most U.S. public libraries. The fiction access situation was far more dismal prior to 1990, when the *Guidelines on Subject Access to Individual Works of Fiction, Drama, Etc.* (GSAFD) was released by the American Library Association. This was soon followed by the first edition of *Unreal! Hennepin County Library Subject Headings for Fictional Characters and Places* in 1991, created by the cataloging staff of Hennepin County (Minnesota) Public Library, longtime advocates of providing subject access to fiction. The first edition was quickly followed by a second, released in 1992.[18] *Unreal!* serves as a companion to GSAFD, and both were important steps toward improving subject access to fiction. But these headings are not applied consistently, and they still are not specific enough to be of significant use. The terms in GSAFD are predominantly genre terms, some of which are so arcane (e.g., Bildungsromans) or vague (e.g., Love stories, Mystery fiction) that they are not particularly useful for readers' advisory, whether self-directed or librarian-directed. Hennepin County's headings for fictional characters and places are useful in many situations, but they still do not address the inadequacies of traditional controlled vocabularies for describing the "aboutness" of fiction. Despite these advances, library catalogs are still not as useful for readers' advisory librarians—and readers themselves—to locate fiction.

As much as we may believe in the need to provide subject access to fiction, cataloging budgets are decreasing in many institutions, and catalogers are often asked to complete more work in less time. Can catalogers balance the detailed work involved in subject analysis and the assignment of subject headings while still meeting local production standards? Two studies that took place in the 1990s attempted to address this issue by analyzing the amount of time required to complete subject cataloging for fiction based on information from book jackets, introductory materials, and publicity materials. Both Susan Hayes and Christine DeZelar-Tiedman found that catalogers could glean enough information from dust jackets and introductory materials to add appropriate subject headings to an item and could assign the subject headings with reasonable speed.[19] Hayes found that one group of catalogers was able to add subject headings to twenty-five items in 7.2 hours, and a second group was able to add subject headings in 6.3 hours; DeZelar-Tiedman's study found that it took approximately fifteen minutes for a cataloger to add subject headings to an item. The growth of shared cataloging since the mid-1990s has likely reduced the burden on individual catalogers at individual institutions. Now, fifteen minutes of one cataloger's time can help produce an enhanced record that can be used by thousands of libraries across the world. Though shared cataloging has caused a decrease in the repetition of cataloging work in libraries, one drawback is that some libraries accept catalog records as presented rather than correct errors or add enhancements for local use.

One option for catalogers interested in providing better subject access to their fiction collections is the use of local subject headings, which are added to downloaded records as an enhancement. Hennepin County's *Unreal!* list began as a locally developed list of subject headings and grew into a commonly accepted addition to the Library of Congress headings. Catalogers can use the 690–699 range of tags in MARC format for locally developed subject headings. These headings should index in most online catalogs and would therefore be fully searchable. Maintaining a comprehensive thesaurus of local subject headings would be a labor-intensive project, so catalogers should be aware of the benefits and drawbacks before beginning such a task. It's a viable option for librarians who feel that the Library of Congress subject headings are not fully meeting users' needs, as it is better to add a local subject heading than to not add a subject heading at all.

Online Catalogs, Web 2.0, and User Expectations

The explosive growth of the Internet since the mid-1990s has changed users' expectations of the services a library's catalog should provide. As we begin to move toward Web 2.0, the chasm between services offered by our library catalogs and services offered by online bookstores continues to deepen. Library catalogs are competing with commercial websites, and commercial websites seem to be winning the battle. Library catalog interfaces tend to be clunky and several years behind the commercial websites, because of lengthy development cycles. Though it is true that most libraries' online catalogs can now display book reviews and cover art, the vast majority do not provide enhanced content such as Amazon.com's wish lists, "Look Inside the Book" feature, or ability to interact with the data and with other users through reviews, social tagging, descriptive lists of materials, or wikis. For example, the Amazon.com recommendation system is a powerful—although occasionally flawed—readers' advisory tool. As of this writing, some libraries are beginning to develop enhancements to their online catalogs that allow users to interact with one another and with the data in the catalog, but this is currently restricted to the very small number of libraries that have the resources and personnel to develop their catalogs beyond the out-of-the-box basics.

There are two Web 2.0 technologies that could have tremendous impact on readers' advisory services in the near future—social tagging and recommendation systems. With a social tagging system, users add tags to materials to describe them in any way they see fit. Many popular social networking websites, such as Flickr (for photo sharing) and YouTube (for video sharing), employ tagging systems to help users locate specific content. Social tagging is based on natural language, which makes it easier to capture appeal factors such as language and story. Amazon .com allows users to add tags to items, which results in a fascinating array of information—and editorial comment—on popular materials. For example, when I looked there were 179 different tags assigned to Dan Brown's blockbuster *The Da Vinci Code*. The fourteen most popular tags were fiction (20), mystery (13), dan brown (11), books (7), suspense (7), religion (6), thriller (5), book (4), crap (4), da vinci code (4), historical fiction (4), art (3), great read (3), and mona lisa (3).

This group of tags illustrates some of the benefits and drawbacks of social tagging systems, as well as where library catalogs intersect with tagging systems. In the list of tags, we see the book's author and its title. We see some widely accepted genre headings ("fiction," "mystery," "historical fiction"), some general terms relating to the subject matter ("religion," "art"), and some editorial comment ("crap," "great read"). Moving further into the list of tags, there are a few more general terms related to the subject matter, including "Christianity," "Catholic church," "Knights Templar," and "codes," as well as plenty more editorial comment, both positive ("danged good fiction," "life-changing") and negative ("craptastic," "unbelievably bad writing"). Although it's certainly true that some of the tags are pointless to anyone but the user who assigned them (e.g., ten tags are simply people's names), many of the tags do add an additional layer of accessibility to the item and can help readers of *The Da Vinci Code* find similar books that match the specific characteristic they enjoyed.

What's more, these tags cover different terrain from the subject headings assigned to *The Da Vinci Code* in its Library of Congress catalog record:

Leonardo, da Vinci, 1452–1519—Appreciation—Fiction.

Art museum curators—Crimes against—Fiction.

Secret societies—Fiction.

Cryptographers—Fiction.

Paris (France)—Fiction.

Grail—Fiction.

Mystery fiction.

Although these subject headings provide important access points to the item, they simply cannot cover as many nuances as users' tags. To me, so much of good readers' advisory service centers around nuances—getting to the little things readers enjoyed about a book and helping them find similar reading experiences.

Common criticisms of tagging are that the vocabulary is not controlled and that social tagging systems often contain spelling errors and inconsistencies in usage. If one of the purposes of the library catalog is to collocate materials, controlled vocabularies will always be necessary. But allowing users to add tags simply provides another layer of information to access—a layer that many of our users will find helpful when trying to locate similar items. The feedback from user tags can also benefit catalogers by helping them assign better subject headings or by providing the information needed to determine which genre collection the item belongs in. The main drawback to social tagging systems in library catalogs is that some users do not understand the purpose of the system and add tags that are not particularly useful (e.g., "Jen's wish list" or "books read in 2006"), but overall the potential benefits far outweigh these drawbacks. If tagging systems can help readers and librarians find similar books, it's certainly worth a try.

Recommendation systems feature prominently on many commercial websites, including Amazon.com. Since the recommendation systems on commercial websites tend to be based on users' purchases or browsing histories, they can be faulty. They can, however, help readers explore items that may be similar to the item they enjoyed. Customers who purchased *The Da Vinci Code* from Amazon.com also purchased *Holy Blood, Holy Grail*, by Michael Baigent; *Deception Point*, by Dan Brown; *Digital Fortress: A Thriller*, by Dan Brown; *Harry Potter and the Half-Blood Prince* (book 6), by J. K. Rowling; and *The Five People You Meet in Heaven*, by Mitch Albom. This is an interesting array of titles; there are two other books by Dan Brown, two best sellers that are seemingly unrelated in subject matter, and *Holy Blood, Holy Grail*—the book *The Da Vinci Code* is reported to be based on.

As a better and more useful example, customers who purchased Marisha Pessl's critically acclaimed literary novel *Special Topics in Calamity Physics* also purchased *The Emperor's Children*, by Claire Messud; *The Keep*, by Jennifer Egan; *The Ruins*, by Scott Smith; *Reading Like a Writer: A Guide for People Who Love Books and for Those Who Want to Write Them*, by Francine Prose; and *Suite Française*, by Irene Nemirovsky. This almost reads like a list of "starred review" literary fiction from any one of a number of literary review journals from the fall of 2006. With the exception of *Reading Like a Writer*, each is a work of literary fiction that received positive reviews from a variety of review sources.

Amazon.com also has a personalized recommendation system for registered users, one based on the user's purchase history as well as items added to the user's Amazon.com wish list. The system allows users to refine their recommendations by rating items they own and indicating interest in items recommended for them. Because the recommendations are based on the user's purchase history, they don't always work. As an example, I purchased a professional wrestling DVD as a birthday gift for my brother. Until I unchecked the box on the recommendation page that said "use to make recommendations," Amazon.com continually recommended wrestling DVDs as items of interest because of my purchase history. Other commercial websites, such as Netflix, also use personalized recommendation systems to help users find similar items based on items they have rented or have indicated an interest in renting.

The major issue with recommendation systems in libraries is patron privacy. Most libraries delete their users' circulation histories after a brief period, and recommendation systems require user histories in order to work properly. One possible work-around would be to strip identifying information from users' histories and maintain only the connections between items. Since there is no human intermediary in a recommendation system, it may not work as effectively as social tagging. All the same, recommendation systems can be a good tool for helping readers explore materials they might not have found otherwise.

Though traditional classification and genrefication will likely continue to be fertile ground for researchers in readers' advisory, researchers should also consider how Web 2.0 technologies are affecting readers' advisory services. How can we maintain the quality of our services in an increasingly virtual, computer-driven world? How can library catalogs stay relevant among flashy corporate websites that regularly add new enhancements? Updates to some of the landmark studies in the use of online catalogs should be conducted to determine if there is a difference between card catalog use in 1986 and online catalog use in 2006. As libraries begin to incorporate Web 2.0 services such as social tagging and recommendation systems into their online catalogs, the results, including both benefits and drawbacks, should be shared. Research into readers' advisory and classification should not only keep pace with current practice but anticipate future practice.

NOTES

1. American Library Association, Subcommittee on Subject Access to Individual Works of Fiction, Drama, etc., *Guidelines on Subject Access to Individual Works of Fiction, Drama, Etc.: Final Report* (Chicago: American Library Association, 1990; 2nd ed., 2000).

2. Library of Congress, Library of Congress Project for Cooperative Cataloging, http://www.loc.gov/catdir/pcc/fictioninfo.html.

3. In 1997, a special issue of *Information Services and Use* contained several of the articles discussed later in this chapter. It is the last known gathering of research on this subject.

4. L. Yu and A. O'Brien, "Domain of Adult Fiction Librarianship," *Advances in Librarianship* 20 (1996): 151–89; Jessica E. Moyer, "Adult Fiction Reading: A Literature Review of Readers' Advisory Services, Adult Fiction Librarianship and Fiction Readers," *Reference and User Services Quarterly* 44, no. 3 (2005): 220–31.

5. Gail Harrell, "Use of Fiction Categories in Major American Public Libraries," in *Guiding the Reader to the Next Book*, ed. Kenneth D. Shearer (New York: Neal-Schuman, 1996), 149–58.

6. Jeffrey Cannell and Eileen McCluskey, "Genrefication: Fiction Classification and Increased Circulation," in Shearer, *Guiding the Reader*, 159–68.

7. Amy J. Richards, "Genre Fiction Classification: A Study of the Durham County Library," Master's paper, University of North Carolina at Chapel Hill, 1999. Available online at http://ils.unc.edu/MSpapers/2535.pdf.

8. Kerri L. Huff, "Genre Fiction Classification: A Continuation Study of Its Reception by Patrons in the Durham County (NC) Public Library," Master's paper, University of North Carolina at Chapel Hill, 2006. Available online at http://ils.unc.edu/MSpapers/3171.pdf.

9. Sharon L. Baker (discussed below) believes that just moving the collection around (Z to A instead of A to Z) can increase circulation because patrons looking in the usual places are now looking at different books; see "A Decade's Worth of Research on Browsing Fiction Collections," in Shearer, *Guiding the Reader*, 127–47. Shearer's and Huff's works show that genrefying the collection has had a long-term impact.

10. For example, Hans Jorn Nielsen, "The Nature of Fiction and Its Significance for Classification and Indexing," *Information Services and Use* 17 (1997): 171–81; Inga-Lill Ekvall and Sibyl Larsson, "EDVIN—A Search System for Fiction Based on the Experience of Users' Needs," *Information Services and Use* 17 (1997): 81–84; L. Yu and A. O'Brien, "Constructing References from the Book to the Reader in Fiction Searching: An Experiment in the Construction of Information Cues from the Reading Context Approach," *Information Services and Use* 17 (1997): 187–99; Rob Hidderley, "Democratic Indexing: An Approach to the Retrieval of Fiction," *Information Services and Use* 17 (1997): 101–9.

11. Jarmo Saarti, "Feeding with the Spoon, or the Effects of Shelf Classification of Fiction on the Loaning of Fiction," *Information Services and Use* 17 (1997): 159–69.

12. Baker, "Decade's Worth."

13. Debbie Denham, "ICT and Reader Development," in *Reading and Reader Development: The Pleasure of Reading,* by Judith Elkin, Briony Train, and Debbie Denham (London: Facet, 2003).

14. Radway discusses this important issue in *Reading the Romance,* discussed in chapter 7 of this book.

15. Yu and O'Brien, "Constructing References," quote from 192.

16. Baker, "Decade's Worth," 142.

17. Ibid., 128.

18. *Unreal! Hennepin County Library Subject Headings for Fictional Characters and Places,* 2nd ed. (Jefferson, N.C.: McFarland, 1992).

19. Christine DeZelar-Tiedman, "Subject Access to Fiction: An Application of the Guidelines," *Library Resources and Technical Services* 40, no. 3 (1996): 203–8, 210; Susan Hayes, "Enhanced Catalog Access to Fiction: A Preliminary Study," *Library Resources and Technical Services* 36, no. 4 (1992): 441–59.

11

COLLECTION DEVELOPMENT AND COLLECTION MANAGEMENT

Although without a print or media collection readers' advisory would not exist, the collection is an often overlooked aspect of readers' advisory services. In this chapter we look at issues related to collection development and collection management, from selection and acquisition to deselection (weeding). Collection management is as much about removing or replacing older books as it is about acquiring new ones.

RESEARCH REVIEW   BY JESSICA E. MOYER

Since collection development has always been a part of libraries, there is no shortage of literature and research about collection development. In this research review section, I strictly limit the selections to those that relate directly to readers' advisory—essentially collection development and management for popular materials, and preferred new materials.

The Quality versus Demand Debate; or, Do We Actually Give 'Em What They Want?

NORA RAWLINSON AND THE BALTIMORE COUNTY PUBLIC LIBRARY

For nearly as long as libraries have been collecting materials, the biggest issue in collection development of popular materials has been the debate of quality versus demand. There are numerous publications in this topic.

In November 1981, Nora Rawlinson reignited the debate with her "Give 'Em What They Want!" article in *Library Journal*.[1] I say reignited because Rawlinson aptly quotes John Cotton Dana (also from the pages of *Library Journal*) from 1896: "Deny your people nothing that the book-shop grants them. Make your library at least as attractive as the most attractive retail store in the community." Clearly this debate has been going on a long time. Rawlinson's article explains how (circa 1981) Baltimore County Public Library (BCPL) selected its popular materials. Her article is a clear, well-reasoned explanation of the (at the time) pioneering collection development policy for popular materials. Modern librarians reading her article today may wonder why it was so controversial. Many of Rawlinson's policies and strategies are in use by modern public libraries, from buying multiple copies of best sellers, to anticipating demand based on previous use, to being aware of books discussed on talk shows and other popular media. Neither then nor now did this mean an unbalanced collection; instead, as Rawlinson explains, "being responsive to demand means providing the classics and perennial favorites as well as that which is currently popular."

BCPL's collection policy was one of the first to state use of circulation statistics for collection analysis. Modern integrated library systems (ILS) readily provide this data, and such data are now used regularly by libraries all over the United States. BCPL also used ILS data to determine the areas of greatest interest to its patrons and increased acquisitions for these high-interest areas, at the same time discarding low-interest titles, especially from the branch libraries. In fact, BCPL's method works best for a larger library system with multiple branches and centralized collection management. Still, many of the ideas and practices can (and have been) adapted to smaller systems or one-building libraries.

John Berry argued the quality side of the debate in 1979, responding to an earlier article about BCPL practices in *Publishers Weekly*.[2] "It is easier to select for demand. It is not hard to build a popular collection." And yet when librarians select for quality, they "have to make those forbidden value judgements." Rawlinson responded to Berry in her 1981 article, arguing that, other than the few easily predictable best sellers, "for the rest of the books, quality is a factor. . . . Once interest is established, then the book must be judged on many of the same standards of quality all librarians use. . . . At BCPL we are simply trying to devise ways of testing public interest so we can focus our efforts." Addressing the issue of interlibrary loan, Rawlinson noted that BCPL was a net loaning library, not a borrower, even after all the changes in their collection. Analysis of the interlibrary loan data found that "the ones sent to other libraries are for popular interest subjects." It looks like BCPL was meeting the leisure reading needs of not just its own patrons but patrons across the state whose own libraries did not have the leisure materials they desired. Rawlinson's article is enjoyable, readable, and reasonable; her arguments are hard to deny. She ends with a quote from the controversial BCPL director, one that may make some librarians cringe, but one they should think hard about too: "Apparently there is a secret desire in many directors to become the Librarian of Harvard University. Commendable, no doubt, but it's very expensive for taxpayers to turn their public libraries into farm teams for Harvard."

"THE DEVELOPMENT AND TESTING OF AN INSTRUMENT . . . ," BY PATRICIA HAMILTON AND TERRY WEECH

An early research contribution to this debate is an article in *Collection Management* by Hamilton and Weech.[3] They developed and tested an instrument to measure the attitudes of libraries about the quality versus demand debate as part of a survey of Illinois librarians. Although their sample was limited to Illinois, they surveyed librarians from all libraries of all sizes across the state, making their results reasonably applicable in other states. By 1986, when this research was conducted, demand was clearly an important part of collection development. There was, however, still a significant desire for quality in selection.

This was an important early study in collection development and the quality versus demand debate. Since more than twenty years have passed since the data were originally gathered, it would be interesting to see this study repeated. Has demand-based collection development increased, decreased, or stayed the same in twenty years? What about quality? Is it still equally valued by librarians?

"'DO YOU HAVE ANY BOOKS ON . . . ?'" BY JOHN BUDD AND CYNTHIA WYATT

In one of the more recent contributions to this debate, Budd and Wyatt studied the holdings of twenty medium-sized public libraries.[4] One of the most valuable sections of this article is the "Background" section in which Budd and Wyatt review the debate since the late 1970s. They are able to provide several years of distance from the raging debate of the 1980s and a nonjudgmental overview of this contentious issue. They also update the work of Shaw on the importance of reviews in selection, and most important, they bring up the issue of centralized selection, an increasingly common practice in twenty-first-century libraries.

Budd and Wyatt identified a list of high-demand titles and a list of high-quality titles using typical library sources such as *Publishers Weekly* and ALA-created lists. They then determined which titles were held in the twenty libraries selected for the study. Their main result was that, of the seventy-nine total titles, a majority were held by all the selected libraries, "which indicates that both quality and popularity are important factors in collection development." They concluded that public libraries consider both quality and demand when making selection decisions. As is no surprise, all the books on ALA's banned books list were held by all libraries, indicating both that banned books are in demand and that libraries make an effort to collect banned titles.

Budd and Wyatt also investigated the relationship between holdings and reviews, focusing on the fifteen less commonly held titles. Six of these had no reviews listed in *Book Review Digest*, which includes all common library review sources. Of the remaining nine titles, some were reviewed in sources unlikely to be read by librarians, and the others received either negative reviews or reviews that indicated the title would be of interest only to a small audience. They concluded that "not only is the presence of reviews an influential element in selection and acquisition . . . but the content of reviews also seems to appear to affect selection decisions." This is a well-designed, well-executed study of an important library issue. It is the type of study and article that any librarian can and should be doing. It makes a real impact on the library world, in terms of both practice and research.

Weeding: Sometimes Books Must Leave the Library

Weeding (also known as deselection or stock retirement, for U.K. librarians) is one of the most important but contentious aspects of collection development. After all the debates about what to buy, we debate even more about what to get rid of. Renee Vaillancourt contributed an editorial to *Public Libraries* on the difficulties of weeding that will resonate with many librarians confronted with the task.[5] "When push comes to shove, weeding a collection that you have helped to build, especially when the library is pushed for space, can be one of the most difficult tasks a librarian has to face. . . . What will become of these books when we relegate them to our book sales, community agencies or dumpster?" All the same, Vaillancourt concludes, "I am a firm believer in regular weeding." As hard as it is, we must do it. And the next several publications will help, from Jacob's eminently practical article to Slote's classic *Weeding Library Collections*.

"WEEDING THE FICTION COLLECTION," BY MERLE JACOB

Merle Jacob wrote one of the best (and shortest) articles on weeding popular materials in 2001.[6] Even though there is little research in Jacob's article it is extremely useful, partly because it is so practical. Jacob tackles the challenging topic by acknowledging that fiction is the hardest area for her to weed. She makes librarians face some hard truths—"Many librarians are just packrats, and they can't bear to throw anything out"—and emphasizes how we absolutely must do it: "You must get rid of the weeds, before they take over the garden." This is an article that every librarian faced with managing a fiction collection (or other popular materials) must read and take to heart. Follow Jacob's guidelines and the weeding process will not be nearly as difficult as you think. She covers every step, from why weed, to formulating a plan of action, to types of books, to how to actually get the books out of the library (don't just throw them in the Dumpster). This article is focused exclusively on fiction and has been written by someone who has been active in readers' advisory for many years. Jacob's advice is not only good but extremely useful, even when it might be hard to take: "Just because a book is in a bibliography may not be a reason to keep it if it never circulates or doesn't fit your community's borrowing needs."

CREW METHOD

Mentioned by Jacob is the CREW Method, a set of weeding guidelines. The CREW Method was first detailed in the *CREW Manual*, by Joseph P. Segal, in 1979. It was revised and updated in 1995 by Belinda Boon and distributed as an ERIC document.[7] Readily available, the *CREW Manual* is especially useful for librarians new to weeding or those needing a refresher on systematic weeding methods. Use it in concert with Jacob's article when weeding popular fiction collections.

WEEDING LIBRARY COLLECTIONS, BY STANLEY J. SLOTE

Weeding Library Collections, by Stanley J. Slote, is one of the most scientific of all practical library publications, not just those on collection management.[8] This may be why it is also one of the lesser-used methods. Librarians using the Slote weeding method eliminate nearly all human judgment, relying on Slote's formulas and data generated from the library's ILS. Slote provides convincing arguments, including excellent data, for using the Slote scientific method of weeding instead of personal judgment and knowledge—as hard it may be to accept for advisors who habitually rely on their personal knowledge of their patrons, community, and collections. Slote's most important finding for advisors: the best predictor for whether a book would be in demand in the future was whether it had circulated in the previous year.

The Responsive Public Library, by Sharon L. Baker and Karen L. Wallace

One single publication touches on all aspects of collection development and management and addresses all the issues mentioned in the previous sections: *The Responsive Public Library,* by Sharon L. Baker and Karen L. Wallace.[9] The entire book is based on Baker's and others' research on readers and public libraries. Although she has not been active in readers' advisory for the past several years, in the 1980s and early 1990s Baker conducted some of the best work on readers and libraries, including her groundbreaking work on browsing, which is still the best on this subject. The influence of her excellent research is evident throughout *The Responsive Public Library;* few other library and information science publications have such a deep foundation in research. In this section I review the chapters of *The Responsive Public Library* individually. This outstanding work seems to have been overlooked in the past few years, but like most of Baker's work it was so far ahead of its time that it is still relevant today.

Baker starts with an overview of what patrons are looking for in libraries, in terms of both collections and services. Citing a variety of research, she concludes that most libraries are not fully meeting these desires and notes that patrons have four options: (1) accept the limitations and stay loyal, (2) voice their concerns, (3) neglect the problem and indirectly express displeasure, or (4) give on up library needs and go somewhere else. Baker believes that marketing can both help patrons know what libraries have to offer and help libraries offer what patrons need in both the short and long term. "Marketing plans can help staff provide collections and services that satisfy patron and library objectives at reasonable costs while attracting public support for future endeavors."[10] Baker encourages libraries to seek marketing partners and lists a variety of options. Her opening chapter concludes with subjects that were considered by a library planning a marketing campaign and maps them to the later chapters in the book.

To develop a marketing plan and provide high-quality services, libraries must "understand the general characteristics and motivations of those who use the library regularly, occasionally or not at all."[11] All three of these groups must be considered when developing a marketing plan, or indeed any library service. In her second chapter, "Know Your Market," Baker gives librarians a head start by providing excellent research-based overviews of the three types of users. She finds that library users have a desire to explore the world around them and to further their education through the less formal channels of library materials. Two particularly important findings for public libraries are that children in impoverished neighborhoods are much less likely to live in print-rich environments or visit the library, and that children who visit the library are much more likely to become regular adult patrons.

All users must have motivation to use the library, and Baker proposes this theory: "Library use occurs when motivation *plus incentives* outweigh inhibitors (costs). . . . In essence patrons are motivated to use the library by their perception of the benefit(s) that use will provide."[12] She lists a variety of patron motivations for library use, from general (gain knowledge) to specific (when our son had leukemia). The degree to which a patron can obtain, when needed, desired materials often affects collection use. Baker notes that, above all, the decision to use or not use the library is a very personal one that the library can only partially influence. She concludes the chapter with five case studies that detail the various motivations for library use and five techniques for gathering reliable data about service populations.

How do libraries go about creating a master plan? Chapter 3, "Creating Your Master Plan," details the process, starting with a sample plan from a North Carolina library. Focused on three aspects of the planning process—participants, themes, and composition—this chapter provides all the help any library needs to develop a plan of its own.

In the chapter "Collection Choices," Baker focuses on three questions: "What elements influence user selections? What mix of products (that is, items in the collection) best meet user needs? How will the life cycles of particular products affect overall demand?"

> The degree of patron satisfaction with collection contents provides one key measure of a library's responsiveness. It also greatly affects levels of library use. When a collection contains dated or otherwise inadequate materials or lacks desired items, community residents may turn to other sources to obtain the information and stories they need. Developing winning collections requires librarians to make wise choices about purchasing, maintaining and weeding materials.[13]

Again drawing heavily on published research, Baker uncovers the key elements that affect patrons' selection process, which are subject, genre, format, quality or excellence, style and appeal, reading, listening and other levels of sophistication, currency, language, packaging, and awareness of the author or title.[14] Because Baker draws from a wide variety of excellent research, her conclusions here can be considered a definitive understanding of which factors have the most impact on patron selection.

In addressing the question of best product mix, Baker reminds us that librarians must make informed decisions about the products available to them. To start, librarians must review their collections in terms of products, looking to identify those heavily used by patrons, those not used by patrons, and items desired by patrons or potential patrons.

On the topic of life cycle, Baker maintains that nearly all items in the library collection travel through several stages before passing out of demand: from introduction (characterized by slow acceptance and limited use), to growth stage (when it can become impossible to meet demands), to maturity (most have already read it), to decline (strong decrease in demand), and eventually to elimination. She notes that some items revive themselves (e.g., when an older book becomes a movie) and return to the growth stage, and some popular items may stay in the maturity stage for many years. Looking at library collections in terms of product life cycles is both innovative and thought provoking and an idea that librarians should consider more often.

There are several costs associated with library use that, for some patrons, may outweigh the benefits. In the chapter "Cost of Collections and Use," Baker observes that "to encourage use by individuals, who weigh their private out-of-pocket, convenience and psychological costs and benefits when deciding whether to use the library, librarians will adopt and refine techniques to keep combined costs as low and the combined benefits as high as possible."[15] In the latter parts of this chapter she details all the possible costs patrons may incur when visiting or using the library and ways to reduce these costs. Many of these relate to collection access and should be of interest to collection managers.

Baker suggests three strategies for price objectives: maximizing use, limiting use, and recovering costs. To maximize use, the library does everything possible to reduce waiting times for materials and limit out-of-pockets costs, in addition to continuing to publicize the benefits of library service. Limiting use entails reducing loan times for popular items or instituting limits on the number of items per patron for popular collections. To recover costs, Baker suggests that libraries seek funding from outside sources and add value-added services such as rental collection of popular materials that duplicate items in the regular collection. Although these ideas have been considered controversial in readers' advisory circles, Baker's well-researched and well-reasoned arguments are compelling.

On the topic of pricing Baker suggests that libraries steer away from tradition (we've always charged five cents!) and instead use either cost-oriented or demand-oriented pricing, noting that costs can be actual out-of-pocket money or nonmonetary costs such as reduced borrowing times. Sometimes libraries need to changes costs, and this should be done carefully. Baker encourages librarians to estimate the effects of the proposed change on use, particularly to survey patrons to gain a sense of attitudes to the possible change. Libraries should also review the history of the effects of such changes and might consider a small pilot program, such as when adding a rental collection.

In "Creating Access," Baker focuses on issues of patron access to the collection, from discovering items, to locating them within the library, to obtaining them, which might take anywhere from a few minutes if the user is in the library and the item is on the shelf to several weeks if the item is popular and on a waiting list. To address these issues, Baker keys in on four questions: "(1) what collection distribution outlets will the library use? (2) how will staff distribute items among these outlets? (3) how will staff distribute items among collections in a single library facility? and (4) how can the interior be designed for maximum distribution effectiveness?"[16]

For distribution outlets Baker details all the possible locations for library stock, from a main library to full-service or mini branches, as well as bookmobiles, deposit collections, personal delivery, and materials by mail. She discusses how each type functions as well as the pros and cons of each possible service point, with many examples. This wealth of research-backed information should be a first stop for any library considering adding (or losing) any of these services. Baker lists many points to consider and emphasizes the need to research and evaluate the service and its potential population before making any changes, as well as reevaluating the service later to see if it is actually meeting patron needs.

In the final section Baker addresses the problems of returning materials. She suggests that to ease patron costs libraries allow materials to be returned to any of their locations, provide after-hours drop boxes that accept all types of materials, make sure hours are convenient for local patrons, and consider reducing or even eliminating late fees. Libraries then must decide how to distribute items among the various distribution points. Again Baker advocates knowing the local community to be sure the collection best meets their needs.

Distribution of items within a single building is one of the most debated issues among librarians. Genrefication or integrated collections and the related issue of browsing are covered in greater depth in chapter 10 of *The Responsive Public Library* (see below) as well as in chapter 9 of the book now in your hands.

Chapter 7 of *The Responsive Public Library*, "Creating Recognition of Collection-Use Benefits," is devoted to marketing or creating recognition of all the benefits of use of the library's collections. Although marketing collections is an extremely important part of the library's mission, it has less effect on both collection development and readers' advisory; I do not discuss it further here beyond noting that it would be extremely useful for developing a marketing plan for any part of the library's collections, since it covers everything from determining the target market to evaluating the results.

Chapter 8, "Collection Evaluation: A Product Analysis Approach," addresses an essential part of creating and maintaining a responsive library. Baker advocates regular and systematized collection evaluation. With modern ILSs libraries cannot use lack of data as an excuse not to evaluate collections, and modern technology also makes the process faster and simpler. Baker suggests that libraries use a four-step approach to evaluation: identify heavily used currently owned items, lightly used or nonused currently owned items, items not currently in the collection but that would likely receive use, and barriers that inhibit collection use. Baker explains the benefit and importance of evaluating each aspect and describes a variety of techniques to collect the necessary data, including techniques with or without ILS capabilities. For many of the techniques she includes charts, tables, or other sample forms to assist librarians working on that particular aspect of evaluation. Baker sees collection evaluation as both a necessary and ongoing process and part of all library services; public services staff can help in identifying both heavily used items and items that are desired but not owned. Collection evaluation should inform budgeting, with materials expenditures matching actual use by patrons. Identifying desired items and barriers to collection should inform both outreach services and considerations of new services.

"Marketing-Based Selection Policies and Practices" uses a balance of objective (gathered during collection evaluation and from the community) and subjective impressions from the selectors. Baker lays out five steps: (1) writing a detailed, synthesized collection development policy; (2) reviewing materials budget allocations to ensure consistency with library goals; (3) establishing a centralized selection unit to purchase routine items cost-effectively; (4) carefully assigning selection responsibilities and thoroughly training selectors; and (5) asking professional selectors to augment their impressions by reviewing objective data collection about collection use. The section on collection development policy is detailed, useful, and guides the staff person charged with developing or rewriting the policy through all the steps, with any prompts and questions to consider along the way.

Drawing on her previous publications, the section on budgets is one of the stronger and more useful in the book. Baker encourages librarians to rethink their budget allocations completely and consider new strategies to increase access to collections even during tough budget times. The section on selecting and educating selectors is both interesting and potentially controversial, since Baker suggests that selectors do not have to be professionally trained librarians, just anyone with subject expertise who is willing to work with the library's collections. Finally, Baker suggests use of three marketing principles: (1) when an item or type of item hasn't been used, don't buy it again without an overriding reason to do so; (2) if an item or type of item has been or is likely to be used heavily, duplicate it or assign a shortened loan period to keep a patron's chances of finding it on the shelf high; and (3) if an item or type of item not now in the collection may be useful to patrons and levels of potential use justify its expense, buy it. Baker encourages librarians to place primary emphasis on purchasing works that support the library's selected services' responses or roles, which may be a more challenging task than it initially appears.

Browsing and the display and arrangement of library collections, along with other passive readers' advisory techniques such as read-alike lists, are the subjects of "Marketing-Based Promotional Policies and Practices." Classification of the collection is the base of these issues, and so I review this chapter in chapter 9. Other sections of Baker's chapter cover promoting the collection through readers' advisory services and outreach for readers' advisors. As usual, Baker's well-supported conclusions, with all evidence drawn from a variety of research, makes this an excellent source for advisors. Those who want to rearrange their collections or add displays or other passive techniques would do well to consult Baker's reference list. Her research is extensive and widespread and includes many excellent research publications from Europe, which are rarely referenced in North American readers' advisory publications.

The rousing and satisfying concluding chapter of *The Responsive Public Library* will inspire librarians to get started immediately on applying her marketing strategies to their libraries.

LIBRARIAN'S VIEW   BY CYNTHIA ORR

The skills and ability to suggest a good match between readers and books are at the core of readers' advisory service, and research into methods and

---

Cynthia Orr recently retired as collection manager of the Cleveland Public Library and has more than thirty years of experience in collection development, public service, management, and readers' advisory service. She speaks at library conferences, teaches for Kent State University's Graduate School of Library and Information Science, and writes for NoveList. She was awarded the 2004 ALA RUSA Margaret E. Monroe Award for service to adults and is a member of the advisory board of Reader's Advisor Online and editor of its blog.

best practices that can aid librarians in performing this service has been covered in other chapters in this book. But training staff to deliver effective readers' advisory service is not enough. If the local library collection is not adequate or appropriate for the particular community served by the library, then the patron cannot be served well. The readers' advisor can use the best tools to identify a perfect list of suggestions for a patron, but if the library does not own the titles or cannot get them quickly, the patron will not be satisfied. Conversely, if the library contains titles that are not used, they also do a disservice to their community. Perhaps this wasn't so true years ago, but in an age of quick delivery, shared catalogs, consortia, and Internet-based interlibrary loan, libraries can afford to lean toward demand rather than concentrating on "core" titles that are never used. This does not mean that quality does not count, but rather, as Sharon Baker says, that "it's the match that counts."[17]

Committing to the building and maintaining of a relevant collection means anticipating patron demand and realizing that timing is crucial. It means responding to patron requests for titles whose popularity was not anticipated and constantly monitoring demand. It means being aware of local news, interests, and titles with regional appeal. And, though this may seem surprising to some, it requires technical expertise to be able to adopt—or even invent—new technologies to allow for continuous improvements in speed and effectiveness of selection. And this cannot be done alone. A successful collection for pleasure readers can result only from a team effort—even if (and maybe especially if) the library uses centralized selection. In the next several sections I discuss each of these issues, as well as weeding and trends and new technologies for collection management.

Selecting and Building a Relevant Collection for Readers

The first step in building a relevant collection is to identify the potential readers in the neighborhood. Selecting new materials that will fit the community requires a real understanding of the population in the library's service area. Selectors can achieve this understanding by studying demographics, by using the information available from circulation records to determine past patterns of demand, by surveying public service staff and the readers who use the library as well as readers who don't, by walking around the locality, and by just plain paying attention.

Detailed information on demographics of a community can be obtained from U.S. census data. The government has made incredible technological strides since the 2000 census. The data were first released on tape for official census bureau affiliates, and then on CD-ROM, but now only a few years later librarians can use the Internet to produce detailed reports of neighborhoods. GIS software can be used to produce thematic maps that display the information in visual format, making it much easier to absorb than columns of numbers. Some useful ways to map library populations include block-by-block data for each branch showing age, education levels, home ownership, income, and ethnic backgrounds of the population. Try mapping preschoolers to see which branch needs more picture books. Or find areas high in home ownership for books on decorating and home repair or gardening. Map residents by language spoken at home to decide on foreign-language books.

Use the library's ILS data to see what circulates in each neighborhood and, if possible, export the data to a spreadsheet and graph it. What percentage of the circulation is AV and how much is print? Of the print circulation, how much is nonfiction and how much is fiction? What percentage is juvenile, young adult, and adult? Which areas of fiction and nonfiction circulate the most? Which areas have the highest loss rate?

Just as important as raw data that can be mapped into extremely useful graphs and thematic maps is talking to people who know what is needed at a particular library branch. This includes branch staff (not just librarians) and library users. Talking to staff and users can reveal what requests are often made but not filled. Formal surveys are valuable, but it can be almost as useful to see what items are returned in a typical day. Analyzing a day or a week of returns shows the successful parts of a collection.

Walking around the neighborhood and talking to residents and people who work there can be quite revealing. Have they been to the library? If not, why not? What would it take to entice them to come? Do they know what the library has to offer? Look at the types of businesses to see what they indicate about the neighborhood. The presence of a bodega is a good sign that materials in Spanish might be popular, for instance. And if materials in another language are needed, signage in that language on the outside of the building is a simple way to let the neighborhood know that they are welcome.

Demographics, circulation data, interviews with staff, surveys, personal observations, photographs, history of the community, and input from residents, workers, local organizations, and politicians can be used to build a profile of each library neighborhood. But demographics change, people move, and populations shift. Don't forget to update profiles regularly.

Once a selector has a thorough knowledge of the readers in a library service area, she must cast a wide net into the world of new books to find candidates for purchase that fit those readers. Then, within a budget that is never large enough, she must choose the titles and quantities of those titles to add to the collection and make sure they are on the shelves when leisure readers come looking for them.

Selection in libraries has changed incredibly just within the span of the career of many librarians working today. It has not been so very many years since the only information available to librarians about books to be published in the future was a paper copy of "Forthcoming Books." This tool—a supplement to *Books in Print*—had an inadequate subject guide and was woefully slow to arrive in the mail. Selection was typically done by routing standard review journals among several librarians, who marked the number of copies in the journal. These titles were eventually ordered from vendors after much clerical work to make sure that titles reviewed in more than one journal were not duplicated.

Though this was sometimes a frustrating situation, at least readers were in the same boat as librarians in those days. Patrons largely heard about new books when bookstores got them onto the shelves or when they read reviews of the titles in magazines and newspapers. But in this age of the Internet everything has changed. The founding of Amazon .com suddenly put prepublication information into the hands of readers, who naturally turned to their local libraries for titles—at first with little success. The advent of blogs, electronic discussion lists and groups, personal websites, and social networks has changed everything in just a few years. In the not-so-distant past, for example, avid readers would get this week's best-seller list delivered to their doorstep along with their Sunday *New York Times*. Now the list is published online on Friday. Readers subscribe to blogs, check favorite authors' websites, read online reviews, join discussion groups, and share what they're reading through such sites as Facebook, MySpace, Good Reads, and LibraryThing. The days of marking book selection in print journals and then adding patrons to a months-long hold list are over. Readers know what new books are coming, and they expect to have them shortly after publication.

Timing is crucial for readers. Reading, though usually done in a solitary setting, is also somewhat counterintuitively a social activity. A reader's first impulse upon completing a book is often to talk to someone about it. Reading groups bring people together to discuss titles, and best sellers are often the topic when friends gather. Readers want to read a book at the same time everyone else is reading it, and librarians should not be surprised by that fact.

Selectors now have powerful technology-based tools to anticipate demand so that titles can be on the shelves when they hit the best-seller lists. This is more complicated and difficult than it may sound, because it involves far more than using the Internet and vendor services or websites to identify potential best sellers before they are published. It requires placing orders for enough copies to deliver an acceptable ratio of holds to titles owned. It requires coordination among selectors, acquisitions, shipping, and cataloging departments to make sure that these high-demand titles are ordered, unpacked, processed, and delivered to the public service departments by street date. It means that public service librarians must keep up with deliveries and check in and shelve titles quickly, or all the effort from the behind-the-scenes departments will be for naught. Holds cannot be filled expeditiously if cataloging records for titles are not available in the library's database far in advance of publication. Once copies are linked with a hold, patrons must be contacted quickly so that popular titles do not sit unnecessarily on hold shelves. And ensuring that books are not sitting in delivery bins or boxes is another part of the equation.

Techniques and Issues for Selectors

Many readers are interested in reading the newest titles they see on various best-seller lists and on bookstore shelves. Librarians who aspire to have high-demand titles on their library shelves by their specified lay-down dates can no longer rely on old techniques. Instead, here are some ways to get ahead of the curve. First, use vendor websites like Baker and Taylor's Title Source III, Brodart's Bibz, BWI's Title Tales, Midwest Tape's website for DVDs and music, or Ingram's iPage to get access to their lists of forthcoming hot titles. Another option is to use vendor websites to do powerful searches, such as for hardcover adult fiction titles with a print run of more than 100,000 that will be published in the next six months. Set up automatic ordering of books by the most popular authors (and don't forget to add them to the catalog so patrons can place holds). Check sources such as PrePub Alert and Buzz Girl from the *Library Journal* and On-Sale Calendar from *Publishers Weekly*.

Another method for anticipating demand is to subscribe to niche magazines for genres. These include titles like *Locus* for science fiction, *Romantic Times* for romance, and *Mystery Scene* for crime. There are many other sources available, including *Historical Novel Review, Books and*

Culture: A Christian Review, Fantasy and Science Fiction, Multicultural Book Review, Black Issues Book Review, and *Bookmarks.* Selectors should not forget the thousands of websites and 'zines fans read as well. Traditionally it has been difficult to keep up with genre fiction because the mainstream media did not do a good job of covering it. Things have improved, but don't forget such useful online sites as Overbooked, Powell's Books, the Sci Fi Channel, the Horror Writers Association, International Thriller Writers Organization, Nancy Pearl's Picks, Mostly Fiction, and online bookseller sites. There are literally hundreds of useful sites, many of which have been listed in Cindy Orr's *RA Bookmarks* on IKeepBookmarks.com.[18]

Information overload is a real problem for selectors, and subscribing to e-mail newsletters and a blog aggregator such as Bloglines is essential to scan for book news quickly. Blogs such as *GalleyCat* (www.mediabistro .com/galleycat/), *Maud Newton* (http://maudnewton.com/blog/index .php), *Reader's Advisor Online Blog* (www.readersadvisoronline.com/ blog/), and *Nonfiction Anonymous* (www.nonanon.com) can be invaluable for keeping up with the world of books. Several of these, including the *Reader's Advisor Online Blog* and *Maud Newton,* do a weekly "roundup" of news, which makes it much faster to stay current on book news.

Selectors should place themselves in the shoes of their patrons as much as possible, and another way to make sure all the bases are covered is to monitor local news and media outlets—preferably before publication. It may be possible to convince the local newspaper's book review editor to alert the library about titles to be reviewed, or to get an author interview schedule from local radio or television stations. In addition to this, there are organs that specialize in listing which books will be discussed in the media. These include *The Get-Ready Sheet,* published by the Mid-York Library System, and *MOTOR: Mentioned on TV or Radio*—both available by subscription—and free websites such as the *Books on TV* section of the *Orlando Sentinel* newspaper, BookTV.org, and Fresh Fiction's *Media Spotlight.*

In addition to anticipating demand, selectors must also be prepared to respond to demand. Again, technology is an essential tool. Most ILSs can deliver information on circulation, number of holds, and number of copies owned. Designing reports that give selectors essential information at a glance is well worth the cost. One example is a purchase alert report that automatically counts the number of copies of a title owned and the number of holds on that title, then calculates the holds-to-copies ratio and ranks titles in descending order of ratio. With this information, a selector can immediately see titles that need additional copies—a very quick way to monitor demand. Another useful report shows titles with holds that have been received but not yet cataloged. This report can be used by catalog departments to move in-demand books to the head of the line for processing.

Most public libraries work hard to anticipate demand, but what about "sleepers" or unanticipated best sellers? In the old days, the only option was to make a quick run to the local bookstore to buy some extra copies, then rush them through processing—and this is still a good backup plan. But here is where knowing your suppliers can be invaluable. Some vendors are good at delivering hard-to-find titles; others have large warehouses and can deliver books in only a day or two if they are ordered electronically. Speed and efficiency are even more important when a title creates unexpected demand.

Many libraries in the old days had a patron suggestion form that allowed users to request a library to purchase a title. Placing this form online and making sure completed forms are sent to selectors immediately can give a fantastic view of what patrons wish the library owned.

As mentioned before, making sure that readers have a good experience at the library is truly a team sport, and selectors should not forget to purchase the readers' advisory tools that public service staff and they themselves need. These include monographs and reference works commonly used by readers' advisors, electronic products that help the readers' advisor and the public, and magazines, including those used most often by fans of particular genres.

Selectors can keep abreast of essential tools for readers' advisory service staff by reading reviews of library tools in *Library Journal, American Libraries,* or *Public Libraries* and by checking catalogs of major library publishers, especially Libraries Unlimited and the American Library Association.

Maintaining the Collection

Selecting and delivering new titles is only part of the picture. The appearance of books is important. Savvy selectors make sure that perpetually popular titles are replaced so that readers who may be new to the title don't have to take a shabby or dirty copy. Covers are important, and librarians should be aware that great covers can make a book. Sometimes mediocre reviews can be outweighed by a beautiful or enticing cover. This means that books sent to be repaired should have their jackets preserved.

Selectors must be aware of needed replacements. Again, library ILS reports can help with this. A report of the most circulated titles can target volumes that may need replacement. Often replacement and duplication of earlier titles in a series needs to be considered when a new title is issued. So, for example, when *Harry Potter and the Deathly Hallows* was announced, many selectors reviewed earlier titles in the series to make sure they had enough stock to meet demand. A variation on this theme is that sometimes an author becomes known for the third or fourth book in a series. When this happens, selectors should be prepared to purchase the earlier books in the series so that readers can start reading at the beginning.

A release in a new format can trigger demand. Many people reread the *Lord of the Rings* books in anticipation of the movies. It is important to be aware of upcoming releases of movies made from books in order to review current stocks for potential replacements or the need for extra copies. One way to do this is to keep up with the blog *Romancing the Tome* (www.romancingthetome.blogspot.com), which is all about literary adaptations.

Another issue to consider is out-of-print but in-demand titles. *Roots*, the classic title by Alex Haley, was out of print for many years until being reissued in 2007. Selectors should be ready to snap up titles like this when they become available. Purchasing used copies may be necessary in the meantime. And then there are new formats for old but still popular titles. For many years it was impossible to get replacement copies of the audio version of *To Kill a Mockingbird*. Subscribing to the discussion group Fiction_L and watching blogs and newsletters is one way to keep up with issues like this.

Weeding: The Other End of the Selection Cycle

In her book *The Responsive Public Library Collection,* Sharon Baker makes the point that many readers love to browse, and it is essential to their selection of new titles. The arrangement of titles and the importance of displays is covered in chapter 10, but another issue arises when library shelves are too full. Browsers want to find a good book to read, but when the library shelves are jammed too full and books become hard to access, it becomes difficult for them to find something they want. This brings us to the necessity of weeding. And even if shelves are not overflowing, weeding is necessary to remove books with outdated information and to maintain balance in the collection.

Weeding used to be a labor-intensive job. Librarians would take standard catalogs of recommended titles and head to the shelves. Each title would be laboriously checked to see if it was in sources such as the *Public*

Library Catalog or the *Fiction Catalog,* and then a decision would be made only after physically checking the book to see when it last circulated. Slote (see above) found the best predictor of whether a book will ever circulate again to be whether it had been checked out in the previous year. How do you know which books fit this criterion? Here is where your ILS can be a huge time-saver and make weeding a more efficient and less painful process. For instance, a weeder can ask for a report that excludes titles added in the past year but includes titles that have not been checked out in a certain period of time. This yields candidates for weeding and greatly speeds up the process. Work with the ILS system to test the report before printing to make sure that the list of candidates to be checked for possible weeding is not too long. Ask for a report that shows titles that have not been checked out in five years. Is this list too short? Try three years.

Weeding is enjoyable for some librarians but can be an overwhelming and stressful burden for others—especially those in understaffed and busy public service areas. One successful approach is to schedule the job for a particular period and carefully plan for a "blitz." Schedule as many staff as possible; make sure to have help that can withdraw, mark, and pack up discards; and stock up on needed supplies such as boxes, book trucks, and anything else that is necessary. Read and put the shelves in order before the day of the project. Ask for volunteers and make it fun by eating lunch together. Divide up the ILS report into sections for each weeder and ask them to record missing items. Some titles have not circulated because they are missing. These should be updated in the catalog after the project.

One issue to consider when weeding fiction is highlighted by research that shows that nearly half of readers choose their next title on the basis of familiarity with the author. When readers find an author they enjoy, they typically look for other books by that author.

Many patrons absolutely hate the idea of libraries discarding books, so it is vital to be discreet. Boxing books and withdrawing them are procedures best done behind the scenes if at all possible, and it is always a good idea to try to find a good home for the books. One possibility is Better World Books (www.betterworldbooks.com), whose mission is to prevent books from being discarded in landfills and which uses its income from sales to promote literacy.

Keeping Up with New Trends and Developing Innovative Methods

Libraries are constantly changing, and the pace of change is accelerating. It is imperative to try new methods in order to continue to improve and keep up with demand. In this section I discuss "floating collections," "browsing collections," and two recent projects under study at the Cleveland Public Library (CPL), where I previously worked as collection manager.

Items in a floating collection "float" to where there is demand and stay in the branch where they are returned rather than the branch that originally purchased them. This approach is interesting in that it lets patron demand determine where titles are ultimately shelved. Positive aspects of floating collections include the saving in transportation costs, increased turnover rates thanks to saved delivery times, decreased processing costs because titles are selected for only one agency, and the elimination of the need for location stamps or stickers. Some negatives are that staff may not know their collections as intimately and that it is possible for a patron to take out all the items in the system on a particular subject and then return them all to one location. Some staff members may feel a loss of pride in "their" collection.

Many libraries have instituted browsing collections, which are a few copies of titles likely to be in demand that are set not to accept holds. This guarantees that browsers who come into the library have a chance of finding current popular titles on the shelves rather than on a hold list. An obvious positive of this approach is that it satisfies browsers, and studies have shown that many library users prefer browsing. On the other hand, occasionally a patron who is waiting on a hold list will find the title on the shelf and be upset.

Since 2005, CPL has worked with vendors to develop detailed profiles for the vendor to use in providing lists of titles to be considered for addition to the collection. Bibliographic records for these titles are loaded into the library catalog weekly with the designation "Being Considered for Purchase." These titles are made available for patron holds. Reviewing the demand for these potential titles has greatly improved the chances of matching books with local patrons. And since CPL is a large system, it is also experimenting with automatic orders for titles that have at least one hold. Improved vendor technology makes detailed profiling realistic, and this approach can be tailored by each library. There are three primary advantages to this approach. Titles are added to the catalog within a week of the vendor learning about them—far earlier than in the past. Patrons can place holds on titles, and they often do within days if not hours. And considering titles on the basis of a profile makes librarians aware of titles that have not been reviewed. Costs associated with this approach are minimal, and since vendors tailor the profiles of titles per library criteria, there is really no downside to this approach.

CPL has also recently created a High Demand Department. As mentioned earlier, it does no good for selectors to identify high-demand titles if they are not received and delivered to the shelves in time for the readers' advisor to be able to give them to patrons when they ask for them. Selectors, using all of the techniques discussed above, identify titles likely to be popular or time sensitive and place them into separate electronic lists. The High Demand Department orders the titles from vendors who can deliver titles using EDI and 9xx ordering, two new technologies that allow for tremendous time (and paper) savings by permitting vendor websites to interact directly to the library ILS to place orders, assign distributions, and invoice electronically.

Working with vendors, the library makes sure that boxes shipped from these special accounts are marked by vendors in such a way that the shipping department can easily identify them as high demand and push them to the head of the line for processing. Since this department receives about two hundred boxes a day, this is an important part of the process. The goal of the technical services division is a forty-eight-hour turnaround for high-demand items, so the High Demand Department also receives and catalogs the items they order. They are able to achieve a quicker turnaround than the regular catalog department since by definition high-demand items are not rare and cataloging records are readily available. In addition, the 9xx ordering process automatically downloads a record when a title is ordered if there is not already one in the ILS. The 9xx procedure creates local order records including distribution of titles by branch, saving thousands of keystrokes for library staff.

Procedures such as these will continue to be developed as long as collection managers and selectors in libraries work diligently with vendors to improve their service continually. It is apparent that many of the newest breakthroughs in efficiency in selection and timely delivery of high-demand titles require close cooperation between departments. For this reason, I believe that it is important, even crucial, for collection development to be located in the technical services area of libraries so that department heads can work together to deal with the difficult technical and coordination issues to be faced. Teamwork, as we mentioned before, is vital.

Conclusion

As we have seen in other chapters of this book, readers' advisors use techniques, skills, and resources to match people with books and books with people. But to do this they must have the books on the shelves at the time they are working with the patron, and they must have the resources that support them in making these matches. This is where the collection development aspect comes in. This has always been true, but recent changes in technology and shrinking library budgets have increased the pressure to deliver books to the shelves ever faster and more efficiently. Selectors must work to anticipate demand and to meet lay-down dates by scanning their environment, understanding their patrons and their needs, and casting a wide net into the universe of books for candidates from which to choose those that fit their particular patrons.

To do this selectors use new, powerful technological tools, including those of vendors, to find and order books and get them cataloged, processed, and out to the shelves quickly and efficiently. They also respond to demand for titles missed, offer patrons a way to request titles, provide staff with electronic and print tools that help them do their job, and provide selectors with tools to help them as well. Collection development includes maintaining the collection, replacing, repairing, and weeding titles, again using the ILS and other tools and reports. They say it takes a village to raise a child. Well, it takes a team of library staff to deliver needed titles to the readers' advisors so that they can do their job of matching patrons to books and books to patrons.

NOTES

1. Nora Rawlinson, "Book Selection at the Baltimore County Public Library Aims to . . . Give 'Em What They Want!" *Library Journal* 106, no. 20 (1981): 2188–90.

2. John Berry, "Leaning toward Quality," *Library Journal* 104, no. 17 (1979): 2013.

3. Patricia Hamilton and Terry Weech, "The Development and Testing of an Instrument to Measure Attitudes toward the Quality versus Demand Debate in Collection Management," *Collection Management* 10 (1988): 27–42.

4. John Budd and Cynthia Wyatt, "'Do You Have Any Books on . . . ?': An Examination of Public Library Holdings," *Public Libraries* 41, no. 2 (2002): 107–12, quotes from 108, 109.

5. Renee J. Vaillancourt, "Weed It and Weep," *Public Libraries* 41, no. 6 (2002): 304–5.

6. Merle Jacob, "Weeding the Fiction Collection: Or Should I Dump Peyton Place?" *Reference and User Services Quarterly* 40, no. 3 (2001): 234–39, quotes from 236, 237.

7. Joseph P. Segal, *The CREW Manual: A Unified System of Weeding, Inventory, and Collection-Building for Small and Medium-Sized Public Libraries* (Chicago: American Library Association, 1979); Belinda Boon, *The CREW Method: Expanded Guidelines for Collection Evaluation and Weeding for Small and Medium-Sized Public Libraries,* rev. ed. (Austin: Texas State Library, 1995), ED 386 195.

8. Stanley J. Slote, *Weeding Library Collections: Library Weeding Methods,* 4th ed. (Englewood, Colo.: Libraries Unlimited, 1997).

9. Sharon L. Baker, *The Responsive Public Library Collection: How to Develop and Market It* (Englewood, Colo.: Libraries Unlimited, 1993); and Sharon L. Baker and Karen L. Wallace, *The Responsive Public Library: How to Develop and Market a Winning Collection,* 2nd ed. (Englewood, Colo.: Libraries Unlimited, 2002).

10. Baker and Wallace, *Responsive Public Library,* 5.

11. Ibid., 11.

12. Ibid., 16.

13. Ibid., 61.

14. Catherine Sheldrick Ross has also written on this in *Reading Matters,* which is reviewed extensively in chapter 2 of this book. Many of Baker's and Ross's findings agree, in part because they were drawing on some of the same sources for their conclusions.

15. Baker and Wallace, *Responsive Public Library,* 92.

16. Ibid., 121.

17. Ibid., 20.

18. IKeepBookmarks.com, *Cindy Orr's RA Bookmarks,* http://ww2.ikeepbookmarks.com/browse.asp?folder=1393282.

12

THE FUTURE OF READERS' ADVISORY

by Neil Hollands and Jessica E. Moyer

It has been nearly twenty years since Saricks and Brown published the first edition of *Readers' Advisory Service in the Public Library*. Two editions later we are still in the midst of a readers' advisory renaissance. As the chapters of this book show, both research about and practice of readers' advisory are more extensive and diverse than they ever have been. Readers' advisory courses are being taught at some of the best library and information science schools in North America.[1] Visit any national or state conference where public librarians are present, and you are likely to find several well-attended sessions on aspects of the practice of advisory. Books and electronic resources to support advisors and readers alike are widely available. Though the form in which people receive advice varies tremendously, access to some kind of intelligent suggestion about what one might read next is at an all-time high.

The long-term success of readers' advisory, however, remains in the balance. Despite advances, the extent and quality of service at any given library is inconsistent. Our steps forward have brought us to the proverbial crossroads. Down the darker path, we could let promotion of readers' advisory waver and dwindle into another fad or at best a surge of interest to be noted with curiosity by library historians of the future. In the other direction, we can continue to consolidate and build upon success, working toward a future when the ability to aid library users in finding works that entertain, educate, and otherwise benefit them will be the first emphasis, the cornerstone of the practice of librarianship.

Neil Hollands is a librarian at Williamsburg Regional Library in Virginia. His first book, Read On . . . Fantasy Fiction *was published in 2007. He is working on a handbook for science fiction and fantasy book groups, and he writes articles and presents at conferences regularly on his passions in librarianship, readers' advisory, and collection development.*

Comprehensive looks at the future of advisory are surprisingly rare. Much of our research has focused on fundamental questions: justifying the existence of this specialty, learning the basics about how readers think about books, and defining basic parameters of service. In practice, our energies have been devoted to getting readers' advisory service off the ground, developing basic tools to aid our practice, and recruiting more colleagues to participate in the process. We have been so engrossed in these fundamentals that few writers have found the time to look at where we have been and where we are going. It is a daunting yet exciting task to attempt a comprehensive look at the future of readers' advisory.

False History, False Future: A Response to Dilevko and Magowan

Readers' Advisory Service in North American Public Libraries, 1870–2005: A History and Critical Analysis, by Juris Dilevko and Candice F. C. Magowan, is ostensibly a history of readers' advisory service in public libraries, but from the book's first sentences it is apparent that "history" is molded to serve the authors' arguments about what readers' advisory service should be.[2] Dilevko and Magowan seek to revise the ways most readers' advisors look at the history of readers' advisory and in doing so lead a reactionary movement toward a future in which advisory is practiced as it was in the past, not as it is in the present. The authors have strong opinions, but ultimately their conclusions are wrongheaded. Because this is both one of the newest works on readers' advisory and the only full-length "history" of the field, there is good reason to address it in some depth. In examining and responding to the strong opinions put forth by Dilevko and Magowan, we can clarify the philosophical bedrock underlying contemporary readers' advisory service, the foundation upon which we can build goals for future practice.

Dilevko and Magowan's central thesis is that contemporary literature has become commodified, concerned only with the profitability of books and their use to cross-promote other products. They believe that beginning in the late 1960s, under the influence of the "Give 'Em What They Want" movement, readers' advisory in public libraries was steadily co-opted by corporate culture. Readers' advisors, they argue, have devolved into little more than marketers (perhaps knowingly, perhaps not) for dumbed-down, narcissistic literature to the detriment of readership for classics and serious nonfiction. Even worse, they claim, our emphasis on appeal factors, technological tools like the *NoveList* database, and categorized book lists is leading to "McProfiling," a de-skilling of the profession that will ultimately lead to our replacement by machines and paraprofessionals.

Let's look a little closer at Dilevko and Magowan's "history" of readers' advisory. The best chapters of their book concern readers' advisory up to 1962. This history will remind thoughtful practitioners that many interesting approaches to advisory have historical progenitors that deserve exploration. If the authors had stopped here and drawn reasonable conclusions—that educational and therapeutic aspects of readers' advisory deserve renewed attention; that systematic reading courses supporting self-education in practical topics might be a good addition to promotion of popular materials; that advisors might find inspiration in historical ideas, such as the belief that every librarian should be a capable readers' advisor—this would be a valuable book for practitioners.

But Dilevko and Magowan have an ideological ax to grind. In grinding it, they make claims that go beyond the boundaries of any evidence. Rhetoric used to promote adult education programs in the early twentieth century is taken as proof of their superiority to modern approaches, but there is little evaluation of how well these programs met educational goals or were received by readers. One cannot help but notice that almost all of these programs were confined to the largest U.S. cities, where some budgets might once have supported full research libraries and staffs may, historically, have been large enough to maintain subject experts.

On this basis, Dilevko and Magowan propose that readers' advisory be remodeled in the fashion of what they consider its glory days, 1917–1962, an era they believe was committed to systematic adult education. In that era, they hold, readers' advisors were subject experts who could separate literary wheat from chaff and design systematic reading courses in subjects that would help undereducated adults "get somewhere." The authors seem to have no argument with early library practices that actively discouraged popular fiction reading.

In their analysis of contemporary readers' advisory, Dilevko and Magowan present egregious examples of abusive practices in contemporary publishing and marketing, then generalize these extremes to larger classes. Because examples of ridiculous cross-media promotion exist, they argue that all contemporary literature is commodified. Because some bookstores and online sellers sell product placements, all best sellers are found fraudulent. Because there are some questionable or overly specialized literary awards, all award-winning books are condemned. And because a few genre books are produced according to publisher rules and templates, all genre fiction is defined as stereotypical. On page after page, "genre titles, bestsellers, celebrity-authored books, and prize-winning titles" are lumped together for condemnation, as if these books were all of one ilk. These extremist positions show a lack of education about contemporary literature. It seems to us that Dilevko and Magowan could use a long talk with a good advisor who could help them discover the many contemporary best sellers, award winners, and genre titles with literary heft.

But therein lies the problem: Dilevko and Magowan wouldn't consult a readers' advisor. Time and again in their analysis, they hold the judgment and interpretive skills of contemporary public librarians *and* readers in contempt. According to them, we make a Pavlovian response to every marketing ploy, drooling on command when confronted with a mass-marketed book. Any attempt by readers to pursue their own agendas is dismissed as narcissistic self-satisfaction driven by unseen commercial forces. This elitism is ultimately self-defeating; one cannot build the future of a public service on a foundation of contempt for the public. Unfortunately, the authors exhibit little knowledge of current public library practice. Worse, they appear not to have talked to the advisors whom they vilify. As a result, they misrepresent those librarians' working methods.

Contemporary readers' advisory, according to Dilevko and Magowan, is dominated by two forces: an extreme version of "Give 'Em What They Want" populism promoted by Charlie Robinson at Baltimore County Public Library that de-skills the profession through knee-jerk promotion of popular culture; and an overreliance on lists and weak technical tools, which they claim leads to the "McProfiling" of readers through the fragmenting prism of appeal factors. Each of these claims deserves a response, for each has a place in current practice and will likely play a role in the future of readers' advisory.

GIVE 'EM WHAT THEY WANT BUT LISTEN TO 'EM FIRST

Though it is true that modern readers' advisory does try to give readers what they want, characterizing contemporary readers' advisory as an extension of Charlie Robinson's classics-bashing, ultra-populist philosophy is wrong. If the authors had talked to more practicing readers' advisors, they would have found that we serve readers with many goals. Good advisors give readers what they want not by buying more copies of the best sellers, as Robinson might have done, nor by forcing a great book on them, as Dilevko and Magowan would do, but by listening to how they describe their reading experiences and desires and then finding a mix of books that is likely to meet those needs. This mix could easily include classics and great books, side by side with best sellers, award winners, and genre titles, since all might appeal to a reader. Where we differ most significantly with the authors is in our insistence that readers should not apologize for their tastes. We disagree most vehemently with the outdated (and rude) practice of shaming people for what they enjoy. We trust readers to know when a book has served a purpose for them. We can suggest new choices without defaming or shunting aside the books that first drew them to reading.

Sometimes, buried deep beneath the wild generalizations, Dilevko and Magowan make some interesting points. Although characterizing all of contemporary readers' advisory as an extension of publisher marketing is wrong, there may be a grain of truth to this assessment. In our general enthusiasm for reading, advisors may become caught up in promoting books that we know have limited charms but will circulate easily. Some books are advertised more than enough without the advisory community adding to their readership. Without violating our tenets of matching book to reader, we can still seek out the best books within all genres at all levels of difficulty and all measures of appeal.

But to characterize readers' advisory librarians on the whole as purveyors of commodified mediocrity is false. We seek out and promote excellent titles, both new and old. We work hard to find audiences for the "long tail" of lesser-known authors and older books that fill the shelves of our buildings. We campaign tirelessly for the excellent low- and midlist authors our readers enjoy upon discovery. The advisors we know certainly demonstrate more awareness of excellent books than Dilevko and Magowan, who in two hundred pages don't have a single kind word for a living fiction author.

DEALING WITH THE READER AS A WHOLE: THE USE OF APPEAL FACTORS

Dilevko and Magowan's next targets are the lists, books, and databases used by readers' advisors. They believe that the categorization of books within these tools fragments the reading public into ever-diminishing subgenres that become target audiences for publishers. Further, they characterize the development of appeal factor theory by Joyce Saricks and others as part of this attempt to mechanically pigeonhole readers. *Any* attempt by advisors to make the practice of finding books easier or more efficient is considered evidence for their characterization of contemporary readers' advisory as a mindless, automated process. They strongly imply that our final goal is the elimination of human librarians altogether.

Again, there are glimmers of truth in this position. There is a potential for librarians to become too engrossed in subdividing books into categories, to collect books into lists just because we can. Although limits on our resources do require that we seek efficiency in providing readers' advisory, readers' advisory should not be reduced to a simple process of pigeonholing readers into categories. Admittedly our tools are works in progress—a mix of high quality and missed potential. But, again, Dilevko and Magowan's characterization of readers' advisory practice is incorrect on the whole. They misunderstand the way appeal factors are used. The language of appeal, when used correctly, attempts to describe the complex totality of a given reader's preferences, to inventory that reader's values, not reduce them to a single category. The goal is not to provide only books that exactly match every single preference but to make sure that the collection of books we suggest to the reader on the whole addresses their interests and needs. A good advisor can use the language of appeal to help the reader understand his or her reading history and how the suggested books match, and sometimes subtly vary from, those preferences.

When the authors turn to case studies of contemporary readers' advisory tools, they again resort to an unfair reductive characterization of advisory service. In their study of *NoveList*, they asked students to use simple keyword searches to generate read-alikes for their favorite novels. After trying one of these novels, the students critiqued the service. The process used for the case study failed to include more complex kinds of searching that are possible with the database and in particular ignored all of the value-added content that *NoveList* contributors have written. Nancy Pearl's *Book Lust* is given similar treatment, its brief, entertainment-focused reading lists subjected to a scholarly critique that is not appropriate for the format or the stated intentions of the book.

More important, both of these case studies lack an important component of advisory: the advisor. A good advisor would use these tools with the reader to help generate ideas, then follow up with further analysis of what appeals to the reader to narrow (and sometimes broaden) the list of future reading possibilities. Dilevko and Magowan might remind us that too many shortcuts result in shoddy service, but their case studies are ultimately tantamount to snacking only on raw ingredients from a chef's kitchen and then complaining about the quality of the cuisine.

Dilevko and Magowan's alternatives to advisory based on appeal factors are generic and impractical. Referring vaguely to "historical resonance" and the "rich and complex totality" of great books, they would offer nothing to readers but the admonition that they take the classics department's word on what is great literature. Their dismissal of appeal factor analysis as nothing more than an efficiency measure begs the question of how they would evaluate works of fiction. Apparently, great works of literature emerge from writers like Athena from the forehead of Zeus. Dilevko and Magowan complain about the de-skilling of librarianship, but they would leave librarians with little to do but pass out a short list of great books to bewildered patrons.

PUTTING THE PAST TO REST

In the end, the lack of reading and readers' advisory research in Dilevko and Magowan's book is telling. The authors don't have a coherent story about how the reading of great books they espouse will create the ends they desire. They quote the research of Catherine Sheldrick Ross but don't seem to understand its significance. Ross identifies many needs served by many kinds of books, including finding "models for identity," "new perspectives and enlargement of possibilities," "confirmation of self-worth," "connection with others and awareness of not being alone," "courage to make change," and better "understanding of the world."[3] To this list of reading benefits and goals we can add the social value of reading books that others have read, the education derived from information woven deftly into entertaining fiction and nonfiction narratives, the challenge of reading books that enhance our vocabularies and our ability to decipher complex ideas, and the needed diversion sometimes provided by light reading.[4] Helping readers in all of these pursuits is the philosophical underpinning of exemplary contemporary readers' advisory. By finding books that fulfill these varying needs, readers' advisors can create the kind of moral education the authors advocate, but without limiting readers to the great classics that will never meet all the needs of all readers. One wonders what a devoted mystery reader like Jacques Barzun or science fiction fan like Isaac Asimov would say if Dilevko told them that genre fiction was ruining their potential.

Dilevko and Magowan believe that Bernard Berelson's 1949 suggestions would make a good guide for libraries. Berelson believed we could measure library success in terms of "social, political, and psychological processes" such as the "promotion of group understanding, the clarification of the goals and values of the society, the encouragement of interest in politics, [and] the development of greater rationality in political decisions."[5] Ross's enumeration of the values of reading provides a clearer path to these goals than anything suggested by Dilevko and Magowan.

When readers find confirmation of self-worth through romances, they enhance their psyches and become more able to participate in the social world. When they get new perspectives from Alexander McCall-Smith's optimistic detective Precious Ramotswe, Michael Connolly's tough guy Harry Bosch, or the clever historical heroes of Dorothy Dunnett, they incorporate or reject the author's and character's philosophies, thus clarifying what they believe should be appropriate goals for society. Through consideration of hypothetical worlds such as found in George R. R. Martin's fantasies or Lois McMaster Bujold's Vorkosigan Saga, they better understand the real world and become more interested in politics and making intelligent political decisions. And yes, if readers want to pursue these same goals through classics instead of genre fiction, contemporary readers' advisory can accommodate that as well.

Finally, Magowan and Dilevko's claim that contemporary readers' advisory practice somehow de-skills librarianship is true only if we cannot identify worthwhile, challenging goals that need to be addressed for continuing improvement of readers' advisory. When we start from our shared values of service, inclusiveness, respect for the interests and needs of all library users, and advocacy of good reading, then a set of ongoing challenges for professional readers' advisors becomes abundantly clear. We have much work to do, but contemporary readers' advisory is on the right track. Instead of retreating to the methods of the distant past, we should continue evolving high-quality services.

A Better Future for Readers' Advisory

Among working librarians, the philosophical backing for readers' advisory—service, inclusiveness of all materials, respect for all users, and advocacy—has a strong consensus. Basic service methods to use when approached by a reader, though still inconsistently implemented, are also a point of agreement. Beyond these fundamentals, however, much remains to be defined in the practice of readers' advisory. As we look to the future, we need better definition of the components of our service and the appeal factors we have placed at the core of its practice. We must continue to promote readers' advisory, both within the ranks of practicing professionals and outwardly, making sure the public is aware of the service. We must expand our reach, finding ways to deliver the service to all potential audiences and provide guidance for all the materials in our collections, not just some of them. We must integrate readers' advisory with other practices, using what we know to inform every aspect of librarianship. We must share the readers' advisory load between libraries, making gains in efficiency by minimizing redundant work and extending the availability of readers' advisory to users in even the smallest of communities. We must become better at documenting the results of service and maintaining ongoing relationships with the individuals whom we serve. There's no shortage of exciting work in our future.

DEFINING OURSELVES, OUR TERMS, OUR AUDIENCE

Better definition of the scope, terminology, and audience of readers' advisory is fundamental to its progress as a discipline. To begin, we need a consistently inclusive definition of the boundaries of advisory. All seem to agree that, when a reader approaches a librarian for advice, readers' advisory is being practiced, but this is only one of the ways librarians make suggestions to readers. Other methods—book lists, themed displays, reading groups, online materials, and supplements to the OPAC, to name a few—are just as important in connecting books with appropriate readers but often receive less emphasis when we discuss methods of practice. Often mislabeled as "passive" readers' advisory, these other means are the most proactive methods of reaching out to the bulk of library users who do not approach service desks.

In addition, if there is one point to be drawn from Dilevko and Magowan's history, it is that contemporary readers' advisory has tended to focus on entertainment and social aspects of reading, at times emphasizing these aspects at the expense of educational and informational goals. The educational function has often been ceded entirely to reference services, but when help is needed to locate materials that can best serve the variety of educational needs—everything from self-guided academic study to bibliotherapy—the roles of readers' advisor and reference librarian should merge to become one.

As practice in the field expands to include audiobooks, films, music, and other formats and materials collected by libraries, even the term "readers'" advisory is too limiting. Since staffing, fiscal resources, and time devoted to readers' advisory are still controversial in many libraries, it behooves us to lay claim to the full scope of activities that advisors perform in our definition of the service. A broad definition of advisory also will make it easier for us to lobby for its inclusion as a basic part of library school education.

When the full scope of advisory activities undertaken by a library is appreciated, and when one remembers that the first mission still most associated with libraries by the public is access to books and other materials, it becomes easy to make the case that advisory is *the* most fundamental of library services.[6] As readers' advisors look to the future, we would be well served to take the advice of Edward F. Stevens, librarian at the Pratt Institute Free Library, who advocated back in 1934 that every member of the staff have the skills to serve as a readers' advisor. Although varied levels of immersion in advisory are possible for different staff members, advisory skills are central to a library's mission. It is a worthwhile goal, then, that every staff member, particularly professionals working at service desks, understand the general practice of readers' advisory and be encouraged to build up depth of knowledge in at least one genre or content area.

In addition to defining the range of advisory methods, we also need to better define our terms. Appeal factors—the many elements that lead readers to choose the books they do—are crucial to readers' advisory practice. As we fine-tune our ability to help readers discern between one book and another, our understanding of appeal factors, both individually and in combination, must become increasingly sophisticated. But, as Neal Wyatt pointed out in a recent *Library Journal* article, we have yet to agree on a common set of basic factors.[7] We use terms like "pacing," "story," "setting," "frame," "style," "language," and "mood" in loose ways, with definitions varying vastly from one advisor to another. In much the same way that it is difficult for readers to articulate the reasons why they prefer the books they do, advisors find it difficult to communicate with each other.

Definitions within our vocabulary of appeal need to become more exact, and broad categories of appeal must be broken down into component parts. There will always be an art to finding the best reading suggestions for any particular reader, but we could use more science in our approach. A more exact vocabulary will pave the way for better communication between professionals and open the door to classification systems that go beyond content-focused subject headings.

Consider, as just one example, the appeal factor of pacing. We are quick to say that a book is "fast paced," but what exactly do we mean? We may mean it has short chapters, brief sentences and paragraphs, or fewer words printed on a page. We could be referring to vocabulary that isn't difficult. We could be saying that the author sticks to linear plotting or that a limited number of subplots makes the book easy to follow. Or perhaps we are referring to a style that avoids digression, or eschews long descriptive passages, or is heavily plot driven. A book with lots of dialogue reads more quickly, as does a book that makes heavy use of action or suspense elements. Series books with elements repeated from earlier entries are fast paced, as are other books that take a familiar, as opposed to atypical, approach to their genre. Point of view affects pacing: multiple narrators, introspective narrators, or unreliable narrators slow the reader down, whereas third-person or omniscient narration that sticks to a central plot speeds the book up. The clarity of the book's intended meaning also affects pacing.

The point is that all of these elements contribute to the pacing of a book. Some may appeal to a particular reader who wants a "fast-paced" book; others may not. When we define the component parts of pacing, it becomes easier to say whether a book will please a given reader. Pacing is one of the easier appeal factors to define; concepts like tone, style, and story are even more difficult to unpack. To meet reader needs, we have plenty of work ahead as we strive to define and use these terms effectively.

In addition to defining our roles and our terms, we must also work to define our audiences. Although it will always be important to treat each readers' advisory "customer" as an individual, we could also benefit by thinking about our audience collectively. Certain classes of readers (e.g., the inexperienced reader, the young reader, or the reader with limited energy for or access to browsing) might need basic advisory service more than others. Conversely, some groups (heavy readers or those who focus on a particular content area or genre) may prefer more emphasis on a different set of services (finer points of distinction within a genre, more focus on lesser-known authors, support of interactive opportunities like book groups). We also lack aggregate data on which appeal factors and genres matter to the largest number of readers. Such data might help us decide where to focus limited time and resources.

CONTINUING EDUCATION WITHIN AND WITHOUT THE PROFESSION

The work of promoting readers' advisory is nowhere near complete, either within the profession or without to the public. If, as we have argued, basic facility with readers' advisory should be a prerequisite skill for any librarian, then it follows that education in this skill should be a standard part of library education. Although the number of readers' advisory courses in library schools is slowly rising, these courses are usually not mandatory and their scope is limited. Those who wish to specialize in readers' advisory typically have only one or two related courses available to them, while specialists in areas such as technology, reference, or administration can often choose from a full range of course work.

Within our libraries, we must identify the ways every staff member can contribute to advisory. Shelvers can give more priority to keeping displays filled and placing some books face out. At the circulation desk, staff should have resources such as book lists at hand and be trained to listen for comments that indicate a need for attention from an advisory expert. Reference librarians can look for advisory opportunities when dealing with information seekers that go beyond the immediate answer to a question. Catalogers can look for ways to promote advisory through the OPAC or through the organization of the collection. These are just some examples of how advisory is a task for the whole library, not just a minor task to be shunted off on specialists.

We have also done a poor job of educating the public about the availability of readers' advisory as a service. A shortage of funds, space, and staff make it rare for a library to offer a separate service desk for advisory, and in an age of diminishing demand for reference service, the wisdom of separating advisory from reference may be questionable. Even the placement of such a desk is controversial, since it may signify to readers that advisory is confined to fiction (or whatever collection the desk is near). But combining advisory with reference at one service point exacerbates an ongoing dilemma: many readers don't know that their vague questions about what to read next are legitimate and welcomed at a help desk.

In response, we must do a better job of inviting the readers' advisory discussion. In an age of competition from other providers of books, from both megastores and online sellers, libraries should seek to differentiate themselves by marketing a strength: our ability to better advise and inform the reader. Some of this can be done by simply relabeling service points and department names from "Reference" or "Adult Services" to "Reference and Readers' Advisory." Instead of emphasizing that libraries have books or that reading is good, promotional campaigns and internal signs should promote our ability to help people choose between the vast numbers of books and other leisure materials now available.

We can demonstrate this ability to help people find books by giving prominent space to displays. These should rotate regularly to show knowledge of and respect for a variety of genres, nonfiction, classics, and mainstream fiction. We should highlight availability of readers' advisory resources like book lists and bookmarks and add new resources regularly, both physically and on the library website. These should promote our understanding of appeal factor concepts, categorizing books by more than traditional methods like genre or subject matter, also including collections of materials that share a common approach to characterization, pacing, language, style, or mood. We should show that our knowledge extends beyond heavily publicized books and authors to include older titles, mid-list authors, and less-marketed new authors. A bookmark, website, newsletter article, or handout can list simple steps on how to find the best books. All of these methods can help readers' advisory increase its presence to library users.

CHANGING THE WAY WE DESCRIBE BOOKS

The best readers' advisors work endlessly to keep up with even a portion of the books and authors available to readers. Sometimes it feels like standing under Niagara Falls with a teacup: at best one gets an occasional sip while the torrent plummets down on top of one's head. No matter how voraciously one reads, one can't serve every reader without relying heavily on secondary resources.

The good news is that the quantity and quality of resources that help us learn about books and writers continue to improve rapidly. New websites, readers' advisory books, and other tools appear every month. But for the average advisor to keep up, and to have full confidence in suggestions about books they haven't personally read, our information sources need to get even better.

We can start with book reviews. The readers' advisory community can wield a great deal of power in this regard because we also form the primary core of readers and contributors to major review journals. There are still many reviews published that focus heavily on plot and too little on other appeal factors. In some reviews, even the genre of the book does not appear. Comparisons to similar authors are lacking. Series information is frequently left out. Information about pacing, difficulty, characterization, language, tone, and style are also incomplete. Review writers should identify specific kinds of readers who might be interested in the book and warn us about levels of language, sexuality, politics, religion, and violence that may offend, or conversely attract, certain readers.

We must continue to add detail to our shared discussion of books and keep on with the work of collecting lists of books that share common traits. Whether we create these lists on our own or through forums like the Fiction_L mailing list, online sharing has been crucial to the growth of readers' advisory. So have other collective tools like the list of book lists maintained by Molly Williams (http://librarybooklists.org) and the Overbooked website maintained by Ann Chambers Theis (www.overbooked .org). Blogs such as Williamsburg Regional Library's *Blogging for a Good Book* (http://bfgb.wordpress.com) or those of Ann Arbor District Library (www.aadl.org) have also proved very useful. More sites like these will always be welcome, especially those that encourage the collaboration of advisors at many libraries. Too often our work is done in isolation. Collaboration can create economies of scale, achieving results that are not possible with the resources of individual libraries.

We should also consider the nature of the lists and advisory books we create. Sometimes we fail to "practice what we preach." Many of our books and lists lack adequate annotations. When included, they often suffer from the same shortfalls that limit the usefulness of reviews. Recent readers' advisory books have shown improvement, becoming more readable in their own right, considering a wider arrange of appeal factors (instead of just a few subgenres), and suggesting more connections between books. Expansion of these trends will make our tools much more useful.

The online databases used by the readers' advisory community are also a work in progress. EBSCO's *NoveList*, Gale's *What Do I Read Next?* Bowker's *Fiction Connection*, and Greenwood's *Reader's Advisor Online* should be complimented for continuing to add features and expand coverage. Commercial booksellers like Amazon.com, BookSense, Barnes and Noble, Powell's, and Fantastic Fiction also continue to explore new ways of looking for books. Databases, however, are always limited by the quantity and quality of detail they contain. In the case of book databases, this means the number and kind of information fields included. Title, author, publisher, ISBN number, page count, and the text of a few reviews are standard in book databases. Most also contain a few basic genre and subject tags. In just a few cases, character names, character types, series information, and settings are available.

Unfortunately, that's where the coverage of most databases ends. This allows only a few substantive connections to be made. Given a favorite title, a database might be able to pull up other books of the same genre, with similar characters, or in common settings. Even these connections, however, are limited. Subgenres are rarely identified and even when present are not applied consistently. Connections regarding other appeal factors, those that create the *feel* of a book—pacing, mood, language, and tone—remain missing entirely. We also have few indications of the quality of a given book, not the critic's kind of absolute judgment but more subjective judgments of the success of books as compared to books of a similar style or their appeal to a particular reading audience.

Expanding databases to include this information will be difficult. Only a careful reader can identify such appeal factors, and even then labeling and categorizing carry a high degree of subjectivity. To attach this kind of information to books, we must develop new measurements—tonal scales that can capture subtle variations and controlled vocabularies that describe noncontent appeal factors. We need large numbers of readers able to apply such measurements consistently; a few paid reviewers could not hope to keep up with publishing volume at this level of detail.

Wiki technologies that allow creation of social taxonomies, such as LibraryThing (www.librarything.com), have great promise in this regard. To improve the quality of our databases, it seems likely that we must find means such as this that allow multiple contributors to work together to build the profile of an individual book. Only a large number of contributors can hope to make such information available for all books. There are great challenges ahead in combining the mass productivity of social taxonomies with the precision of more carefully controlled databases, but the potential benefits are enormous. With enough information contributed to databases by advisory professionals, it becomes thinkable that high-quality readers' advisory could become an automated process, nothing less than the application of an artificial intelligence that understands the full scope of the enormous topic of literature.

SPECIAL DELIVERY: TAKING THE SERVICE TO ITS AUDIENCES

Another frontier for the future is the targeted delivery of services to readers. The basic model for readers' advisory service traditionally begins when a patron approaches a librarian and asks for help in choosing a new book. Proactive advisors have expanded that model by finding nonintrusive ways of approaching browsers in the stacks. Resource collections, book lists, and displays have been used to reach out to readers reluctant to engage with librarians. This makes a fine starting point for readers' advisory service, but new models and methods are proliferating, and still more creative approaches would be welcome.

One promising approach to readers' advisory, pioneered by Williamsburg Regional Library in Virginia and Lincoln City Libraries in Nebraska, is the use of reader profile forms, both on paper and online, to collect a full inventory of a reader's history and preferences. This approach obtains more information than can be gained in an interview or conversation and is less obtrusive to the patron, but it allows the advisor to work asynchronously with full access to resources in developing a thoughtful list of suggestions. Though some readers like to engage with a librarian, many prefer this more anonymous approach. An important side benefit is the full documentation of the readers' advisory transaction gained by using the forms.

The nature of many readers' advisory encounters—discussions held briefly in the stacks—makes documentation of advisory difficult. Advisors know when they have helped a reader find a desirable book, but such successes are fleeting and difficult to share with others. Since much of readers' advisory originates in reference or adult service departments and the boundary between advisory and other questions taken at these desks is subjective, even keeping a simple count of advisory questions is not easy. As a result, most documentation of the benefits of readers' advisory is anecdotal, and even these anecdotal examples have not been collected or summarized.

This lack of documentation is problematic. In the internal competition for positions, funds, space, and time resources, it can be difficult to make an evidenced case for readers' advisory. It also makes it difficult for librarians to maintain a relationship with a reader over time or to share the work of supporting a reader. Only the librarian who originally helps a reader can remember what information was exchanged, and even these memories are likely to be spotty.

The use of reader profile forms that are then kept on file (with patron consent) is a good start toward solving the documentation problem. The profiles can be filled out by the patrons or used by the librarian when conducting an advisory consultation. If use of these forms is consistent, the library can keep a basic count of the number of readers served while building a file (in either hard copy or digital form) that can be used to maintain an "institutional memory" of the reader.

Throughout this volume, examples have been given of fundamental research about readers' advisory that is needed. These deficits in our knowledge limit advancement of the service. As we seek to improve advisory in the future, better means of documenting our impact and maintaining good relationships with readers become increasingly important. We need better data, for instance, about how displays enhance circulation, how annotated book lists get used, and what kind of follow-up service readers find desirable. We need to find out if some authors really are "sure bets" for frequent recommendation. When we have generated hard proof that those given readers' advisory service are happier, on the average, with the books they select than readers who browse without help, it will be easier to advocate for expansion of the service.

READERS' ADVISORY INFORMING OTHER LIBRARY PRACTICES

Finally, if readers' advisory is indeed central to library practice (as we argue it is) and if advisory service has made true advancement, we must begin thinking about how readers' advisory can inform other library practices.

In many libraries, for instance, readers' advisors are already noticing shortfalls in their collections or are on the lookout for good read-alikes for certain popular authors. They use information they gather in readers' advisory practice to inform intelligent collection development. It is easy to see a future in which such arrangements are made more formal.

Readers' advisory should also inform technical services. As our understanding of appeal factors continues to improve, readers' advisors need to work with catalogers to get more advisory information into records in library OPACs. Records for fiction in particular do not currently provide adequate information to help readers make decisions. We must find ways to make catalog records include more measures of appeal than the few simple subject headings they contain now. Annotated book lists, review sources, discussion guides, web links, reading maps, and read-alike suggestions are just a few of the items that could be linked directly to records in the catalog.

Circulation departments can also benefit from the knowledge of advisors. The circulation desk is still an essential point of contact between most readers and the library. We must prepare and help those who work at these desks to provide basic advisory service. Beyond that, even more creative approaches might be found to building advisory into circulation functions. For instance, we might find ways to put new recommendations for regular advisory customers directly on hold. Perhaps a "serial" hold could be devised, in which the next book in a series or a favorite author's chronology could automatically be placed on hold for a reader when the previous item was returned. Outreach done by the library to reach homebound or other distant patrons can benefit from the application of advisory methods.

Boundaries between readers' advisory and reference services require further exploration and clarification. Do all reference librarians need basic advisory skills? (We would argue that, yes, they do.) It might become a standard part of the reference interview to ask if a patron would be interested in fiction, nonfiction, or other media related to his query. Offers to provide bibliographies, author information, or series information could become a standard part of ready reference. As they did in the first incarnation of readers' advisory service, reference librarians could bring their content knowledge and subject expertise to the task of devising educational programs.

Finally, as noted in chapter 4, advisory is spreading from reading into other media: audiobooks, movies, and music. As experience, better budgets, and years of collecting have improved these resources, more libraries now have media collections with enough breadth and depth to allow librarians to help users explore and broaden their horizons. We need to study how appeal factors change in each medium and how patterns of use (such as the reduced time commitment needed to try a CD or DVD) change the way we approach practice. With new sets of reference and support materials to master, these collections will provide new opportunities and challenges to advisors.

Readers' advisory can also inform programming decisions at a library. At Williamsburg Regional Library, for instance, through advisory we have learned that we have an unusually large audience for historical fiction and British writers. These interests, in turn, have generated ideas for successful programs. Advisory information should help libraries decide which new book groups to offer and which authors to invite. Conversely, any programming event is an opportunity to connect back to the collection, displaying books or offering lists of materials that event attendees might want to check out.

We have listed just some of the ways readers' advisory could expand to inform other areas of library practice. Finding the readers' advisory role of every library employee is a fundamental step toward a future of whole library readers' advisory.

Conclusion

Readers' advisory is at the core of library practice, the place where the interests of library users, the totality of the library collection, and the skills of the librarian meet. When practiced in a broad and inclusive way, advisory can affect the results of every person who uses the library. The energy we put into making advisory successful pays dividends in every aspect of library practice.

Contemporary readers' advisory practice is built on a solid philosophy of service, inclusiveness, respect for the interests and needs of all library users, and advocacy of the best materials. We have made great progress in putting that philosophy into methods of practice. The potential for further improvement, however, is almost limitless—there is work here for as many librarians, researchers, and writers as will take up the challenge. Those of us who work in readers' advisory are lucky enough to be active in a field during its renaissance. If we continue the work, we can look forward to even greater future success.

NOTES

1. See, for example, Jessica E. Moyer and Terry L. Weech, "The Education of Public Librarians to Serve Leisure Readers in the United States, Canada and Europe," *New Library World* 106, nos. 1/2 (2005): 67–79.

2. Juris Dilevko and Candice F. C. Magowan, *Readers' Advisory Service in North American Public Libraries, 1870–2005: A History and Critical Analysis* (Jefferson, N.C.: McFarland, 2007).

3. Catherine Sheldrick Ross, "Finding without Seeking: The Information Encounter in the Context of Reading for Pleasure," *Information Processing and Management* 335, no. 6 (1999): 793–95; "Making Choices: What Readers Say about Choosing Books to Read for Pleasure," *Acquisitions Librarian* 13, no. 25 (2001): 5–22; Ross, Lynne E. F. McKechnie, and Paulette M. Rothbauer, *Reading Matters: What the Research Reveals about Reading, Libraries, and Community* (Westport, Conn.: Libraries Unlimited, 2006).

4. See Jessica E. Moyer, "Learning from Leisure Reading: A Study of Adult Public Library Patrons," *Reference and User Services Quarterly* 46, no. 4 (2007). Available online at http://rusq.org/2008/01/06/learning-from-leisure-reading-a-study-of-adult-public -library-patrons/.

5. Bernard Berelson, "Reply to the Discussants," in *A Forum on the Public Library Inquiry: The Conference at the University of Chicago Graduate Library School, August 8–13, 1949*, ed. Lester Asheim (New York: Columbia University Press, 1950), 64.

6. See Cathy De Rosa et al., *Perceptions of Libraries and Information Resources* (Dublin, Ohio: OCLC, 2005). Available online at http://www.oclc.org/reports/2005perceptions.htm.

7. Neal Wyatt, "An RA Big Think: The Concept of Appeal Is on the Table, and Readers' Advisory Librarians Are Revolutionizing It," *Library Journal* 132, no. 12 (2007): 40–43.

INDEX

Page numbers followed by n (e.g., 197n13) indicate the presence of full bibliographic information in an endnote. Titles of books are in italics. Title of articles and chapters in books are in quotation marks. Specific discussions of chapters in books are listed under the author of the chapter and the title of the book.

Jessica E. Moyer is a graduate of the University of Illinois, Graduate School of Library and Information Science, where she earned both MS and CAS degrees. Since graduation she has worked as a reference and instruction librarian at Richland Community College and SUNY Oneonta. Currently she is a full-time doctoral student at the University of Minnesota–Twin Cities in the Literacy Education doctoral program. Jessica also teaches part time at the College of St. Catherine in the Information Management program and the Master of Library and Information Science program. Jessica is the author of several articles on readers, reading, and readers' advisory services published in *Reference and User Services Quarterly, New Library World,* and *Readers' Advisor News.* She has presented her work at the Library Research Round Table's 4 Star Research Forum at the 2005 ALA Annual Conference, and at the 2003 and 2004 BOBCATSSS symposiums. Jessica currently serves as a member of the editorial boards of *Reference and User Services Quarterly* and *Booklist Reference Books Bulletin* and is a chair of the 2008 RUSA Awards committee. Jessica reviews fiction, audiobooks, reference books, and professional reading for *Booklist* and fiction for *Library Journal.*